Buddhist China

KUAN-YIN.

(*From painting by a Chinese monk.*)

BUDDHIST CHINA

By Reginald Fleming Johnston

Author of
Lion and Dragon in Northern China
From Peking to Mandalay
Twilight in the Forbidden City
Confucianism and Modern China

Buddhist China © 2008 Soul Care Publishing

All rights reserved. No part of this book may be used or reproduced or transmitted in any manner whatsoever, transmitted electronically, or distributed by any means without the written permission of the publisher.

Library and Archives Canada Cataloguing in Publication

Johnston, Reginald Fleming, Sir, 1874-1938
    Buddhist China / by Reginald Fleming Johnston.

Includes index.
ISBN 978-0-9680459-3-0

    1. Buddhism—China. 2. Buddhism—China—History. 3. Buddhist shrines—China. 4. China—Civilization—Buddhist influences. I. Title.

BQ624.J64 2010   294.30951   C2009-907109-6

Published by Soul Care Publishing
Vancouver, B.C. Canada

Cover Picture byMark Linden O'Meara

诸恶莫作
众善奉行
自净其意
是诸佛教

Abstain from all evil,
In all things act virtuously,
Be pure in mind:
This is the religion of the Buddhas.
-From the Commandments Sutra.

做好人
行好事
读好书
说好话

Do good deeds;
Read good books;
Speak good words.
-Inscription carved on rock near
Buddhist monastery of Ku-shan,
Fuhkien Province.

ABBREVIATIONS
B.N.   Bunyiu Nanjio's Catalogue of the Chinese Translation of the Buddhist Tripitalca. (Oxford, Clarendon Press, 1883.)
E.R.E.   Encyclopedia of Religion and Ethics, edited by James Hastings. (Edinburgh, T. & T. Clark.)
Har.   The Hardoon edition of the Chinese Buddhist "Canon." (See Preface.)
J.R.A.S. Journal of the Royal Asiatic Society.
S.B.E.   The Sacred Books of the East, edited by Max Muller. (Oxford, Clarendon Press.)

PREFACE

The early chapters of this book deal with the origin and development of some characteristic features of Mahayana Buddhism, especially in respect of the forms assumed by that branch of the Buddhist system in its Chinese environment. The sixth and seventh chapters are concerned with religious pilgrimages in China, and with those sacred mountains which are the homes of Chinese monasticism arid the radiating centres of Buddhist influence. Of these favoured seats of religious activity, the six last chapters contain detailed accounts of two which are taken as typical namely, the holy mountain of Chiu-hua, in the province of Anhui, and the holy island of Puto (Pootoo), off the coast of Chehkiang.

An accomplished writer on Oriental Art-the late Ernest Fenollosa has observed that "a very large part of the finest thought and standards of living that have gone into Chinese life, and the finest part of what has issued therefrom in literature and art, have been strongly tinged with Buddhism." The truth and justice of this remark will not be gainsaid by those Western students who have succeeded in finding their way into the treasure-house of Chinese poetry, or have fallen under the potent witchery of Chinese landscape painting. Those of China's foreign friends who long to see not only the political regeneration of this great country, but also a brilliant revival of creative activity in art and letters, can hardly fail to take a keen and sympathetic interest in the fortunes of that wonderful creed, or system of creeds, which for at least fifteen centuries has exercised so powerful an influence artistic and philosophic no less than religious and ethical over the heart and mind of China.

It is too soon yet to say whether the forces set in motion by the Revolution or rather the forces of which the political revolution was one of the manifestations will bring about the total collapse of Buddhism in China. Judging from the present activity of the Buddhists themselves, it seems more likely that what we are about to witness is not a collapse, but at least a partial revival of Buddhism. Those Western observers who fancy that the Buddhist religion in China is inextricably associated with old-fashioned and discredited political and social conventions in general, and with the corruptions of the Manchu dynasty in particular, have a very imperfect knowledge of Chinese history and of the past relations of Buddhism with the Chinese body-politic.

Buddhists had no cause to regret the overthrow of the Manchus, to whom they were bound by no ties of sympathy, gratitude, or self-interest; and if the rulers of the New China honourably adhere to their declared policy of complete religious freedom, there is no reason why the Buddhists should not look forward to taking a distinguished part in the future progress of their country in respect of its social, artistic, and spiritual interests.

It may be that the present activity of the Chinese Buddhists has been inspired to some extent from Japan, as for example in the matter of the recent creation of a central organization (the Fo-chiao Tsung Hui) which has been established for the purpose of protecting the legitimate interests of the Buddhist faith. But the admirably-edited Buddhist magazines, the Fo-tisueh Ts ung-pao and the Fo-chiao Yueh-pao, which have made their appearance during the past year, furnish ample evidence that the movement (which is very largely a reform movement) is genuinely and fundamentally Chinese; and this is confirmed by the fact that the creation of the Tsung Hui itself (which might be described as a National Buddhist Synod or Representative Church Council) has met with the hearty approbation of Buddhists in all parts of the empire, and that in many localities branch Councils (composed, like the parent Council, of both laymen and ordained monks) have been already successfully established.

Though it is too early to say whether this movement will lead to any permanent results, it is certainly not of mushroom growth; nor can it be said to be a mere by-product either of revolutionary excitement or of reactionary caprice. Evidence of this may be found in the fact that during the past decade an influential group of Chinese Buddhists has been quietly at work producing a new complete edition of that prodigious collection of Buddhistic literature which is usually but inaccurately referred to as the Chinese Buddhist Canon. This great work, having occupied a large staff of editors and printers for several years past, has been quite recently (1913) brought to a happy conclusion.

Perhaps the most prominent among the learned and able Buddhists whose names are honourably associated with this undertaking is a native of the district of Ch'ang-shu, in Kiangsu. He entered the Buddhist monkhood at the age of twenty-one, and was given the monastic name of Tsung-yang. He is a man of varied culture, has travelled widely in both China and Japan, and is a writer of vigorous prose and graceful verse. Like all true Buddhists, he shows him self tolerant, charitable, and courteous towards those whose religious beliefs are different from his own. He belongs to the Monastery of Ch'ing-liang, on the Wu-mu-shan a mountain not far from Soochow; but since 1903 his various duties have required him to reside in Shanghai, where he and his colleagues have been the guests of well-known Shanghai residents Mr and Mrs S. A. Hardoon.

If it is mainly through the inspiring influence of a small group of enthusiastic monks and laymen that the republication of the "Canon" has been successfully carried out, the thanks of all Buddhists, and of all students of Buddhism, are also due to Tsung-yang's munificent hosts and patrons, who not only provided accommodation for him self and his colleagues, amid the flowers and trees that are dear to the hearts of all Buddhists, but also ensured the success of this very costly undertaking by their generous donations and financial guarantees. The completed work, which is frequently referred to in the following pages under the name of the "Hardoon" edition of the Buddhist scriptures, deserves to find its way into the hands of all serious students of Chinese Buddhist literature.

The author is glad to record his grateful appreciation of the unvarying courtesy and hospitality extended to him by the abbots and monks in whose romantic mountain-homes he has spent the happiest days of his fifteen years sojourn in China. Whatever may be the ultimate fate of Buddhism, he earnestly hopes that neither his kindly hosts nor their successors will ever be driven away from the quiet hermitages which they so justly love; and that it may continue to be China's glory and privilege to provide, amid the forests and crags and waterfalls of her cloistral mountains, homes or resting-places for all pilgrims to the shrines of truth and beauty.

R. F. J.
WEIHAIWEI,
15th April 1913.

TABLE OF CONTENTS

I.	**The "Three Religions" Of China**	1
	The Sage Fu Hsi	2
	The Alter of Heaven	3
	Religious Freedom	4
	Religion and Morals	6
	Ancestor-Worship	7
	Taoism	9
	Buddhism	10
	Buddhism as a Religion	11
II.	**Buddhism Under Asoka And Kanishka**	14
	Asoka	16
	Buddhist Missions	16
	The Mahayana	18
	Asvaghosha	19
	Buddhist Patriarchs	21
	Buddhist Chronology	22
	Council of Kashmir	22
	The Buddhist Canon	24
III.	**Early Buddhism And Its Philosophy**	26
	The "New" Buddhist	26
	Sources of Dogma	27
	The Mahayana	29
	Teachings of Buddha	32
	The "Silence" of Buddha	33
	A Parable	33
	The "Chariot" Passage	34
	Soul-Theories	36
	Personality	39
	The False Ego	39
IV.	**The Ideals Of Hinayana And Mahayana**	41
	Buddha and Miracles	42
	Brahma	44
	Salvation by Faith	45
	Buddhist Ethics	45
	Nagasena	47
	Bodhisatship	49
	Selflessness	50

	Arahantship	52
	Altruisn and Egoisn	53
	Self-Renunciation	54
	Celestial Bodhisats	56
	The Two Vehicles	57
	Self-Culture and Self-Sacrifice	57
V.	**Buddhist Schools And Sects In China**	**60**
	Bodhidharma	60
	Mysticism in East and West	61
	Buddhist Subdivisions	64
	Famous Religious Leaders	65
	Vinaya School	66
	Amitabha	67
	Amidist	68
	Amitabha	70
	Buddhist Heavens	71
	Rebirth in Paradise	74
	Kuan-Yin	74
	The Pure Land	75
	Amidist Creed	79
	The Beatific Vision	80
	Holy Name of Amitabha	80
	Time and Space	83
	Buddhism Independent of History	84
	The White Way	88
	Nirvana	88
	Symbols and Parables	90
VI.	**Pilgrimages And The Sacred Hills Of Buddhism**	**91**
	Chinese Civilization	91
	Pilgrimages in Christendom	92
	Chinese Pilgrimages	94
	The Canterbury Tales	94
	Religious Fanaticism	97
	Pilgrim-Seasons	98
	Confucian and Buddhist Shrines	99
	Struggles of Early Buddhism	100
	Defeat of the Taoists	101
	The Four Famous Hills	104
	The Four Elements	105

	The Eight Mountains	108
VII.	**"The Pilgrim's Guide"**	**109**
	Buddhism in Practice	109
	Buddhist Teachings	112
	Etiquette for Pilgrims	113
	Host and Guest	114
	Warnings to Pilgrims	115
	Follow Good, Eschew Evil	117
	Forbearance and Patience	120
	Be Content With Little	120
	Avoid Covetousness	122
	Hospitality in China	122
VIII.	**Ti-Tsang Pusa**	**124**
	The Vow of Ti-Tsang	124
	The Treasure House of Ti-Tsang	127
	Ti-Tsang Sutra	127
	Redemption of Mankind	128
	Story of the Brahman Girl	129
	The Mother of Buddha	131
	P'u-Hsien Pusa	133
	"Evil Poison"	134
	The Lord of Fate	136
	Use of Images	137
	Faith in Ti-Tsang	138
	Filial Piety	139
	Yama	140
	Evil Not Eternal	142
	Buddhist Demonology	143
	Buddhism and Hinduism	146
	Mahayana Mysticism	147
IX.	**The Prince-Hermit Of Chiu-Hua And His Successors**	**150**
	The Hermit's Death	151
	Kingdom of Hsin-Lo	152
	Korean Kingdoms	153
	Wizards and Buddhist Monks	154
	The Poet and the Hermit	155
	Pilgrim-Routes	158
	The Tea of Chiu-Hua	158
	"Half Way to the Sky"	160

	Confucian Hostility	161
	Chou Pin on Buddhism	162
	Prospects of Buddhism	163
X.	**Monks And Monasteries Of Chiu-Hua**	**165**
	Buddhist Mummies	165
	Mountain Clubs and Colleges	166
	Imperial Patronage	169
	Prayers to Ti-Tsang	169
	The Shrine of Ti-Tsang	171
	Austerities of Buddhist Monks	173
	The Tower of Heaven	174
	Strange Hermits of Chiu-Hua	175
	Wang Shou-Jen	176
	Mountain Lovers	179
	Poets of Chiu-Hua	180
	A Wizard of Chiu-Hua	181
	The Rain Maker of Chiu Hua	182
	Southern Slope of Chiu-Hua	183
XI.	**Puto-Shan And Kuan-Yin Pusa**	**187**
	Gutzlaff at Puto-Shan	188
	Early European Visitors	189
	Chusan Islands in Chinese History	192
	Buddhist History of Puto	195
	Buddhism and Catholicism	196
	The Little White Flower	197
	The Great Bodhisats	198
	Sex of Kuan-Yin	199
	The Mother of Buddha	201
	Marichi	203
	Story of Kuan-Yin	204
	Religious Faith	206
	The Emblems of Kuan-Yin	208
	Iconography	209
	The Dea Syria	211
	Kuan-Yin as a Fish-Goddess	211
	Extension of Cult of Kuan-Yin	212
	Buddhist Austerities	214
	Sutras Written in Blood	215
	The Sacred Cave	217

	A Story of Kuan-Yin	219
	Idolatry and Symbolism	220
	Filial Piety	221
	Use of Prayer in Buddhism	222
	Prayers of the Jhana School	224
	A Buddhist Prayer	224
XII.	**The Monastic History Of Puto-Shan**	**227**
	The Diamond Rock	227
	Relics of Buddha	229
	Buddhist Ordination	229
	Morals of Chinese Monasteries	231
	The Arrival of Egaku	232
	The Sea of Water-Lillies	234
	A Monk of Puto	235
	The Temples of Puto	236
	Monastery of Universal Salvation	239
	Imperial Patronage	240
	A Famous Monk	241
	Japanese Pirates	243
	Feng-Shui	244
	Imperial Edicts	245
	Death of Wu Ching-Luan	247
	The Coming of the Red-Hairs	249
	Dutch Marauders	249
	Departure of the Monks	251
	Restoration of Monasteries	252
	Edict of K'ang-Hsi	254
	Religious Policy of K'ang-Hsi	256
	The Empress-Dowager	257
XIII.	**The "Northern Monastery" And "Buddha's Peak"**	**258**
	Rock Inscriptions	259
	"Northern Monastery" Founded	259
	The Story of a Bell	260
	The Abbot Pieh-An	263
	"The Rain of the Good Law"	264
	The Laughing Buddha	265
	The Four Kings of Heaven	266
	Mei-Li and the Guardian Kings	267
	Interior of Monastery	269

Monastery of Buddha's Peak	271
Solar and Lunar Deities	272
The Buddhist Dead	273
Fauna of Puto	275
Poets of Puto	277
Incorruptible Riches	278
Two Strange Visitors	279
The Praises of Buddha	280
XIV. Index	**283**

Reginald Fleming Johnston

I. The "Three Religions" Of China

Within the grounds of one of the most famous Buddhist monasteries in China Shaolin in Honan may be seen two stone tablets inscribed with pictorial statements of a doctrine that is familiar to all students of Chinese religion and philosophy the triunity of the San chiao, or Three Doctrinal Systems of Buddhism, Confucianism, and Taoism. On one of these tablets, the date of which corresponds to the year 1565 of our era, there is the incised outline of a venerable man holding an open scroll on which a number of wavy lines like tongues of flame converge and blend. The old man's draperies are symmetrically arranged, and his crouching figure is skillfully made to assume the appearance of a circle, the centre of which is occupied by the open scroll. The whole drawing is surrounded by a larger circle, which signifies ideal unity and completeness, or represents the spherical monad of Chinese cosmological philosophy. The other tablet, which is more than seven hundred years old, is of a less symbolical or mystical character. It shows us the figures of the representatives of the three systems standing side by side. Sakyamuni Buddha occupies the place of honour in the centre. His head is surrounded by an aureole, from which issues an upward-pointing stream of fire, and beneath his feet sacred lotus-flowers are bursting into bloom. On the left of the central figure stands Lao-chun, the legendary founder of Taoism, and on the right stands China's "most holy sage" Confucius.

The words which are ordinarily used to sum up the theory of the triunity of the three ethico religious systems of China are San chiao i t'I — the Three Cults incorporated in one organism or embodying one doctrine.[1] The idea has found fanciful expression in the comparison of the culture and civilization of China with a bronze sacrificial bowl, of which the three "religions" are the three legs, all equally indispensable to the tripod's stability.

Such teachings as these are abhorrent to the strictly orthodox Confucian, who holds that the social and moral teachings of Confucius are all that humanity requires for its proper guidance; but they meet with

---

[1] 三教 一体九流 一源百家 一理万法 一门

ungrudging acceptance from vast numbers of Buddhists and Taoists, who, while giving precedence to their own cults, are always tolerant enough to recognise that Confucianism, if somewhat weak on the religious side, is strong and rich on the ethical side. They find an echo, indeed, in the hearts of the great majority of the Chinese people, who show by their beliefs and practices that they can be Buddhists, Taoists, and Confucians all at the same time.

The Sage Fu Hsi

A vivid and picturesque statement of this truth is contained in a quaint little story which is told of a certain sixth-century scholar named Fu Hsi. This learned man was in the habit of going about dressed in a whimsical garb which included a Taoist cap, a Buddhist scarf, and Confucian shoes. His strange attire aroused the curiosity of the Chinese emperor of those days, who asked him if he were a Buddhist. Fu Hsi replied by pointing to his Taoist cap. "Then you are a Taoist?" said the emperor. Fu Hsi again made no verbal answer, but pointed to his Confucian shoe?. "Then you are a Confucian?" said the emperor. But the sage merely pointed to his Buddhist scarf. It is a far cry from the sixth century to the twentieth. The China of to-day has crossed, for weal or woe, the threshold of a new era. What has been true of the Chinese in past ages will not necessarily continue to be true in future. Will the three cults continue to form "one body," or will they fall apart? If they fall apart, will each maintain a separate existence of its own, or are they one and all destined to suffer eclipse and death? Who will be the Fu Hsi of the centuries to come? What are the symbols that will replace the cap and the shoes and the scarf that Fu Hsi was proud to wear? And who let us ask with bated breath is to take the place of Fu Hsi's imperial master?

These are gravely important questions for China, and their interest for Western nations is far from being merely academic. The forces that mould the character and shape the aspirations of one of the greatest sections of mankind cannot be a matter of indifference to the rest of the human race, whose future history will be profoundly affected, for better or for worse, by the nature of the ideals and ambitions that inspire the constructive energies of the makers of the new China.

Reginald Fleming Johnston

The Alter of Heaven

If the ultimate fate of the "three religions" were dependent on the degree of respect now paid to them by some of the more zealous spirits among China's foreign-educated reformers, we should be obliged to prophesy a gloomy ending for all three. Taoism is treated as a medley of contemptible superstitions, and multitudes of its temples, with their unquestionably ugly clay images and tinsel ornaments, are falling into unlamented decay. Buddhism meets with scant courtesy, and is threatened with the confiscation of its endowments and the closing of some, at least, of those beautiful monasteries which during the happiest centuries of China's history were the peaceful refuge of countless poets and artists and contemplative philosophers. The moral sovereignty of the "uncrowned king" -Confucius totters on the edge of an abyss which has already engulfed a throne more ancient, if not more illustrious, than even his -the imperial throne of China. There are rumours that the state subsidies hitherto granted at regular intervals for the upkeep of the great sage's temple and tomb at Chu-fou will perhaps be withdrawn, and that in the state schools and colleges reverence is no longer to be paid to the canonised representative of Chinese civilization and moral culture. There are signs that not even the holiest sanctuary in China is to remain inviolate: for the whisper has gone forth that the silent and spacious grove that surrounds the Altar of Heaven that marble index of a religious system which even in the days of Confucius was hallowed by the traditions of an immemorial antiquity is to be adapted to commercial uses and turned into an experimental farm.

Among the guiding spirits in the destructive and constructive work undertaken since the overthrow of the Manchu dynasty are men of fine ability, unquestioned patriotism, and earnest zeal for their country's welfare; but many of them have been so bewitched by the glamour of Western methods, and so impressed by the material successes of Western civilization, that they have lost all touch with the spirit of the traditional culture of their own race. The iconoclastic tendencies of to-day have not been guided by the will of the people for the will of the people has not yet found a means of making itself known and felt. They have not sprung into activity in obedience to the voice of China for the voice of China has not yet been heard.[2]

Yet perhaps, after all, the prospects of the "three religions" are not quite so dismal as a glance at the present state of affairs might lead us to suppose. That the iconoclastic activity of to-day will be succeeded sooner or later by a reaction in which all the traditional conservatism of the Chinese race will take a strenuous part, is one of the few prophecies with regard to China's future which may be uttered with reason able confidence. The reaction will itself be succeeded, no doubt, by further oscillations, more or less violent, before China can hope to attain that condition of stability and peace without which there can be no permanent reconstruction of her shattered polity; but we need not be surprised if the China that emerges victorious from the political chaos of to-day is found to have quietly gathered up and loyally preserved many of the traditions of imperial China which the triumphant Revolution was supposed to have torn in fragments and trampled under foot.

Religious Freedom

It is improbable, on the whole, that the reorganised Chinese State will show hostility to the religious idea as such; it will not, we may assume, waste its strength in a foolish and necessarily futile attempt to suppress the religious side of man's nature. The religious problem that will face the country's rulers will probably narrow itself down to this: Is the Government to encourage the people to make their religious emotions and interests flow in certain specified directions, either by the "provision of religious education in the State schools or by the official support of a State cult; or is religion to be regarded as n private concern of the individual, with which the State has nothing whatever to do so long as the religious beliefs or practices of any given individual do not lead him into conflict with the ordinary law of the land? It seems probable, judging from present indications, that it is the second alternative which will be accepted by the rulers of the new China. Already we find that the declared policy of the republican pioneers is to grant toleration to all religions, native and foreign, but to show special favour to none: and this policy is not unlikely to become a permanent feature of the Chinese constitution.

---

2 Written in January 1913

But though China will probably accept the principle of complete separation between the State and all organised or institutional religion, and will (it may be suggested) be perfectly right in so doing, it is not therefore to be assumed that the Chinese Government (or Governments) will cease to exercise a paternal supervision over the people's morals. If that were so, the chasm between the old China and the new would indeed be a bridgeless one. There has always been an intimate connection between ethics and statesmanship in this chosen land of moral philosophers, in spite of the fact inevitable in China as elsewhere that practice has not always conformed to precept. A Chinese Government which disclaimed full responsibility for the moral welfare and guidance of the people, or which confined its activities in this direction to the occasional amendment of its penal code, would be regarded as having definitely cut itself adrift from the most sacred traditions of past ages, and would have to face the hostility of all the conservative sections of Chinese society.

The separation between religion and politics will not necessarily, in China, affect the traditional intimacy between politics and morals. In spite of the references to supernatural powers and agencies, and to religious ceremonies, in the old-fashioned Chinese proclamations and rescripts, it is undoubtedly the fact that in China the distinction between creed and morals or perhaps we should say their separability has for ages been tacitly recognized. The view that sound morality is impossible except in alliance with a definite religious creed, belief in which is therefore an essential condition of good citizenship, is a view which has never been accepted by Chinese thinkers or rulers. It is a curious and instructive fact that while in the West under the influence of a privileged and intolerant Church ethics and institutional religion are regarded, or were till recently regarded, as inseparably linked together, in China the association has been rather between ethics and politics. This is part of the practical outcome of the national recognition of Confucius as the supreme Teacher. It is in Confucianism that we find the closest approach to a fusion between ethical and political ideals, and it was Confucius who, while showing a genial tolerance towards the tenets of popular religion, recommended his disciples to consider and minister to the ascertainable needs of men before perplexing themselves over the problematical demands and requirements of the gods.

Buddhist China

Religion and Morals

According to the educational theory which in parts of Europe has for some time dominated the relations between religion and the State, definite religious instruction forms no necessary part of the content of ethical education and has no vital relation to moral conduct; but it is usually agreed, nevertheless, that respect should be paid to the religious idea, and to spiritual interpretations of life, and that tolerance should be shown to all forms of religious expression.[3]

This is no place for an enquiry into the justice or adequacy of such views, but that they are in entire harmony with the letter and spirit of Confucian teachings is a fact which, if it were fully realized, might go far towards bringing about a permanent reconciliation between the moral and educational and to a great extent even the political aims of the "progressive" and the conservative parties in China. It has long been recognized that Confucianism is an ethico-political rather than a religious cult[4]. Such definitely religious elements as the system contains, including those resulting from the elevation of Confucius to quasi-divine rank, might be got rid of, or might be ignored by the State, without gross violence being done to any deep-rooted popular prejudices; for the ritual solemnities that took place at regular intervals in the Confucian temples were always the affair of the emperor and his officials, and their suppression would not interfere with any cherished religious customs or practices of the people. Thus the Chinese Government which retains Confucianism as a basis for moral training need have no fear that it will be convicted of having betrayed the cause of political progress or of giving

---

3 Cf. the speech by the French deputy at the Moral Education Congress held in London in September 1908. Canon Lilley has more recently (August 1912) told us that in France ee a new sense of growing religous need is everywhere making itself felt throughout the national life." This is very probably true: man's religious instincts will not suffer themselves to be extinguished at the bidding of a political party. But a revival of religion does not necessarily imply a revival of belief in a theological system or a readiness to subscribe to definite credal formulas. The French intellect once emancipated from ecclesiastical domination in spiritual matters is not likely to return of its own accord to a condition of spiritual servitude. France is restless because she is realizing the insufficiency of a civilization which concentrates its whole attention on material interests and is contemptuous of the needs of the spirit. As for China, she, too, will discover, sooner or later, that Western civilization, in spite of its outward splendour and its alluring promises, is but too prone to pamper the body and starve the soul; though whether China will find it impossible to satisfy her spiritual needs except by throwing away her own spiritual heritage and adopting that of another race, is a different question.

4 It is true, no doubt, that Confucian statesmen have been guilty from time to time of persecuting Buddhism and other cults which were, or were believed to be, irreconcilable with Confucian teachings; but such persecutions have been undertaken on political and social grounds, not with the aim of crushing religious opinions as such.

State support to any organized system of religious worship or belief; and such a Government will assuredly gain the glad support of all who wish to see the evolution of China proceeding, so far as is reasonable and practicable, along the lines of its own immemorial past.

Ancestor-Worship

If it were our task to undertake a full treatment of religious conditions and prospects in China, a special chapter would have to be devoted to the consideration of the weighty problems arising out of the so-called worship of ancestors, which is in many respects the most deeply-rooted religious cult in China. This cult is independent of Confucianism, though it may be said to have grown and prospered under the protection of the Confucian system, and to have received a certain amount of qualified approval from the great sage himself. Ancestor-worship would not necessarily lose its hold on the people if Confucius were dethroned; and though it will doubtless undergo various modifications and adaptations, and will be seriously menaced by the gradual disintegration of the present organization of society, in which the family rather than the individual is regarded as the social unit, it nevertheless seems likely to last, in one form or another, quite as long as any other religious cult at present competing for the popular favour. There are superstitions connected with ancestor-worship which the spread of education and of scientific knowledge will infallibly sweep away, but the essential ideas at the root of the cult are sound and healthy, and their forcible removal would constitute the severest moral catastrophe which could befall the Chinese people.

Buddhist China

ARCHWAY AT THE PI-YÜN TEMPLE, WESTERN HILLS.

ARCHWAY AT THE WO-FO TEMPLE, WESTERN HILLS.

Reginald Fleming Johnston

Taoism

But if Confucianism and the cult of ancestors shorn of their superstitious accretions-- may still be destined to play an active and beneficent part in the moral guidance of China, what expectation is there that anything but ignoble decay awaits their rivals? With regard to Taoism, let us admit at once that as an organized religion with temples and a priesthood it is already moribund. Taoist wizardries shrink from contact with the gleaming lances of the knights of modern science, and already excite the ridicule of those who once came to marvel and to revere. The opening of every new school nowadays may be said to synchronize with, if not to be the direct cause of, the closing of a Taoist temple. The priests of the cult are not only ceasing to enjoy the respect of others, they are losing confidence in themselves and in the potencies of their gods and demons. An enlightened China may be Confucian, it may possibly be Buddhist, it may "worship" its ancestors, it may be agnostic or rationalistic, but it will certainly not be Taoist. The venerable system of philosophic mysticism from which modern Taoism claims descent is still, indeed, of interest and value to thinkers of the present day, and it may be admitted that the fantastic musings of Taoist sages and mountain-roaming hermits were not wholly unproductive of strange discoveries in certain unfrequented by paths of psychology and natural science. Yet the disappearance of Taoism as a distinct cult will not be a thing to be regretted by the friends of China. If its teachings contain a good deal that is true, they also contain much that is crude and false. The false may well be cast aside and forgotten, the true will in due time be claimed and classified by science and philosophy. As for the ethics of popular Taoism, as distinct from the lofty teachings ascribed to Lao-tzu, they contain very little that is original, very little of value that may not be found in Confucianism or in Buddhism.

There is only one way in which Taoism can hope to survive the shocks and changes of the coming years, and it will be by treading the narrow path of humility and self-sacrifice. Taoism must throw away its gaudy trappings and relinquish its claim to be "a way of salvation." It must be content to play the humbler parts of a handmaid to art and poetry and a guardian of folklore and romantic legend. The fear has been expressed of late that the triumph of Western civilization in China will involve the irremediable decay of the country's literature and art: indeed many have found reason to doubt whether China has not already ceased to be a producer of beautiful things and a foster-mother of artists and poets. So pessimistic a view as this is hardly justifiable; but the future leaders of China's artistic development will be doing an injustice to themselves and an injury to the aesthetic and spiritual instincts of their race if they turn contemptuously away from a wonder-working fountain whence the poets and artists of their country have drawn copious draughts of inspiration for a period of nearly two thousand years. In the imaginative literature and art of China Taoism has had an influence which is not unworthy of comparison with the influence wielded in Western art by the Greek mythology, or by the ideals of medieval chivalry, or by the legends associated with the beginnings of Christianity. The Greek gods stepped down from their thrones on Olympus long ago, but in performing this act of humiliation they were fitting them selves to become the occupants of new thrones in an ideal world of poetry and romance. In a similar ideal world the divinities and wild-eyed mountain-wizards of Taoism may find themselves not quite forlorn, and though their clay images may be trampled into mud and their temples levelled with the ground, they may still find themselves in a position to take an honourable share in the creation or evocation of the dreams and visions of the painters and poets who will guide the fortunes of a Chinese literary and artistic renascence.

Buddhism

If Confucianism and Taoism are only to survive on condition that they cease to claim the honours and privileges usually accorded to religion, what is to be said of the prospects of Buddhism? It is true that Buddhism itself has often been denied the name of a religion, and that many people prefer to regard it as a system of philosophy. With regard to this point, it is enough to say that the Indian sages of the time of the Buddha would have been puzzled if they had been asked to draw clear lines of distinction between philosophy and religion. We may well hesitate to give Sakyamuni the name of philosopher and deny him that of religious teacher; while if we concede the latter title as the more appropriate, we must also admit that it would be difficult to exclude the name of the founder of Buddhism from any comprehensive history of Indian philosophy.

As to the form of Buddhism which prevails in China, perhaps we may fairly say that it is not only both a religion and a philosophy, hut that it embraces many religions and many philosophies, and that these are not always consistent with them selves or with one another. Chinese Buddhism has drawn its doctrines from many sources and from many schools of religious and philosophic thought. India, Central Asia, Persia, China itself, have all contributed to the final result, but no religious genius has yet undertaken the colossal task of fusing the various elements into one homogeneous system. The Chinese Tripitaka has sometimes been called the Bible of the Buddhists; but it should rather be described as a miscellaneous library, in which the Buddhist, the moral philosopher, the psychologist, the metaphysician, the student of comparative hierology, the historian, the collector of folklore, and the lover of poetry and romance, may all find ample stores of the kind of literature in which they take delight. There are many highly-cultivated members of polite society in China who would deny with some vehemence that they were Buddhists, and who yet take a deep and intelligent interest in various aspects of Buddhistic philosophy; and there are many people of fine literary discernment who never enter a Buddhist temple except from curiosity or to inspect its artistic treasures, and who will never theless admit that they take a keen intellectual pleasure in much of the fine work bequeathed to Chinese literature by some of the saints of the Buddhist Church.

Buddhism as a Religion

These considerations are enough to convince us that even if Buddhism collapses as a religious system ("system of religions" would describe it better), it may still continue to wield an.-immense though perhaps impalpable influence over Chinese thought. Indeed it may actually regain some of the influence which it has been gradually losing over cultivated minds when it shakes itself free from the worthless superstitions with which the need of satisfying the crude religious instincts of an ignorant populace has forced it into more or less grudging alliance. Moreover, the fact must , not be overlooked that Buddhism has taken a part no less distinguished than that of Taoism in constructing the channels through which have flowed, for many past centuries, some of the main currents of the Chinese artistic and poetic imagination. Neither the pictorial art nor the poetry of the Chinese can be properly understood or adequately appreciated without a sympathetic knowledge of Buddhism and Buddhistic lore; and there is no proof that Buddhism as a fountain of artistic and poetic inspiration is exhausted.

But it would be rash to assume that even as a religion, in the ordinary sense of the word, Buddhism has run its course. Confucianism and Taoism, as we have seen reason to believe, must abate something of their loftiest claims (or the claims that others have made on their behalf) if they wish to maintain a strong hold on Chinese hearts and minds; but it is not quite certain that Buddhism must follow their example. Access to Western fountains of wisdom has not resulted in the disappearance of the Buddhist faith from Ceylon or Siam or Burma, and even in so progressive a country as Japan we find that several schools of Buddhism are at present showing signs of renewed vitality and vigour. It would be rash to attempt to prophesy, in these days of convulsion and transition, what the future may have in store for Buddhism in China; but that the subject is one of interest and importance few students of religion or of world-politics will feel disposed to deny. A Christian theologian of our own day has recently observed that Buddhism is the only religion in the world that can be regarded as "a serious rival to Christianity[5]. If this be so, then for that reason if for no other it is incumbent upon the peoples of the West to form some correct notions about the history and present condition of Buddhism in that country which, in spite of the attractions of rival faiths, contains a greater number of Buddhists than any other country in the world.

An attempt will be made in these pages to introduce the Western reader to some of those aspects of Chinese Buddhism with which he is least likely to be familiar, and to conduct him on imaginary pilgrimage to some of those great monasteries which long have been, and still are, the strongholds of Buddhist influence among the Chinese people. It may be that he will return without having formed any exalted conception of the fitness of Buddhism to take a dignified part in the future development of Chinese civilization. Yet his pilgrimage will not have been wholly in vain if it enables him to enter into partial communion with that mysterious entity which has baffled and bewildered so many Western minds and has so often been declared inscrutable the Soul of China. For it is a fact that few of us can hope to gain true insight into the spiritual core of Chinese

---

5 Rev. J. A. Selbie in the Expository Times, April 1912.

culture until we have followed in the footsteps of the great poets and painters of T'ang, Sung, and Ming, and have wandered as they did among the beautiful mountain-homes of monastic Buddhism. There we must cast aside so far as it is humanly possible for Western men and women to do so all occidental preconceptions and prejudices, and try to hear with Chinese ears and to see with Chinese eyes. Only then will stream and wood, crag and waterfall, cast over us the same spells that they cast over China's hill-roaming painters and minstrel-pilgrims. Perhaps when we are watching a browsing deer that refuses to take fright at our approach, perhaps when, on some lonely mountain-slope, we are listening to the deep, soft note of a monastery-bell, we may see a little way into the secret of the intense love of the poets and painters of China for rock-throned pagoda and forest-guarded hermitage, and learn how it was that they acquired their wonderful knowledge of the ways of those wild animals that flee in dread from the dwellers in the plains, but come without fear to share food or shelter with the Buddhist monks whose homes are in the quiet hills.

II. Buddhism Under Asoka And Kanishka

Buddhism had already passed through its main doctrinal developments before it succeeded in establishing itself as one of the three religions of the Chinese people. Before we can hope, therefore, to understand the history and present position of the Buddhist religion in China we must know something of its varying fortunes in the land which gave it birth. Buddhist China is unintelligible without some acquaintance with Buddhist India. Sakyamuni Buddha is now believed to have died in or about the year 483 B.C. Under the patronage and personal support of the emperor Asoka (whose reign probably extended from 264 to 231 B.C.) the religion founded by Sakyamuni consolidated its position in the Gangetic valley, where it had originated, and extended its influence to other countries both in India and beyond its borders. Buddhism, in fact, became a missionary religion, and its missionaries proved themselves as intrepid as they were zealous. It is to be gathered from one of the Asokan edicts that the emperor formed ambitious plans for the peaceable conversion not only of various Central Asiatic states, but also of Syria, Egypt, Macedonia, and Epirus; and though the teachings of the Buddhist preachers seem to have made but little outward impression on the religious thought of the lands which lay within the Greek sphere of influence, there is ample evidence that Asoka's missionary zeal was largely responsible for the victorious march of the Buddhist religion through the Himalayan states, including Kashmir and Gandhara, as well as through southern India and Ceylon.

PART OF THE ARCHWAY AT THE PI-YÜN TEMPLE.
(*For stereoscopic view of detail.*)

Buddhist China

Asoka

By this time Buddhism possessed its canon and its formulated doctrines, though the religion to which Asoka gave his enthusiastic support was if we may judge from his famous rock and pillar edicts little more than a refined and undogmatic system of practical ethics. Filial piety and respect towards teachers and those in authority; kindness and courtesy to dependents, tenderness and pity for the weak, hospitality and charity towards the stranger and the traveller, sympathy and consideration for all living creatures; truthfulness and honesty in word arid deed; self-control, gratitude, fidelity, liberality, and purity of heart; toleration for the beliefs of others, and avoidance of all hatred and uncharitableness in act, thought, and language such are the essential doctrines of Asokan Buddhism, and as far as they go they are ^entirely consistent with the ethical teachings of Sakyamuni himself.

Buddhist Missions

Whether Asoka's missionaries reached China or not is a difficult question to answer. All we can say is that they may possibly have done so. A Chinese tradition says that Buddhism appeared in China about the year 217 B.C. Moreover, the Buddhistic literature and monastic chronicles of China contain numerous references to Asoka himself, who is declared to have been the founder of a vast number of pagodas, some of which were erected on Chinese soil[6].The stories of Asoka and his Chinese pagodas are no doubt fabulous, but it is possible that the legends which associate his name with the early propagation of Buddhism in China may contain a measure of truth. Asoka died about the year 231 B.C. The self-styled "First Emperor" of China (Ch'in Shih-huang), the builder of the Great Wall, reigned from 221 to 210, and it was about the year 213 that this Monarch's policy, which might perhaps be described as Political Futurism, culminated in the "burning of the books." It is not inconceivable that these books which are believed to have embraced all existing literature except works relating to medicine, agriculture, and divination --included some Buddhist tracts. For though there is reason to believe that the canon had

---

6 Even the Shan States are supposed to have had a share of the Asokan pagodas. See Sir George Scott's article on " Buddhism in the Shan States" in J.E.A.S., Oct. 1911, p. 921.

not been reduced to writing at that early date, it is by no means certain that portions of the scriptures did not already exist in literary form; indeed, if there were no literature of any kind, it is difficult to explain the success of the missionary propaganda in India and Ceylon. There is a passage in a Chinese historical work which distinctly states that Buddhist books had been widely circulated for a long time, but disappeared when the Ch'in dynasty established itself on the throne. On the other hand, some of the Asoka legends bear a suspicious similarity to those relating to the Indo-Scythian king Kanishka, and it is possible that there has been some confusion of names and events. Whether this be so or not, there is good reason to believe that Kanishka or one of the other monarchs of his race had diplomatic and other relations with China; and if (as high authorities maintain) Kanishka reigned in the first century B.C., it is possible that he or an early successor may have had something to do with the facts underlying a well-known story of a Chinese embassy to the Yueh-chih in the year 2 B.C.

Very soon after Asoka's death his empire began to break up. Buddhism continued to prosper, but in adapting itself to the needs of the tribes and nations of Central Asia it was obliged to submit to various far-reaching compromises. The pressure which it had to encounter was not from external forces only. Some of the old schools of Buddhist thought which had been treated as heterodox and kept in subordination in pre-Asokan days found fresh sources of strength and support among multitudes of the new converts. Outside India the orthodoxy of the Pali canon (fixed in the third century B.C.) was exposed to the contempt or neglect of heterodox schools, which showed a disposition to gather materials for a new canon of their own; while within the limits of India itself there was a gradual obliteration of the old lines of demarcation between Buddhism and the other systems of Indian religion. In Ceylon, indeed, Buddhism has maintained itself as the religion of the country ever since its establishment there in the Asokan age, and Burma (which embraced Buddhism in comparatively recent times) is still devotedly attached to the religion of its choice; but in India Buddhism allowed itself to be gradually absorbed by more strenuous rivals, and it is only in Brahmanical Hinduism that a few traces of its influence may still be found[7]. The process of absorption may be said to have lasted till the twelfth century of our era; indeed, if we regard Nepal as part of India, we may say that the process is not yet quite complete.[8]

The Mahayana

But it is not the obscure history of the decline of Buddhism in India that claims our attention here. Our concern is rather with that wonderful system known as the Mahayana a system which in some respects is so different from the Buddhism of the Pali canon that many students have been tempted to question its right to claim more than a nominal association with the teachings of Sakyamuni, and have tried to trace its characteristic doctrines to sources that were neither Buddhistic nor Indian.

The term Mahayana Great Vehicle was adopted by the followers of the new doctrines to distinguish their own system from primitive Buddhism, to which they gave the name of the Hinayana, or Small Vehicle. The Hinayana was so called because, according to its opponents, it was capable of conveying to the "other shore" of Nirvana only those rare individuals who by their own strenuous exertions had earned for them selves the prize of salvation; whereas the Great Vehicle offered salvation to all beings in all the worlds. The two names are convenient designations of the rival systems, though it should be noted that the term Hinayana was not accepted by the canonical Buddhists as a correct description of their own school, for which a more correct term would be Theravada -the School of the Elders or Presbyters.[9]

A great impetus, if an indirect one, is believed to have been given to the spread of the Mahayanist doctrines by the conversion to Buddhism of the powerful Indian ruler already mentioned the Kushan king Kanishka. Very little is known at present of the details of this monarch's reign: even the extent of his dominion is uncertain. It has been supposed that he ruled over a loosely-confederated empire which included not only North-

---

7 Buddhism wasted away after rival sects had appropriated every thing from it that they could make any use of." E. Hardy, quoted by Mrs Rhys Davids, Buddhism, p. 28.

8 Buddhism in India did not owe its extinction to Brahmanical persecutions. The belief that such was the case has been given up owing to lack of evidence. It undoubtedly suffered severely, however, in the last stages of its career from the iconoclastic fury of the Mohammedans. The decay of Buddhism was also largely due to the influence of the Yogacharya, or Tantric Buddhists, who from about the sixth century of our era began to admit Saivite deities into what now may be called the Buddhist pantheon. This helped to obliterate the characteristic features of Buddhism, which thus gradually ceased to maintain itself as a separate religion.

9 The Theravadins were also known as the Haimavantas, or (to use the Chinese term) Hmeh-shan-pu the School of the Snowy Mountains.

Western India, but also portions of Afghanistan, Parthia, Gandhara, Kashmir, and parts of what is known to-day as Chinese Turkestan. A passage in Hsuan Tsang's book of travels implies that his influence extended even to the western confines of China[10]. It has recently been questioned, however, whether Kanishka's direct rule extended beyond India, Gandhara, and Kashmir; reasons have been given for the belief that it was not Kanishka himself, but a line of allied kings of the same Kushan race, who reigned in the northerly regions[11].

Asvaghosha

In any case the name of Kanishka is a great one in the history of Buddhism, for it was he who is believed to have summoned the great Buddhist Council of Kashmir. The names of various patriarchs and doctors have been handed down in connection with the traditions relating to the king's religious activities, the most famous being Parsva, Vasumitra, and Asvaghosha. Unfortunately for the cause of historical accuracy, it is hardly possible to make any very positive statements about the part taken by these venerable figures in Buddhist developments, for there were several Vasumitras and several Asvaghoshas. All we can say is that, according to one Buddhist tradition, a monk named Vasumitra became president of the Council of Kashmir [12]; that, according to another tradition, a monk named Asvaghosha was sent to the court of a king, who may have been Kanishka, in accordance with the peace conditions imposed by that monarch after a successful war with a neighbouring Indian ruler; [13] that an Asvaghosha probably took a prominent part (perhaps as vice-president) in Kanishka's Council; that this may have been the Asvaghosha who figures in the lists of Indian patriarchs which have been preserved by the Buddhists of China; and that a writer named Asvaghosha (of uncertain date) was the author of certain religious treatises in which some of the

---

10 See Watters, Yuan Chwang ii. 124.

11 See J. Kennedy in J.R.A.S., July 1912, pp. 665

12 Paramartha's Life of Vasubandhu (Har. xxiv. vol. ix. pp. 115-118) gives Katyayani-putra as the name of the president.

13 This is recorded in the Life of Asvaghosha, by Kumarajiva, Har. xxiv. vol. ix. p. 112. The same authority gives us the foolish story about the six starving horses which (with ample supplies of food in front of them) refused to eat in order that they might give their undivided attention to Asvaghosha's sermons. (Hence the name Asvaghosha, Chinese Ma-miny, which means Horses neighing.)

Mahayanist doctrines may have found literary expression for the first time.[14]

All this is very vague, and the vagueness is increased by the unfortunate fact that the chronological position of Kanishka himself is still a matter of controversy. In view of the importance of the religious movements which took place in his time, it is much to be hoped that the fresh literary and archaeological material recently discovered in Khotan and the neighbouring regions of Turkestan will produce evidence whereby the matter will be put beyond the reach of further dispute. The beginning of Kanishka's reign has been assigned by some scholars to the first century B.C., and by others to the first, the second, and even the third centuries of the Christian era. Between the earliest and the latest dates which have been suggested there is a difference of no less than three hundred and fifty-six years a fact which is sufficient to indicate the chaotic state of Indian chronology. At present the best authorities hold that the reign began either in 78 of our era or in the first half of the first century B.C. According to one high authority, the so-called Vikrama era, which is dated from 58 B.C., commenced with the year of Kanishka's accession; according to another, that era had a religious origin, and was dated from the convocation of the great Buddhist Council.[15]

The view that Kanishka reigned in the first century B.C. is supported by the tradition preserved by Hsuan Tsang concerning Buddha's alleged prophecy that a king named Kanishka would reign four hundred years after his death[16]. The "prophecy" was no doubt manufactured after the event, but it is of interest as giving the belief, at the time it was recorded, of the number of years that had elapsed between the death of Buddha and the accession of Kanishka. If Buddha died in 483 B.C. and Kanishka

---

14 A Japanese scholar (M. Anesaki) has described the Mahayanist Asvaghosha as " the Buddhist Origen," and ascribes to him the first systematization of the Buddhist Trinitarian (trikaya) theory. The reference is to AsVaghosha's Awakening of Faith, which English readers should consult in Suzuki's translation. This is the Ch'i-hsin-lun referred to below.

15 Mr V. A. Smith formerly held (see his Early History of India, 2nd ed., 1908, pp. 239.) that Kanishka began to reign in the first half of the second century of our era, probably in the year 120 or 125; but more recently, in his History of Fine Art in India and Ceylon (1911), he pronounces himself in favour of the year 78 of our era. Dr J. F. Fleet, than whom there is no higher authority on Indian chronology, maintains that Kanishka's reign began with the so-called Vikrama era in 68 B.C. The view quite recently put forward by Mr J. Kennedy (J.R.A.S., July and October 1912) is to the effect that Kanishka's reign began a few years earlier than this; that the Buddhist Council was held in his reign, in the year 58 B.C.; and that the Vikrama era is dated from that event.

16 Watters, Yuan Chwang, i. 203.

commenced his reign in 58 B.C. or a few years earlier, it seems that the "prophecy" was correct within twenty-five years.

Buddhist Patriarchs

It is doubtful whether Chinese Buddhistic writings can give us much help in solving the chronological problem, yet an examination of the list of the patriarchs through whom the Ch'an (Dhyana) Buddhists of China trace their spiritual descent from Sakyamuni may perhaps be found suggestive.

These Chinese Buddhists say that Buddha died in a year which corresponds to 949 B.C., and that the first and second "patriarchs" were Mahakasyapa and Ananda, who died in 905 and 867. If these dates were correct, we should have to assume that Ananda, though he was Buddha's own cousin and intimate disciple, survived the Master by no less than eighty-two years! Coming lower down the list we find that Asvaghosha (twelfth patriarch) died about the year 330. Asvaghosha in his turn was succeeded by Kapimala, and Kapimala by the celebrated Nagarjuna (fourteenth patriarch) who died in 212 B.C. Obviously all these dates are unreliable; indeed we cannot feel sure that we are touching solid ground till we come to the illustrious name of Bodhidharma, with whom the Indian patriarchate came to an end. The arrival in China of Bodhi dharma or "Tamo," as the Chinese call him about the year 520 of our era is a well-attested fact; and there is no reason to doubt that the death of Tamo, who was the twenty-eighth Indian and first Chinese patriarch, is correctly placed by the Chinese monkish chroniclers about the year 528.

The correction of all the dates in the list of patriarchs would be a hopeless task. The initial error in the date assigned to Buddha's death is of itself sufficient to vitiate all the subsequent chronology. It is not impossible, however, that though tradition has gone astray in the matter of dates, it has correctly preserved the names of the patriarchs and the order of their succession. According to the Chinese chronology the lives of the twenty-eight patriarchs (949 B.C. to 528 of our era) covered a period of 1,477 years. Each patriarch, therefore, must have survived his predecessor by an average period of about fifty-two years. It is hardly necessary to point out how improbable it is that so long a period as this can have elapsed between each of the successive deaths of twenty-eight patriarchs. But a different solution of the question at once suggests itself when we assume that Buddha's death took place not in 949, as the Chinese say, but in 483. That this was the true date of the death of Buddha is the conclusion at which Western scholars have recently arrived, and we are justified in assuming it to be approximately correct[17]. The lives of the twenty-eight patriarchs, then, extended over a period not of 1,477 but only of 1,011 years. Now, if we calculate the average length of each patriarchate on this new basis, we find that it is no more than thirty-six years. This is not impossibly long, especially when we assume (as we are entitled to do) that each patriarch made a point of selecting a youthful successor in order to preserve an analogy between the physical succession of father and son and the spiritual succession of teacher and disciple.

Buddhist Chronology

If we now test our new scheme of dates by assigning to Asvaghosha the chronogical place which he ought to occupy on the assumption that each patriarchate lasted thirty-six years on an average, we arrive at once at the interesting discovery that Avaghosha's death may be placed in the year 51 B.C. We cannot, of course, place much reliance on the accuracy of a date arrived at in this arbitrary manner; but it is in exact conformity with the requirements of the tradition concerning Asvaghosha's relations with Kanishka and the part taken by him in the work of the Council of Kashmir, and it is in equally precise agreement with the new theory that the Council was held in 58 B.C.

Council of Kashmir

The solution of the chronological problem will no doubt enable students of Buddhism to speak with more confidence than is possible at present concerning the early history of the Great Vehicle. But the once-prevalent theory that the rise and expansion of the Mahayana school was directly due to the personal support of Kanishka, and to the labours of the Council of Kashmir in compiling a new Sanskrit canon which was to supersede the Pali canon, must be abandoned. There is no evidence that the Council tampered in any way with the existing canon or even that it was Mahayanist in sympathy. On the contrary, there are strong reasons for believing that it was a Hinayanist council, and that one of its principal

---

17 See Dr J. F. Fleet's article in J.R.A.S., 1912, p. 240. Arguing in favour of the year 483, he says: (There is, of course, no means of attaining absolute certainty. But I think that this result cannot be bettered,"

objects was riot to promote but to check the expansion of the Mahayanist heresies. If Hsuan Tsang's account is to be trusted, it is clear that earnest Buddhists of the old school (or rather the Sarvastivadin branch of the old school) were alarmed by the doctrinal confusion that existed throughout the Buddhist world, and that they therefore induced the king who has been called the Clovis of Buddhism to summon a Council in defence of the interests of their own type of orthodoxy. Various places were suggested for the meeting of the Council, and Kashmir seems to have been selected partly for the significant reason that "it was surrounded with hills as a city is surrounded by its walls," and could only be entered by a single pass; and that in this secluded region the Council (or rather the committee of monks who carried out the literary and editorial duties imposed upon them by the Council) would not be liable to be disturbed by heretics and schismatics[18]. The Council seems to have occupied itself mainly with religious discussions and debates which were subsequently reduced to writing in the form of Sanskrit commentaries[19]. The editorial work is said to have been entrusted to Asvaghosha, who was specially invited to Kashmir for the purpose; and the principal result after twelve years of literary labour was the great philosophical compilation known as the Mahavibhasha[20]. Hsuan Tsang tells us that the approved treatises were engraved on sheets of copper, which were enclosed in stone caskets and buried under a stupa some where near the modern Srinagar. When this was done an edict was carved on stone whereby it was forbidden to remove the sacred literature from Kashmir. One of our authorities makes the very significant observation that these measures were taken with a view to the

---

18 Paramartha, Life of Vasubandhu, Har. xxiv. vol. ix. p. 116. The reference is to the king's proclamation issued after the Council had completed its labours. See also Watters, op. cit. i. 271.

19 See J. Takakusu, J.R.A.S., 1905, p. 415.

20 See Paramartha, loc. cit.; Watters, op. cit., i. 271, ii. 104. The commentaries are included in the Chinese Tripitaka (so-called) under the section of Hsiao Sheng Lun the Abhidharma of the Hinayana. See J. Takakusu in J.R.A.S., 1905, pp. 52, 160-162, and 414-415; also his article in the Journal of the Pali Text Society, 1904-5, on The Abhidharma Literature of the Sarvastivadins." He observes that "all arguments about the Council and its works will be valueless until the Mahavibhasha an encyclopedia of Buddhist philosophy is trans lated into one of the European languages." For the Chinese version, see Har. xxii. vols. i.-viii. (B.N. 1263). The Chinese attribute the Mahavibhasha to the I-ch ieh-pu, which is one of their names for the Sarvastivadin school (also known as Hetuvada) of the Hinayana. Another Chinese name for the school was Sa-p o-to.

protection of orthodox religion from the corrupting and destructive influences of hostile schools and the Great Vehicle[21].

The Buddhist Canon

It is clear, then, that it is erroneous to speak of the Council of Kashmir as having given "official authority and a sacred canon" to the Mahayana form of Buddhism[22]. Indeed it is not strictly accurate to apply the term "canon" to any collection of Buddhist writings except that which was apparently fixed in the third century B.C. or earlier, and was reduced to writing (in Pali) in the first century B.C.[23] All we can say with regard to the so-called Mahayana canon is that the Mahayana schools recognize certain works as more sacred or more authoritative than others, and that each of the sects into which the Mahayanists divided themselves in China and Japan based its teachings on a limited number of sutras carefully selected from the available accumulations of sacred literature. Thus each school or sect practically constructed a miniature canon for itself, and the sanctity or canonicity of any individual work in the so-called Chinese Tripitaka varies with the sectarian standpoint from which it is regarded[24].

---

21 恐余部及大乘汉壤此正法 Paramartha, Life of Vasubandhu, Har. xxiv. vol. ix. p. 116 (6). I am inclined to believe that it was the fame of the Council and the general recognition of the value of its literary labours that impelled some Mahayanist writers of a later age to pretend that the Council had been attended by Mahayanists as well as by Hinayanists. The strange story of Vasumitra, recorded by Hsuan Tsang (see Watters, Yuan Chwang, i. 271), reads like a Mahayanist writer's invention; and it is a significant fact that while, according to one tradition (probably the most reliable) the Council was attended by arahants only (that is, Hmayanist (saints"), another tradition asserts that it was also attended by an equal number of bodhisats (that is, Mahayanist " saints").

22 The words quoted are those of Mr J. Kennedy in J.R.A.S., 1912, p. 674.

23 See Max Muller, S.B.E., vol. x. pp. xx.-xxii. xxxiv.-xliii.; Rhys Davids, S.B.E., vol. xxxv. pp. xxxvii.-xl., vol. xxxvi. pp. xv.-xvii.; and Dialogues of the Buddha, pt. i. pp. ix.-xx., pt. ii. pp. 77-8.

24 To a very limited extent the same eclectic tendency was shown by some of the Hmayana schools also. Rhys Davids points out that several of these schools "had their different arrangements of the canonical books, differing also, no doubt, in minor details " (Dialogues of the Buddha, pt. i. p. xix.).

Reginald Fleming Johnston

STŪPA AT THE PI-YÜN TEMPLE.

III. Early Buddhism And Its Philosophy

The "New" Buddhist

It is a matter of common knowledge that some of the doctrines of the Mahayana (not to mention its ritual practices) bear a remarkable resemblance to some of the teachings of Christianity. This is one of the reasons why the question of the date of Kanishka is of considerable interest and importance to Western enquirers. It seems reasonable, at first sight, to suppose that if certain important features of Buddhism, which are also characteristic of Christianity, did not develop until the time of Kanishka or later, and if the reign of that king belonged to as late a period as the first or second century of our era, then the Mahayana must have borrowed from Christianity. One critic has been venturesome enough to assert that Avaghosha and the apostle St. Thomas actually became personally acquainted with one another at the court of St. Thomas's supposed Indian patron, Gondophares, or Gondophernes, and that such Christian elements as are to be found in the Mahayana were therefore the result of the intercourse between the Christian apostle and the Buddhist patriarch[25].

The problem of the nature of the relationship between Christianity and Buddhism is not to be explained by any such airy suggestion as this; and, indeed, the evidence adduced in favour of this particular theory is worthless. On the whole there is something to be said for the view that the resemblances between Christianity and the "New" Buddhism (as the Mahayana has been called) are not due to borrowing either on one side or the other, but to the fact that both had access to the same sources of doctrinal inspiration sources which in themselves were not specifically either Christian or Buddhist. It is now a matter of common knowledge that

---

25 See the late T. W. Kingsmill's article, which contains several rash and questionable statements, in The Anglican (a missionary periodical published in the Far East), June 1909, pp. 22 ff. Mr Kingsmill, Dr Richard, and Professor Arthur Lloyd all seem to assume that the AsVaghosha who wrote certain Mahayanist works such as the Sraddhotpada-sastra (the Chinese Ch i-hsin-lun, B.N. 1250) must have been no other than the Asvaghosha who attended Kanishka's Council and helped to edit the commentaries. As we have already seen (p. 27), there were several Asvaghoshas (or several persons who wrote under that name), and it is at present impossible to distinguish between them all or to assign them to their proper dates. See Mr Anesaki's article in E.R.E., ii. 159, and T. Suzuki's Awakening of Faith (Chicago: 1900), pp. 6-17.

Christianity and Mithraism were in many respects amazingly alike; yet the best authorities assure us that at the root of those two religions "lay a common Eastern origin [Persian and Babylonian] rather than any borrowing.[26]" 1 If this be so, we need not consider ourselves under any obligation to look for evidence of borrowing when we come across strange similarities between Christianity and the Mahayana, whose common features are probably less striking than those which were shared by the religions of Christ and Mithras.

Sources of Dogma

That the Mahayana doctrines were not of Christian origin is frankly admitted to-day even by some who might have felt tempted to give Christianity the benefit of the doubt. A well-known Anglican missionary in Japan, writing on Buddhist and Christian origins, remarks that "we cannot always trace an actual contact; it is perhaps enough to recognize the fact that these thoughts were in the air.[27]" According to another writer, a missionary in China, "it is getting clearer every day that these common doctrines of new Buddhism and Christianity were not borrowed from one another, but that both came from a common source.[28]" This writer believes that the common source was Babylonian, and that "from this centre those great life-giving inspiring truths were carried like seeds into both the East and West, where they were somewhat modified under different conditions.[29]"

We may, then, admit the possibility that some of the characteristic doctrines shared by Christianity and the Mahayana such as the efficacy of belief in divine or superhuman saviours incarnating them selves in man's

---

26 Dr Grant Showerman, "Mithraism" (Encycl. Brit., llth ed.). Mgr. Louis Duchesne, in his Early History of the Christian Church (Eng. trans., 1910, i. 396), admits that "the religion of Mithras contained elements in theology, morality, ritual, and in its doctrine of the end of all things bearing a strange resemblance to Christianity."

27 Lloyd's Creed of Half Japan, p. 340. Prof. Percy Gardner holds similar views of the alleged borrowing by Christianity from the pagan mysteries. " Ideas are propagated from school to school and teacher to teacher less often by the direct borrowing which comes of admiration than by the parallel working of similar forces in various minds. When ideas are in the air, as the saying is, men catch them by a sort of infection, and often without any notion whence they come."

28 Dr Timothy Richard, The Awakening of Faith, p. xiii.

29 It would be a mistake to give undue emphasis to the Babylonian theory, yet the history of Mithraism, Manichaeism, Mandaeism, and certain early Gnostic cults such as that of the Ophites, shows us how far-reaching the Babylonian-Assyrian influence undoubtedly was. " Babylonia/ says Mr J. Kennedy (J.R.A.S., 1912, p. 1005), "with its mixed populations, had been for centuries the exchange-mart of the popular religions, and this process was in full swing at the commence ment of the Christian era."

form for the world's salvation were partly drawn from sources to which the builders of both religions had equally ready access. We may accept the view that each of these creeds incorporated certain ideas which had long fascinated the religious imagination of a considerable portion of south-western Asia. Yet while we recognize the palpable truth that Buddhism in the course of its expansion in foreign lands absorbed some alien beliefs which were important factors in determining the course of its subsequent development, we are by no means obliged to assume that there was a dissolution of continuity between the old Buddhism and the new. In spite of the differences and contrasts that undoubtedly exist between the primitive Buddhism of the Pali canon and the mature (or, as some would say, degenerate) Buddhism which we find in the later Mahayanist schools, we are not obliged to accept the conclusion that the two Buddhisms are separated from one another by an unbridged and fathomless chasm. We should be warned against any such conclusion by our knowledge of the fact, vouched for by the Chinese pilgrims, that for many centuries after the new teachings had risen into prominence (shortly after or shortly before the beginning of the Christian era) the adherents of the two systems studied their scriptures side by side within the great religious university of Nalanda, and lived harmoniously together in many monasteries. Even in the matter of language there was no real cleavage. The rather prevalent idea that Pali was exclusively the sacred language of the Hinayana and that Sanskrit was exclusively the sacred language of the Mahayana is far from being strictly accurate, though it is true that by the adoption of Sanskrit as their literary vehicle the Mahayanist doctors were better able to move away from the strict orthodoxy of the Pali canon than if they had been obliged to adhere to the Pali language.

It may not be always possible to trace every link in the evolutionary chain, and in some cases it is quite conceivable that the evolution would never have taken place had not the Buddhist organism reacted to stimuli from a non-Buddhist environment; but it would be difficult to point to many characteristic doctrines of the Mahayana of which at least the germs cannot be traced in the earlier or later speculations of the Hinayanist schools.

The Mahayana

The student of Buddhism is obliged at an early stage of his investigations to recognize two important facts. One is that the Mahayana is not a single homogeneous system with a definite formulated creed. It is erroneous to ascribe its foundation to any single man or even to any single group of religious teachers [30]; and the uniformity which was lacking at the commencement was never achieved at any subsequent period. The Mahayana includes a large number of schools and sects, each of which, as we have already noticed, compiled its own canon; and some of these sects came to differ from one another much more widely than the early Mahayanists differed from some of the Hinayanists of their own time. The other important fact, the significance of which is less generally recognized, is that the Hinayana itself was subdivided into various schools which, though they all professed adherence to the canon, and all regarded it as their ultimate authority, did not always agree in their interpretations of its meaning [31]. These schools were not the result of a disintegration of Buddhism; rather were they a proof of its vitality. Eighteen is the traditional number of the schools that had come into existence before A3oka's time, and in name at least they existed for many centuries after his death. As late as the year 559 of our era we hear of a monastery which contained representatives of all the eighteen Hinayanist schools a very remarkable testimony to Buddhist tolerance [32].

The schools of the Hinayana debated among themselves many questions of great philosophical and religious importance which Buddha was supposed to have answered enigmatically or not at all, and they were founded as much on attempts to penetrate the mystery of the Master's cryptic silence as on varying interpretations of his spoken word. It is in the discussions of these schools, orthodox and unorthodox, not in Babylonian poetry or prophecy or in the missionary activity of a St. Thomas, that we must look for the ultimate sources of the principal streams that flow into the ocean of Mahayanist belief. As for that ocean itself, let us admit that if it is fringed with many a sheltered inlet and quiet haven, it also contains

---

[30] Dr Timothy Richard describes the Asvaghosha of the Ch i-hsin-lun as "the founder" of the Mahayana (The Awakening of Faith, p. xiv., and The New Testament of Higher Buddhism, pp. 37, 38, and 50). With regard to some of the theories and suggestions of Dr Richard and Mr A. Lloyd, see the author's article on " Buddhist and Christian Origins " in The Quest, October 1912.

[31] See above, p. 35, footnote 2.

[32] See Journal of the Pali Text Society, 1904-5, p. 67.

Buddhist China

wreck-strewn rocks and perilous shallows and profound waters that no man can fathom. But which of all the streams that issue from the fountain of the religious thought and emotion of mankind does not flow at last into an ocean that is very much like this?

No attempt can here be made to follow the intricate windings of Mahayanist speculation, but a brief glance at certain aspects of Buddhist thought in a few of its successive stages will help us to understand the point of view here set forth.

The records of primitive Buddhism leave unanswered many interesting questions relating to the beliefs of the historical Buddha, but their testimony leaves no room for doubt as to the general trend of his teachings. He taught his disciples to discard what he conceived to be false and harmful ideas concerning the human personality or "soul," and to pursue a definite method of self-culture and self-discipline which would lead to the annihilation of sorrow, the extinction of the "three-fold fire" of delusion, desire, and malevolence, and the attainment of the passion less serenity of "arahantship." Certain ultimate problems with which philosophy loves to grapple and which some other religious teachers profess to have solved through "revelation" were deliberately set aside by Buddha as having nothing to do with his system and outside the scope of his teachings.

PAGODA, WESTERN HILLS.

ARCHWAY IN GROUNDS OF OLD SUMMER PALACE, WESTERN HILLS.

Buddhist China

Teachings of Buddha

It is not to be supposed, indeed, that Buddha who, let us remember, was a philosopher in a nation of philosophers ignored the existence of such ultimate problems. On the contrary, it is clear that he had himself deeply pondered many profound questions which for frankly-stated reasons he refused to discuss with his disciples[33]. It is one of the canonical texts that tells us the story of how Buddha once plucked a few leaves from a tree and asked his disciples whether these leaves which he had plucked, or all the leaves on all the trees of the neighbouring grove, were the more numerous. "The leaves on all the trees of the grove," they said, "are far more numerous than those in the hand of the Holy One." "Even in such measure," said Buddha, "are the things which I have learned, and have not communicated to you, more numerous than those of which I have spoken. And why, my disciples, have I not spoken to you of these things?[34]" And he goes on to explain that it is because the subjects on which he maintains silence have no relation to the truths which it is his mission to impart the truths concerning sorrow and the cessation of sorrow and have no bearing on that process of self-discipline whereby he would have his disciples achieve the destruction of passion, illusion, and ignoble desire, and attain the inward illumination and perfect peace which culminate in Nirvana.

The canonical books contain many stories similar in significance to that about the leaves of the trees. Among those which are accessible to English readers may be mentioned the passages dealing with the questions of Potthapada to each of which Buddha makes reply: "that is a matter on which I have expressed no opinion[35]"; the questions of Vacchagotta, whose problems are greeted by Buddha with perfect silence;[36] and the questions of Malunkyaputta, who insists eagerly and almost rudely that Buddha should either solve the problems propounded or frankly confess his ignorance yet the Master does neither.[37]

3333 " We can scarcely help forming the impression that it was not a mere idle statement which the sacred texts preserve to us, that the Perfect One knew much more which he thought inadvisable to say, than what he esteemed it profitable to his disciples to unfold"
(Oldenberg, Buddha, Eng. trans., 1882, p. 208).
34 See the Samyutta Nikaya, as quoted in L. de la V. Poussin, Bouddhisme, p. 58.
35 See Rhys Davids, Dialogues of the Buddha, pt. i. pp. 254-5.
36 See Olderiberg, op. cit., pp. 272-3.
37 See Oldenberg,, op. cit., pp. 117-122; Warren,, Buddhism in Translations, 1906, pp. 274-6.

Reginald Fleming Johnston

The "Silence" of Buddha

Buddha's "silence" about matters on which he knew that speech would only lead to misunderstandings may be compared with the somewhat similar attitude of another Asiatic sage who lived in Buddha's own time, though neither was known to the other. Confucius was born about twelve years after Buddha, and survived him about four years[38]. We are told that a disciple once pressed him for an answer to the question as to whether the dead retain consciousness. Like Buddha, but not for Buddha's reasons, Confucius declined to give a direct reply. He merely observed that if he said "yes," this might lead to unnecessary extravagance in sacrifices and funerals, and thus the living would be neglected for the sake of the dead; and that if he said "no," filial piety might decay, and the bodies of the dead might be treated with disrespect. Hence he left the problem unsolved[39]. Perhaps a more remarkable passage is that in which his disciple Tzu-kung spoke of the difference between the ready frankness with which Confucius expounded his social and ethical principles and the reticence which he observed in discoursing about metaphysical subjects and the law of God[40]. According to the Chinese commentators, this passage means that Confucius spoke freely to all his disciples on such subjects as he thought were suited to their capacities, but only allowed a chosen few to share his thoughts on problems of a deeper kind[41].

A Parable

We might define the attitude of Buddha towards the ultimate problems on which he kept silence by the use of a simple parable. The way of Buddha is a road along which all who wish to accept him as their guide may travel safely to the supreme blessedness of sainthood the ineffable

---

38 Buddha, c. 563 to c 483 B.C.; Confucius, 551-479 B.C.

39 Confucius would have agreed with our own philosopher Caird, who warned us that "the belief in immortality may easily become an unhealthy occupation with a future salvation, which prevents us from seeking for salvation here " (The Evolution of Religion, 1893, ii. 243).

40 T'ien-Tao. The passage occurs in Lun Yu, bk. v. ch. xii.

41 Both Buddha and Confucius would have approved of the words of Plotinus " Readers of Chinese literature will remember that the founder of Taoism (whose great and lonely figure is but dimly visible through the mists of the Tao-te-ching) was even less willing than were Confucius and Buddha to discuss matters which were beyond the reach of verbal analysis. ("The Tao which can be expressed in words is not the eternal Tao; the name which can be uttered is not its eternal name.") Gf. Sextus-Pythagoricus: " Wise is the man who even in silence honours God, knowing why he is silent "; and St. Augustine: (si dixi non est quod dicere volui." " Of Thee," says Hooker in his fine prayer, our fittest eloquence is silence."

state of the arahant. But there are pleasant meadows and seductive gardens within sight of the road, and amid the trees and flowers there are winding pathways that lead into many a trackless forest and deadly morass. Beyond these there rises a many-pinnacled range of glorious mountains, whose snowy peaks seem to touch the heavens, and whose shining cliffs are a perpetual challenge to the stout-hearted way farer. "I long," he says, "to explore those forests and to scale those mountain heights." "Yes," says his guide, "there are wonderful secrets hidden in those dark forests, and there is a splendour in those distant hills. But if you step aside to wander among those trees and flowers, and to solve the mystery of forest and mountain, you will lose sight of the road which I have made for you. Who will lead you safely through those fens and marshes and over those pitiless crags? Where will you, in your stumblings, come across another path that will bring you safely to your journey's end?"

A fair reply would be that bold and enquiring spirits have always risked the danger of failure and disaster in the past and will continue to do so in the future. So long as there are heights that remain unsealed, the dauntless spirit of man will try to scale them. The fact that Buddha discouraged his disciples from attempting to find a way to the shining pinnacles that looked down upon them from afar off did not have the result of keeping Buddhist philosophy in the plains. High up among the snows of thought, adventurous Western mountaineers have found the footsteps of Buddhist explorers who reached those heights long before them: and perhaps there are some glittering peaks that have yielded their secrets to none but Buddhist climbers.

If Buddha discouraged his followers from ascending the perilous heights of metaphysical speculation, there was one question of pressing interest which could not be ignored, though it was a subject on which both speech and silence were liable to mislead. This was the question of the existence or non-existence of a permanent entity in human personality.

The "Chariot" Passage

It must be admitted at once that the ordinary soul-theories current in Buddha's own time were by him uncompromisingly rejected. There are several passages in the sacred books which, if they correctly embody the belief of Buddha himself, seem to indicate not only that he rejected all soul-theories that had been held or suggested in the past, but also that his teachings were incompatible with any soul-theory that human ingenuity might excogitate in the future. Such is the well-known "chariot" passage at the beginning of the Milinda Dialogues[42], which seems to leave us no way of escape from the conclusion that just as a chariot is merely a name given to a collection of wheels, spokes, pieces of wood, and other materials, put together in such a way as to make them serve a certain useful purpose, so a man is nothing but a bundle of skandhas[43] or integration of grouped "elements" (sensations, perceptions, and the like), and ceases to exist when those "elements" fall apart[44].

An even more uncompromising passage is to be found in one of the works belonging to the Chinese translation of the Hinayana Abhidharma[45]. It describes a visit paid by a certain king to a learned monk[46].

"I have come," he said, "to ask you about a matter which perplexes me. All the other monks I have visited are full of words, but they tell me nothing to the purpose. You, I am sure, are an exceptional monk, and will readily solve my difficulty. What is it your majesty wishes to know?" asked the monk. "I want you to tell me," said the king, "whether the soul is or is not distinct from the body." "That is a question which admits of no reply," said the monk. "This is not fair," said the king; "why will you not give me a plain answer to a plain question?" "Well" said the monk, "it is my turn to be the questioner. I, too, am in doubt about something. All the other kings whom I have questioned are very talkative people, but your majesty is an exceptional monarch, and I believe you will readily give me a straight answer." "Ask your question," said the king. "I want your

---

42 See S.B.E., xxxv. 43-5. For Chinese versions, see Har. xxiv. vol. viii. pp. 45, 54.

43 The skandhas (Chinese wu-yun) are the five aggregates " which compose a living being (see Warren, Buddhism in Translations, pp. 487-96). A somewhat similar idea found its way into Taoist specula tion (see L. Giles, Taoist Teachings, 1912, p. 23).

44 The " chariot " passage is not quite so conclusive against the soul-theory as the unwary reader may suppose. To use the words of James Ward in his Realm of Ends, 1911, pp. 101-2, "The whole is more than the sum of its parts that is the cardinal characteristic of evolution as understood by the pluralist. A unity that is not more than its constituent elements is no real unity at all: it is only a formal or mathematical whole. All real synthesis entails new properties which its component factors in their previous isolation did not possess." Cf. also Dr Sanday in his Personality in Christ and in Ourselves, 1911, p. 20: "There is a Self within the Self. There is a something within us which is not either foot or hand or eye, which is not either reason or emotion or will, but which binds together all these various organs and faculties in one. For personality we want something more than the mere congeries of thoughts and impulses and appetites and passions which go to make up the individual man."

45 See Har. xxii. vol. x. p. 108 (B.N. 1267).

46 The names of king and monk (Pi-lin-t o and Lung-chun) are suspiciously like Milinda and Nagasena (Ndga is the Chinese Lung), from which it might be inferred that this story comes out of the Milinda Dialogues. But it does not appear in the Pali original as translated by Rhys Davids; moreover, in the Chinese version of the dialogues the names of king and monk are given as Mi-Ian and Na-hsien.

majesty to tell me what the mangoes in your palace-garden taste like. Are they bitter or are they sweet?" "I haven t any mango-trees in my garden," said the king. The monk looked at the monarch with a severe countenance. "This is not fair, your majesty," he said. "Why don t you give me a plain answer to my question?" "But," said the king, "how can I tell you about the taste of my mangoes if I have no mango-trees in my garden?" "Well, it is just the same in the matter of the soul," said the monk. "There is no such thing: so what was the use of asking me whether it was distinct or not distinct from the body?"

Soul-Theories

Those of us who feel rather crushed by the climax to this quaint little dialogue may console ourselves with the reflection that the monk was only voicing the opinion of a school though that school was for a long time regarded as the citadel of orthodoxy. Buddha himself is never represented as having disposed of the soul question in so thorough-going a fashion as did the monk with his analogy of the non-existing mangoes. A foremost exponent of Buddhism has told us that this religion "stands alone among the religions of India in ignoring the soul.[47]" Would it not be more accurate to say that Buddhism ignored the soul as a quasi-material entity which had its dwelling in the physical body and flew away from it at death? That Buddha denied the existence of this kind of soul and therefore rejected all the soul-theories which found popular support in the India of his day is undeniably true; but there is much to be said for the view that he had a loftier soul-theory or rather self-theory of his own.

---

[47] Rhys Davids, Dialogues of the Buddha, pt. i. p. 242. He adds that " the vigour and originality of this new departure are evident from the complete isolation in which Buddhism stands, in this respect, from all other religious systems then existing in the world." Cf. also ibid., pp. 188-9.

Reginald Fleming Johnston

HSI-YU MONASTERY, CHIHLI.

TOMBS OF MONKS, HSI-YU MONASTERY.

Buddhist China

A story which gives us a hint of Buddha's true meaning is that which tells us how the wandering ascetic Vaccha asked what became of the Tathagata after death that is, what is the state of the sage who has passed away from ordinary human life after having attained Nirvana. Does Nirvana (a blessed state attainable in this life) result, after death, in total extinction, or does it lead to a different state of being? To this question Buddha replies by telling Vaccha that he is trying to probe a very deep mystery which only the wise can comprehend. "You will hardly understand it," he says, "you having different views, endurance, inclinations, efforts, and teaching." But he attempts a veiled explanation; and after declaring that everything material will be left behind at death, says that the Tathagata "when thus liberated from the category of materiality, is deep, immeasurable, difficult to fathom, like the vast ocean.[48]" 1

A very similar story is told about the king of Kosala and the learned nun Khema. The king asks the nun whether the Tathagata the liberated sage who has attained Nirvana and has passed away from earth does or does not still exist. The nun replies that it is not correct to say of the Tathagata that he still exists; nor is it correct to say that he does not exist; nor is it correct to say that he both exists and does not exist. After some further discussion the nun observes that the great ocean is deep, immeasurable, unfathomable. The being of the Tathagata can no longer "be gauged by the measure of the corporeal world; he is deep, immeasurable, unfathomable as the great ocean."

That this reply of the nun Khema was recognized as thoroughly orthodox is shown by the care taken to represent Buddha as having given her words the stamp of his approval; for the story goes on to say that the king repeated his question in an interview with Buddha himself, and that the Master's reply was word for word identical with the reply previously given by the nun[49].

---

[48] See the Aggi-Vacchagotta-sutta, quoted by Dr. F. Otto Schrader in the Journal of the Pali Text Society (1904-5), pp. 165-6, and by Warren, op. cit., pp. 123-8. Dr Schrader has ably argued against the theory that, according to Buddha's own teaching, Nirvana was followed by annihilation. He observes that "we are not entitled to say that Buddha denied the soul, but only that for him duration in time was duration of a flux and not immutability in any sense, not the stability of a substance." The doctrine of anatta (no soul) "embraces the five khandas or constituent parts of nature, not more. ... It was the Buddha and no one else who made the doctrine of anatta a moral principle, and that not by denying the Absolute One, but presupposing it as the true self, the only reality."

[49] See Oldenberg, op. cit., pp. 278-80. It is interesting to note that Western mystics also speak of in vastissimum divinitatis pelagus navigare.

Personality

We must beware of supposing that these comparisons of the deceased Tathagata with the "deep immeasurable ocean" indicate nothing more than a kind of vague pantheism, and imply the utter extinction of the human personality. The crux of the whole problem is this very word "personality." If we knew what personality was, we should possess a key that would unlock some of the deepest mysteries before which humanity stands baffled. It is in vain to probe the secret of Buddha's deepest thoughts on this subject; yet perhaps the meaning of such passages as those above quoted will become clearer to us when we compare them with the utterances of some of those Western thinkers who (often unknown to themselves) are Buddha's philosophical kinsmen. "Couldst thou annihilate thyself for a moment," said Eckhart, "thou wouldst possess all that God is in himself.[50]" According to the mystic's psychology, as an eloquent writer of our own time tells us, it is an error to regard consciousness of self as the measure of personality. "The depths of personality are unfathomable, as Heraclitus already knew; the light of consciousness only plays on the surface of the water.[51]" It is of interest to find here a parallel drawn between the real (as distinct from the phenomenal) personality and the deep ocean precisely the same parallel as that employed by Buddha. "So far is it from being true," continues the English thinker, "that the self of our immediate consciousness is our true personality, that we can only attain personality, as spiritual and rational beings, by passing beyond the limits which mark us off as separate individuals. Separate individuality, we may say, is the bar which prevents us from realizing our true privileges as persons."

The False Ego

These words are, I believe, in entire consonance with the authentic thought and utterance of the Buddha. It is very necessary, no doubt, to guard against the rash application to the philosophical notions of ancient

---

50 Eckhart's position, like that of the writer of the Theologia Germanica and such mystics as Blake (annihilate the Selfhood in me"), is perhaps nearer to that of the Upanishads than it is to the position of Buddha. It is very necessary to avoid reading into Buddhism meanings which are Vedantist and not Buddhist; yet Dr Coomaraswamy is undoubtedly justified in his remark that " through all Indian schools of thought there runs like a golden thread the fundamental idealism of the Upanishads the Vedanta." He is right to make no exception of Buddhism,, for the golden thread is not missing from the woven fabric of Buddhist thought.

51 Dr W. R. Inge's Christian Mysticism (2nd ed.), p. 30. Of. also Underhill, Mysticism, pp. 507-8, et passim.

Buddhist China

India terms which have acquired a special significance in Western thought; but it may nevertheless be confidently maintained that there is a close association between the Buddhist idea of a personality liberated from the phenomenal ego and the belief of Western mystics and others in a transcendental self freed from the limitations of temporal individuality[52].

Speaking of the false ego, "a half-way abstraction of the ordinary understanding, a bastard product of bad metaphysics and bad science," the English writer last quoted observes that Christianity from the very first rejected it[53]. It is an instructive fact that several centuries before the birth of Christianity this same "bastard product of bad metaphysics "had already been rejected and cast out by the great thinker who founded Buddhism.

---

[52] As Mr G. R. S. Mead observes in a recent essay (The Quest, iii. G69), it would be convenient if we " could have some satisfactory term to distinguish the transcendental or spiritual self (what is sometimes called the mystical I), the fundamental being or life beyond subject and object,, from the ever-changing me which Buddhism insists quite rightly on regarding as the impermanent ego." The Buddhist view of the ego is close to that of several prominent thinkers of our own day, besides those mentioned in the text. Cf. } for example, F. C. S. Schiller (the apostle of Humanism) in his Riddles of the Sphinx, 1910 ed., pp. 275-6.

[53] Dr VV. R. Inge,, Personal Idealism and Mysticism, 1907, p. 103.

IV. The Ideals Of Hinayana And Mahayana

The reflections contained in the foregoing chapter may help the reader to understand the significance of the statement that the numerous schools of the Hinayana were founded partly on the results of the discussions of questions to which Buddha was supposed to have given enigmatic replies, and partly, also, on different interpretations of his mysterious silence. It was further pointed out that in the discussions and disputes of the Hinayana schools, orthodox and unorthodox, we may trace the origin of most of the characteristic beliefs of the Mahayana[54]. Let us now glance briefly at the growth of three of those beliefs the belief in the divinity of Buddha, the belief in the efficacy of faith, and the belief in saviour-bodhisats.

The beginnings of the gradual process of the deification of the great Indian teacher may be traced in the earliest records of primitive Buddhism for the trustful reverence shown towards their much-loved Master by all his disciples w r as not far removed from religious adoration. We may cite the enthusiastic words of the disciple Sariputta.

"Now the venerable Sariputta came to the place where the Exalted One was, and having saluted him, took his seat respectfully at his side, and said: Lord! such faith have I in the Exalted One, that methinks there never has been, nor will there be, nor is there now any other, whether wanderer or brahmin, who is greater and wiser than the Exalted One that is to say, as regards the higher wisdom[55]. "

The Master meets his disciple's enthusiasm in a spirit of gentle irony. "You have burst forth into a song of ecstasy, Sariputta," he says, "but how do you know that there never has been and never will be any greater or wiser teacher than I am?" And then in the Socratic manner he cross-examines Sariputta on the meaning of his words, and compels him to admit that he does not really know "the hearts of the Able Awakened Ones that have been, and are to come, and now are. He only knows the lineage of the faith."

In another canonical dialogue we hear of a "young householder" who went to Buddha and begged him to empower one of his disciples to

---

54 See above, pp. 40-42.
55 Rhys Davids, Dialogues of the Buddha, pt. ii. p. 87.

perform a miracle, that thereby all the people might recognize him as their lord. "This is a prosperous place," he said, "crowded with people devoted to the Exalted One. It were well if the Exalted One were to give command to some brother to perform, by power surpassing that of ordinary men, a mystic wonder." If Buddha would do this, he added, it would increase the devotion with which the people regarded him[56]. But the Master refuses to perform common miracles or to empower others to perform them; the greatest and most wonderful thing that can be shown even by a Buddha is the way that leads to arahantship, the self-discipline that ends in the extirpation of the roots of all sorrow[57].

Buddha and Miracles

This dialogue contains one of the most deservedly famous of Buddhist stories that which narrates how a certain monk by the exercise of miraculous powers ascended to the various heavens ruled over by the gods of the Hindu pantheon, in the hope of obtaining from those mighty beings an answer to a profound metaphysical problem. One after another, all confessed their inability to solve it, each group of deities referring the monk to the group that was "more potent and more glorious than we. They will know it."

---

[56] Dialogues of the Buddha, pt. i. p. 276.

[57] " As usual; the Buddha is represented as not taking the trouble to doubt or dispute the fact of the existence of [miraculous] powers. He simply says that he loathes the practice of them; and that a greater and better wonder than any or all of them is education in the system of self-training which culminates in Arahantship. There is no evidence of a similarly reasonable view of this question of wonders having been put forward by any Indian teacher before the Buddha." Rhys Davids, op. cit., pt. i. p. 272. In this connection it is of great interest to note the new attitude which some Christian theologians are beginning to take up with regard to the "miraculous" aspects of Christianity. Miracles, says the Rev. J. M. Thompson, "are a useful means of rousing and reviving popular religion of a lower type. But to any high religious experience they are most often a hindrance and a distraction. So we may sum up the case by saying that the critical conclusion, miracles do not happen, finds a welcome waiting for it in the religious experience (miracles do not matter. And faith is set free to reconstitute its world with greater sincerity both towards history and towards religion." Through Facts to Faith, 1912, p. 75. Cf. the Rev. A. C. Headlam's observation that Jesus of Nazareth disappointed some people because He would not work any conspicuous miraculous sign. There was no thaumaturgic display such as the Messiah, according to them, might be expected to make. He would not let them make Him king the reason, of course, being that He had a far higher and more spiritual aim than anything that they understood " Miracles: Papers and Sermons, p. 49 (Longmans, Green & Co.: 1911).

PAGODA AT HSI-YU MONASTERY, CHIHLI.

Buddhist China

Brahma

After passing through all the heavens from the lowest to the highest, he comes at last to the gods of the retinue of Brahma; even they, however, like all the lesser gods, confessed their ignorance. "But there is Brahma, the great Brahma," they said, "the Supreme One, the Mighty One, the All-seeing One, the Ruler, the Lord of all, the Controller, the Creator, the Chief of all, appointing to each his place, the Ancient of days, the Father of all that are and are to be! He is more potent and more glorious than we. He will know it[58]."Then the monk approaches the great Brahma, arid once more states his problem; but the great Brahma, anxious to escape the humiliation of confessing that there are mysteries beyond the reach of even so mighty and glorious a god as himself, tries to evade the question. When the monk insists upon a direct answer, Brahma at last takes him aside and makes an admission which he was ashamed to make in the presence of the assembled deities. Even he, the great Brahma, the Controller, the Ancient of days, the Father of all that are and are to be, is unable to solve the problem. He bids the monk go to Buddha, and chides him for having vainly sought an answer from the mere gods. "Go you now, return to the Exalted One, ask him the question, and accept the answer according as he shall make reply."

The Buddhists, let us remember, did not deny the existence of the Hindu gods, but they regarded them as limited in knowledge and power, as liable to rebirth in a lower sphere, as unemancipated from change and illusion, and as debarred (so long as they remained gods) from the attainment of supreme wisdom and felicity. To all such beings Buddha, and indeed every arahant, was immeasurably superior, for arahantship is a state which far transcends in glory the highest of the heavens, and to which the greatest of the gods cannot aspire. But to withhold the title of god from a being that is wiser and greater than all the gods is to place an arbitrary limitation on the idea of god head; therefore the elevation of Buddha to a loftier sphere than that assigned to Brahma, the mightiest of the known gods, had an inevitable result which might easily have been foreseen. The problem of the Mahayanists was to deify Buddha without depriving Buddhahood of what may be termed its superdivinity; and the

---

58 Dialogues of the Buddha, pt. i. p. 281.

obvious solution was so to exalt the conception of godhead as to make it include the conception of Buddhahood.

Salvation by Faith

We may say, then, that the deification of Buddha, though it is a characteristic feature of the Mahayana, was already implicit in the dogmatics of the primitive Buddhists. Similarly, the notion of the efficacy of faith a notion which in certain Mahayanist sects has become all-important is easily traced to Hinayanist origins. Sariputta's "song of ecstasy,[59]" already referred to, is simply a declaration of faith in one who is described as the greatest and wisest of teachers. Here, indeed, we have no hint of the later doctrine of salvation by faith alone. Perhaps one of the earliest passages in which this doctrine is suggested is to be found in the Milinda Dialogues, which are Hinayanist but extra-canonical that is to say, they were not put together until after the canon had been closed. One of the questions which King Milinda puts to the monk Nagasena is as follows:

"'You people say, Nagasena, that though a man should have lived a hundred years an evil life, yet if, at the moment of death, thoughts of the Buddha should enter his mind, he will be reborn among the gods. This I don t believe. And thus do they also say: By one case of destruction of life a man may be born in purgatory. That, too, I cannot believe.'

"'But tell me, O king, would even a tiny stone float on the water without a boat? '

"'Certainly not.'

"' Very well; but would not a hundred cart loads of stones float on the water if they were loaded in a boat?'

"'Yes, they would float right enough.'

"'Well, good deeds are like the boat.'"[60]

Buddhist Ethics

This little fragment throws an interesting light on certain popular Buddhist beliefs of the time. It indicates that when the book was written the ordinary lay Buddhist looked forward to a re-birth in one of the age-long but not eternal "heavens" rather than to the more exalted state of

---

[59] See p. 57.
[60] S.B.E., xxxv. 123-4.

Buddhist China

Nirvana. There is, indeed, reason to believe that even in Asoka's time this was in full accordance with the unwritten Buddhism of the lay masses as distinct from the canonical Buddhism of the cloistered philosophers[61]. Neither "heaven" nor "purgatory" was a Mahayanist invention or innovation[62]. The passage just quoted shows us, however, that the king was not prepared to swallow certain tenets of popular Buddhism without a grimace: indeed he, the unconverted layman, shows himself actually more orthodox more in sympathy with the philosophical Buddhism of the canon than his monkish preceptor. Like Buddha himself, he disbelieves, for example, in the efficacy of death bed repentance. According to strict Buddhist teaching, there is no way of escape from the law that as a man sows, so shall he reap. Man is master of his fate, but the past cannot be annulled, any more than it can be lived over again. The effects of the past live in the present, and the future will be moulded by the thoughts and acts of to-day[63]. No "unearned" supernatural grace, no priestly absolution, no magical rites or sacramental ceremonies, can accelerate the attainment of a state of blessedness: nor can their absence retard it[64]. But from the passage quoted it is clear that there was already a falling away from the uncompromising sternness of primitive Buddhist ethics, and that the doctrine of salvation by faith alone had already become popular. That the Milinda Dialogues were composed at a time of doctrinal confusion is plainly indicated by the incomplete and evasive manner in which the monk Nagasena attempts to deal with the ethical problem raised by the king a problem, be it noted, which in one form or another has perplexed the minds of many to whom Buddhism is a sealed book. What the king found it difficult to believe was that a man who has lived a life of consistent sinfulness could win salvation merely by fixing his thoughts on Buddha during the last moments of his ill-spent life. If Buddha himself had been asked to deal with this point, he would have solved the difficulty by simply denying the truth of the alleged fact. Such a man, he would

---

61 Of. Asoka's Rock Edict, vi., and also the Rupnath Edict.

62 As eternal punishment is not taught by Buddhism in any of its forms, it is inaccurate to speak of Buddhist " hells." The Chinese term ti-yu is more appropriately rendered by the word " purgatory."

63 " We are spinning our fates. Every smallest stroke of vice and virtue leaves its never so little sear. . . . Nothing we ever do is in strict literalness wiped out." Thus spoke William James, echoing the teachings of Buddha.

64 It is hardly necessary to say that strict Buddhism would regard as gravely erroneous and immoral all such doctrines as that which condemns the unbaptized infant to an eternal (i limbo " and to exclusion from participation in the beatific vision. For the teaching of Catholic missionaries in China 011 this point, tee Father Wolferstan, Catholic Church in China, 11)09, pp. 405-6.

have said, is not saved that is to say, the inexorable law of retribution will not cease to work at the mere bidding of a tardy repentance. If the sinner has in very truth undergone a fundamental change of character, if his repentance is not due merely to fear or to a temporary quiescence of evil impulses owing to physical weakness or pain, then in his next life he will assuredly find himself in a less miserable and ignoble state than if no such fundamental change of character had taken place; but no death-bed repentance, however sincere, can save him from the necessity of expiating the wrong doing or wrong-thinking of the past. In some such way as this, we may assume, Buddha would have dealt with the problem of King Milinda. The monk Nagasena, however, evades the real point at issue. Instead of expounding the orthodox doctrine of "karma," he merely draws a rather inconsequential analogy between good deeds and a boat ignoring the fact that it is the alleged efficacy of faith, not the efficacy of good deeds, that is in question.

Nagasena

Now if we turn to the Chinese version of the Milinda Dialogues a version which was not made till the fourth or perhaps the fifth century of our era we find a much bolder and more explicit statement of the doctrine of the efficacy of faith than we have found in the Pali original. The first part of the Chinese version of the above-quoted dialogue agrees with the Pali that is to say, the king expresses his disbelief in the doctrine that the life-long sinner who turns religious on his death bed will for that reason be transported to heaven, and Na-hsien (Nagasena) in his reply makes use of the illustration of the stones and the ship.

"The ship is strong," he goes on to say," and will bear the weight of many large stones. So with a man and his sins. He may have a wicked nature, but if only he will once direct his thoughts earnestly towards Buddha,[65] he will not enter purgatory, but will be re-born in heaven. But the man who has done evil and is ignorant of the word of Buddha[66] is like the small stone that sank, he when he dies must descend to purgatory."[67]

---

[65] 一时念佛

[66] 不知佛经

[67] For the two incomplete Chinese versions of Milinda, see Har. xxiv. vol. viii. pp. 43 ff. (B.N. 1358). The dialogue quoted will be found on p. 50. . It is of course impossible to say from what text of Milinda the Chinese translator worked. It certainly differed from the Pali text now known (see S.B.E., xxxvi. Introduction).

Buddhist China

When it is remembered that this passage is taken from a work which belongs to the Hinayanist section of Buddhist literature, it will be realized that the doctrine of faith, though certainly inconsistent with the teachings of the historical Buddha, is not one which can be regarded as the exclusive property of the Mahayana[68].

We are forced to a similar conclusion even in respect of the most characteristic of all the Mahayanist teachings the important doctrines relating to the saving or redeeming power of the bodhisats. But it is in the peculiar emphasis given to the theory of the bodhisats that we must recognize the most pronounced contrast between the doctrinal systems of the smaller and the greater Vehicles; and some insight into the rival conceptions of arahantship and bodhisatship is essential to a clear understanding of the relative positions of the two great branches of Buddhist thought.

Sakyamuni taught that the ideal at which each man should aim is arahantship. An arahant is one who has travelled along the Eightfold Path that leads to peace, insight, and wisdom, and has emancipated himself from the "bonds" of doubt, delusion, sensuality, hatred, egotistic hopes and desires, pride, self-righteousness, ignorance. The arahant sums up in himself all the qualities and characteristics of the ineffable state of sambodhi the perfection of tranquil joy, passionlessness, harmony, enlightenment. Having once attained this mountain-summit, this clear pool beyond the jungle, this "island amid the raging waters," this "home of tranquillity," this blissful state of Nirvana, the arahant will never again be subject to the pains and sorrows of phenomenal existence. He has reached the "other shore" (to use a common Buddhist expression), and is saved for all eternity. This state of salvation, according to Sakyamuni, each man must reach through his own efforts. Buddha himself was merely the Master of Wisdom, under whose guidance men were to tread the Path. "Betake yourselves," he said, "to no external refuge. Hold fast to the truth as a lamp. Hold fast as a refuge to the truth. Look not for refuge to any one besides yourselves.[69]"

---

68 Salvation by faith is the distinguishing feature of what we may call the Amidist theology (see below, pp. 92 ff.).

69 Maha-parinibbana suttanta, S.B.E., xi. 38. In some important respects the Buddha would have found himself in much closer sympathy with Pelagius and Caelestius than with the orthodox Augustine, as is clear from his teaching that man is to rely on himself for his own spiritual development, and that he has in his own nature inherent capacity for moral progress. Moreover like Pelagius, a thousand years after him the Buddha was not in favour of an extreme asceticism. Pelagius was unconsciously repeating the wise counsel given long before by the Buddha when he said, " corpus non frangendum sed regendum est"

Bodhisatship

Mahayana Buddhism, on the other hand, discredits or dethrones the ideal of arahantship, and sets up, as much more worthy of reverence, the ideal of bodhisatship[70]. The bodhisat is one who contains within himself the essence, or rather the potentiality, of perfect knowledge. He is one who has registered a solemn vow (pranidhana) that he will become a Buddha for the sake of the world's salvation; but his approach to Buddhahood may be described as asymptotic, for he abstains from participation in eternal blessedness so long as there remains in the universe a single being who is still enmeshed in pain or misery. The arahant, complains the Mahayanist, saves no one but him self. He is like one who has been confined with others in a dungeon, and who, having found a secret way of escape, hastens to set himself at liberty, while callously leaving his fellow-prisoners in darkness and captivity. The bodhisat, on the contrary, is the embodiment of supreme unselfishness. Freedom and Nirvana are within his reach, but he will not avail himself of the fruits of his virtue and wisdom until all beings that exist in all the worlds have passed before him through the gateway that leads to liberty and utter bliss. The bodhisat may be said to possess in a supreme degree both the selfless benevolence as well as active goodness. He has solemnly dedicated him self to the service of all beings who stand in need of succour; and his infinite charity and compassion are such that he will suffer the most atrocious torments for aeons of time that is, through count less successive re-births if thereby he may save souls from pain. "I wish," he says, "to be food for the hungry, drink for the thirsty." He would fain become "a soother of all the sorrows of all creatures." He would be "a balm to the sick, their healer and servitor, until sickness come never again." He utterly resigns all thoughts of self. "My own being and my

---

[70] The word bodhisat (bodhlmttva essence of perfect enlightenment) is represented in Chinese by four characters, which in modern Pekingese are read p u-t i-sa-t o. This clumsy term is almost always written by Chinese authors in the abbreviated form p u-sa. In spoken English the letters p and t before a vowel are usually pronounced with a slight aspirate; the sound of the two Chinese characters p u-xa may therefore be appropriately rendered in English by the word pusa. Hence in these pages this word will be used to represent the Chinese transcription of the Sanskrit word bodhisattva. Similarly, in the case of the sacred hill or island which forms the subject of chapters xi.-xiii., the name Potala or Potalaka, which is represented in Chinese by characters bearing the Pekingese sounds p'u-t'o-lo-chia, and usually appears in the abbreviated form p'u-t'o, is rendered in this book by the word Puto. The first syllable of this word should be pronounced (approximately) as an Englishman would pronounce poo, as in the case of the first syllable of the word pusa. Apart from the two words Pusa and Puto, nearly all Chinese terms and names employed in this volume are transcribed in strict accordance with the system known as Wade s.

pleasures, all my righteousness in the past, present, and future, I surrender indifferently, that all creatures may win to their end.[71]" He would even commit sin, and take upon himself the inevitable consequences of sin, if by so doing he could alleviate the present or future sufferings of another. "It matters little if I am condemned to hell," he says, "if only I may save this sinner or assuage the misery of that suffering soul."

Selflessness

Mahayanist literature contains many fanciful stories analogous to the legends of the Christian saints which are intended to illustrate the self-sacrificing activity of those who have taken the vows of a bodhisat. One of these legends tells us of a monk who came, with begging-bowl in hand, to the house of a certain rich man. While he was waiting at the entrance he saw a tame goose enter the house and swallow a beautiful jewel. Of this incident the monk was sole witness. When the lord of the house entered the room he noticed that the jewel had vanished, and promptly assumed that the monk was the thief. Greatly enraged, he fell upon him with blows and curses. The monk endured his castigation with patience and in silence, when suddenly a servant appeared and reported the sudden and unexpected death of the goose. "Beat me no more!" said the monk. "I saw the goose swallow the jewel." "Why did you not tell me that at once?" asked the astonished master. "I was afraid that the goose would be killed," replied the monk. "Now it is dead I am free to speak.[72]"

---

71 The Bodhicharydvatara of Santi-Deva, trans, by L. D. Barnett (The Path of Light, p. 45: Wisdom of the East series).

72 I am unable to assign a date to the first appearance of this Chinese story, which occurs in a commentary on the Fo-i-chiao-ching. It is noteworthy that another version of the story is to be found in Arabic literature of the eighth century of our era. There we read of two Mohammedan " sceptics" who were unjustly accused of having stolen certain gems. It was known to the supposed culprits that the gems had been swallowed by an ostrich, and had they informed their accusers of this fact they would have escaped a flogging that nearly cost them their lives; but rather than make a statement which would endanger the life of the ostrich they preferred to suffer innocently in its place (E.R.E., ii. 189).

IN THE SHANG-FANG HILLS, CHIHLI.

PAVILION AT HSIAO HSI-T'IEN ("LITTLE HEAVEN"), CHIHLI.

Buddhist China

It is hardly necessary to say that such stories as these are not supposed to be taken too literally. They are fables, told for purposes of edification. The good Catholic is not expected to regulate his daily life in accordance with the ascetic practices of an Antony or a Suso; nor is the good Buddhist expected to conduct himself as though the interests of mankind were subordinate to those of dumb animals.

Arahantship

The Mahayanist ideal of the bodhisat who devotes himself, with utter disregard of his own interests, to the service of others certainly seems, at first sight, to be a loftier ideal than that of the Hinayanist arahant, who apparently has no higher aim in view than his own salvation; and if this conception of the relative ethical positions of the two systems is the true one, we shall be obliged to admit the justice of the claim of the Mahayanists that their system is the nobler of the two. But the matter is not to be disposed of so easily. In the first place, we must take note of the fact that the theory of bodhisatship is not peculiar to the Great Vehicle. In the Hinayana, bodhisatship is recognized as the state which immediately precedes the attainment of Buddhahood. Gotama himself is represented as having been a bodhisat up to the moment when, under the sacred Bo-tree, he became the "Awakened One." In the second place, no adherent of canonical Buddhism would admit that an arahant is entirely occupied with his own salvation and is careless of the interests of his fellow-men. On the contrary, the ideal of universal love and benevolence is inculcated in the canonical books in many beautiful and striking passages which unquestionably enshrine the authentic message of primitive Buddhism[73].

---

[73] In a recent translation of the Dhammapada (The Buddha's Way of Virtue, Wisdom of the East series, 1912) the following version of ch. xii. verse 166 appears on p. 45: " Even for great benefit to another let no man imperil his own henefit. When he has realized what is for his own good, let him pursue that earnestly." If this were the correct interpretation of the original Pali, and if the text as thus rendered were in accordance with the ethics of Buddhism, some of the strictures of the Mahayanists would be fully justified. But I strongly suspect that the translators have misapprehended the true meaning of this passage. Max Muller (S.B.E., x. 46) observes that attha (lit. "object") must here be taken in a moral sense, "as f duty rather than as advantage. " He therefore translates: (let no one forget his own duty for the sake of another s, however great; let a man, after he has discerned his own duty, be always attentive to his duty." It may be observed that all the various Chinese versions of the Dhammapada seem to have been made from texts which are not now in existence. The passage now under discussion is not exactly paralleled in any of the Chinese versions; but none of the Chinese passages which may be said to correspond to it can be made to bear the meaning ascribed to it in The Buddha's Path of Virtue. (For the Chinese books which correspond to the Dhammapada, see Har. xxiv. vols. v. and vi. [B.N. 1321, 1353, 1365, 1439]). According to the true canonical doctrine, the Buddhist seeks his own good, but is also bound to seek the good of others. (Ubkinnam attham carati; attano ca parassa ca, quoted by Mrs Rhys Davids, Buddhism, p. 121.)

Arahantship is "the state of one who possesses worthiness" worthiness of a kind that cannot be reconciled with any form of selfishness.

"Even as a mother watcheth over her only child," says the Sutta-Nipata "so let our hearts and minds be filled with boundless love for all creatures, great and small; let us practise benevolence towards the whole world, and let us set ourselves utterly free from all ill-will and enmity."

Elsewhere we read that "all the means that can be used as bases for doing right are not worth one-sixteenth part of the emancipation of the heart through love. That takes all those up into itself, outshining them in radiance and in glory.[74]"

Altruisn and Egoisn

Of all the passages in which Buddha is represented as having taught the duty of charity, perhaps the most interesting to Western readers is that in which he chides his disciples for neglecting to tend the sick. He closes his remarks with words which a French Catholic scholar describes as vraiment remarquables[75]: "If there be one of you who would wish to cherish me, let him go and cherish his sick comrade.[76]"

In finding fault with the Hinayanist ideal, the Mahayanist failed to realize that a selfish being could not become an arahant. Arahantship, as we have seen, consisted in a spiritual exaltation which transcended the limitations of temporal individuality. In what intelligible sense can a system which aims at the elimination of the phenomenal ego be described as egoistic? It is true, indeed, that the candidate for arahantship strove for the full realization of what we must call his transcendental self; but self-realization in the highest sense is far removed from selfishness, and, indeed, it necessarily involves self-sacrifice. The arahant could not have reached full spiritual development if he had failed to act in accordance with the principle that each man forms part of a spiritual whole of which all his fellow-men are also parts, and that to serve them is to enrich, while to neglect them is to impoverish, his own higher self. Whether it is

---

74 The Iti-vuttaka, 19. The translation is by Mrs Rhys Davids, op. cit., p. 229. Cf. also her remark on p. 243: The Buddha who devotes his life to helping mankind was termed, not Saviour, but Omniscient (sabbafmu) Buddha, To understand all, says a French epigram, is to forgive all. The Buddhist goes further; to understand all, is not only to forgive, but to give to give one's self through insight into other's need." Cf. also E.R.E., v. 234.

75 L de la V. Poussin, Bouddhisme, 1909,, p. 7.

76 Of. Matthew xxv. 40; and Al Ghazzali (T-$e Alchemy of Happiness: Wisdom of the East series), p. 104.

possible to bring about a reconciliation between altruism and egoism is a question which is still debated by Western philosophers. Herbert Spencer called it "the crux of all ethical speculation." We are assured by some that the altruistic and egoistic tendencies of human nature are "divergent developments from the common psychological root of primitive ethical sentiment," that both are unavoidable, and that they are ultimately irreconcilable. No higher category can be discovered, we are told, whereby their rival claims may be finally adjusted.[77] On the other hand, there are thinkers who argue eloquently in favour of the opposite and far more cheering view that "there is no self-expenditure without self-enrichment, no self-enrichment without self-expenditure. The ideals of self-culture and self-sacrifice, so far from being hopelessly contradictory, are inseparable, and unrealizable except as two aspects of the same process.[78]"

This, we may assume, is the view of twentieth-century Christianity at any rate, it is that of one of the most brilliant writers and thinkers in the Church of England to-day. Very similar was the belief of some of the old Roman philosophers. The Stoics, we are reminded by a recent authority, conceived an ideal of self-realization or self-culture which "was not and could not possibly be purely selfish or self-regarding, just because the self which the Stoic endeavours to realize is essentially the universal, and not what we should call the individual self at all.[79]"

Self-Renunciation

That self-advancement and social service, or if we prefer the extreme terms egoism and altruism, are not eternally opposed to one another, but are ultimately reconcilable, is the view which seems destined to prevail[80]. This being so, it is perhaps regrettable that those Buddhists who were

---

77 A. E. Taylor, Problem of Conduct, 1901, p. 183.

78 Dr W. R, Inge, Personal Idealism and Mysticism, 1907, p. 105.

79 James Adam, The Vitality of Platonism, 1911, p. 141.

80 It is hardly necessary to refer to the familiar speculations of such writers as Comte, Schopenhauer, Herbert Spencer, and Sir Leslie Stephen (Science of Ethics} on this subject. A more recent work by Delvolve (Rationalisme et Tradition) contains some brilliant suggestions; and the following remarks by James Ward in his Realm of Ends (1911) are significant: "Extreme as the selfishness of many may still be, and rare as is any whole-hearted enthusiasm for humanity, yet the progress already made is amply sufficient to show that the direction in which it has moved and is still moving points towards the ultimate conciliation of self-interest and the common good. This progress may seem small, partly because to us the time it has taken looks immense, and partly because it still falls indefinitely short of the ideal that we entertain " (p. 133).

dissatisfied with what they took to be the narrowness and selfishness of the ideal of arahantship did not content themselves with giving it a new and higher interpretation in the light of what they believed to be their own loftier conception of ethical values. Instead of doing this, they set it aside as morally contemptible, and replaced it by a new ideal of utter self-renunciation. The virtuous man was no longer to aim at arahantship, but at bodhisatship that is to say, he was to purge himself from the slightest taint of self-love or self-regarding interest, to devote himself, without the faintest thought of reward, to the service of all creatures, to sacrifice on behalf of others all personal ambitions, hopes, and desires, and to extend boundless sympathy and measure less love to all suffering beings.

The new ideal was a sublime one, but it was not without its practical disadvantages; and it necessarily produced momentous changes in the moral and religious outlook of the zealous Buddhist. The activities of the would-be arahant, however arduous they might be, were nevertheless believed to be within the scope of every man of properly disciplined will; arahantship, that is to say, was rooted in normal human nature, and therefore had an abiding ethical significance for ordinary humanity. The bodhisat, on the contrary, tended to draw ever farther and farther away from the world of mankind. "A being capable of purely altruistic actions alone," as Nietzsche said, "is more fabulous than the Phoenix." It is true that in the early days of the Mahayana the title of bodhisat was bestowed upon many saints of the Church who were known to have lived on earth as human beings, exceptional only in respect of learning and sanctity; and even at the present time the vows of a bodhisat are taken every year by scores of newly-ordained monks, who thereafter (at least in China) are respectfully addressed by their disciples and novices as ta-pusa ("great bodhisat"). But the speculative fancy of the Mahayanist creed-makers very soon created a broad line of demarcation between those humble persons who were merely stumbling along the stony paths of the preliminary stages of bodhisatship, and those serene and majestic beings, the bodhisattvas mahasattva[81], incalculable in number, who, having employed themselves for immeasurable ages in the merciful work of bringing suffering souls to salvation, were now invisible to mankind (except on the rare occasions when they incarnated themselves in human form), and were in direct personal communion with the supreme Buddhas. These great

---

81 The Chinese pusa maha-sa.

bodhisats, exalted far above ordinary humanity, gradually came to be regarded as partakers of the super celestial nature of the Buddhas themselves; indeed, in the view of some of the mystical schools of the later Mahayanists, all the Buddhas and all the bodhisattvas find ultimate unification in the Dharmakaya or Absolute One[82].

Celestial Bodhisats

Thus the human characteristics of the great bodhisats gradually disappeared in a blaze of celestial glory. From the twilight of mere humanity they emerged into the radiance of divinity. From being heroes among men they became the divine companions, and practically the equals, of the deified Buddhas[83]. Already in the first century of our era, and perhaps earlier, the bodhisats had come to be regarded as divine beings to be worshipped, rather than as supermen to be respected and imitated. Later dogmatic developments were associated with the idea of salvation by faith. According to the tenets of certain Mahayanist schools which to-day enjoy greater prosperity and influence than any others in China and Japan, the Buddhist who wishes to qualify for salvation need do no more than cultivate in himself an attitude of unquestioning faith in a divine saviour a celestial bodhisat who will receive his soul and conduct it to a blissful home in Paradise. The accumulated merits of the bodhisats are supposed to be so superabundant that each bodhisat is able to transfer immeasurable quantities of surplus merit to the account of sinful men, whose salvation is thus due not to any works or merit of their own, but solely to the merit transferred to them by the bodhisat who has endowed them with his saving grace. This theory of diverted merit, which nullifies the old law of retribution and directly contradicts Buddha's own teaching that each man must work out his own salvation, is one of the few Mahayanist doctrines

---

[82] The Dharmakaya is literally c Body of the Law," as distinct from Sambhogakaya the supramundane Body of Bliss, in which the Buddhas appear to the eyes of the saints, and Nirmanakaya the Illusory Body, in which the Buddhas appear to the eyes of men. A full discussion of the doctrine of the Trikaya or Three-fold Body of Buddha cannot be attempted here. The reader is referred to L. de la Vallee Poussin's contributions to Hastings E.R.E., and to his article in J.R.A.8., 1906, pp. 943 ff; and also to Suzuki's Outlines of Mahayana Buddhism. In connection with the Nirmanakaya, it may be noted that docetic tendencies made their appearance in Buddhist speculation at an early date, especially in the teachings of the heterodox or semi-Mahayanist Mahusanghika school (see Anesaki's article on "Docetism" (Buddhist) in E.R.E., iv. 835 ; and L. de la Vallee Poussiu, Bouddhiwne, p. 259).

[83] In Nepalese Buddhism there is a tendency for the bodhisats to be elevated to a position even more exalted than that of the divine Buddhas "bearing the same relation to the Buddhas as Sakyamuni bore to the arahants" (L. dela V. Poussin, E.R.E., i. 96).

which are not traceable to any source in primitive Buddhism[84]. In such forms of Buddhism as these, of which more remains to be said in succeeding chapters, there is an obvious tendency for morality to be subordinated to faith; and Buddhism, if it becomes more of a religion as the term is commonly understood is apt to become less effective as a practical guide of life.

The Two Vehicles

Yet it would be unjust to ignore the great beauty of many of the religious imaginings of the Mahayanists and the splendour of many of their conceptions. More catholic in its sympathies and interests than the older system, more accommodating to the weaknesses of human nature, less rationalistic in its ethic, the Mahayana undoubtedly owed much of its success to the fact that it could make a strong appeal to the religious emotions. In charging the arahant with being over-mindful of his own development and salvation and with ignoring the moral and spiritual condition of his fellow-men, the Mahayanists were hardly fair. But it must be admitted that the ethical content of the ideal of arahantship was peculiarly liable, from its nature, to suffer from undue compression or distortion in times of moral stagnation or decay. Like all other systems of self-culture and self-discipline, the way of arahantship, though well worthy of being trodden by the most magnanimous of saints, was nevertheless one which could be usurped by ignoble adventurers and made to subserve the unholy purposes of a mean-spirited selfishness.

Self-Culture and Self-Sacrifice

Perhaps both Hinayana and Mahayana were perilously liable to be exploited by extremists the one system, under unfavourable conditions, might seem to sanction the exaltation of an ideal of glorified selfishness;

---

84 The doctrine is practically identical with the Roman Catholic teaching concerning the theory of indulgences. The "virtue of indulgences/ says a Catholic writer, "outflows from the infinite merits" of Christ, the Virgin, and the Saints, "whose merits, heing superfluous in their own offering of the satisfaction due to divine justice, have remained in the spiritual arid common treasury of the Church " (Philip Hold's Catholic Doctrine and Discipline (London, 1896) p. 257). This theory of the " Treasure of the Church " (which consists primarily of the " merit and satisfaction " of Christ, but includes also the superfluous merit and satisfaction of the Blessed Virgin and the Saints") represents a comparatively late development of Catholic doctrine. It was not confirmed by the Pope (Clement VI.) till 1350, though it appeared more than a century earlier in the Summa, Theologiae of " the Irrefragable Doctor," Alexander Halensis, an Englishman.

the other set up an ideal of altruism which could never be realized under earthly conditions. On the whole, it can hardly be denied that the Mahayanists would have deserved greater honour than they have received at the hands of the moralists of later ages, if instead of unjustly denouncing arahantship as essentially selfish, they had resolutely set themselves to solve one of the most important and perplexing of all moral problems by showing us how the two ideals of arahantship and bodhisatship in other words, self-culture and self-sacrifice might be reconciled and made one. It is not difficult to see the lines on which such a reconciliation might take place. The arahant is one who has aimed at and has attained self-realization, whereas in bodhisatship all considerations of self are utterly quenched and destroyed. The difference seems immeasurable; but if we are careful to remember the distinction which Buddhism draws between the false personality and the true between the impermanent ego and the transcendental self- may we not say, after all, that the two ideals are essentially the same?

Reginald Fleming Johnston

TEMPLES ON THE SHANG-FANG HILLS, CHIHLI.

V. Buddhist Schools And Sects In China

To follow the varied fortunes of the numerous Mahayanist sects that have flourished on Chinese soil is a task which we may well leave to the religious historian. We, as mere pilgrims in the Buddhist China of to-day, must content ourselves with little more than some general knowledge of the Buddhism that enters into the lives of the religious laity at the present time and the Buddhism that is professed in the great mountain-monasteries.

The lines of sectarian demarcation are now almost obliterated or perhaps it would be truer to say that the great Dhyana (Chinese Ch'an) school has so extended its boundaries that in Buddhist China (or at least in Chinese monastic Buddhism) there is comparatively little territory left for it to conquer. It should be observed, however, that in some respects the victory of the Ch'an school has been more apparent than real. It was not the Ch'an alone, but rather the Ch'an in alliance with the Amidist schools[85], that victoriously encroached upon the territories of its rivals.

Bodhidharma

The Ch'an doctrines are supposed to be traceable to Buddha himself, and to have been handed down through twenty-eight patriarchs, of whom (as we saw in an earlier chapter[86]) Asvaghosha was the twelfth, Nagarjuna the fourteenth, and Bodhidharma the twenty-eighth. The last-named (P'u-t'i-ta-mo in Chinese, usually shortened to Tamo) arrived in China in the year 520, and seems to have died about nine years later. His Chinese home was the famous monastery of Shao-lin, situated at the base of the Shao-shih mountain, near Loyang, in the province of Honan. This monastery, which was founded in the last quarter of the fifth century of our era, is still the beautiful habitation of a group of Buddhist monks, but its once splendid buildings are now to a great extent ruinous. One of its greatest treasures is the stone in front of which Tamo is said to have sat in silent meditation. It is this Indian sage, this searcher of hearts and scorner of books, who is regarded as the founder, in China, of the Ch'an or

---

85 See pp. 92 ff
86 See above, pp. 29-32.

Contemplative school of Buddhism. "You will not find Buddha in images or books," was the teaching of the venerable Tamo. "Look into your own heart: that is where you will find Buddha."

Mysticism in East and West

The Chinese word for "heart," it should be noted, has a very complex significance, and we often come across religious or philosophical passages in which the word might more appropriately, though even then inadequately, be rendered by "mind.[87]" The Chinese term is hsin, and this may be regarded as the key-word of the Ch'an Buddhism which has for many centuries dominated Chinese religious thought. In reading the lives of the great Ch'an patriarchs and abbots we frequently meet with the curious expression shou hsin yin "to transmit, or to receive, the seals of the heart." This expression is used to denote what we might describe as the apostolical succession. Just as a civil magistrate when vacating his post hands over the tangible and material seals of office to the official who is to succeed him, so the Ch'an abbot when about to die transmits to his successor in religion the intangible and spiritual "seals of the heart."

Tamo's system has been described as "the Buddhist counterpart of the Spiritual Exercises of St. Ignatius Loyola "[88]; but there are other Christian saints and mystics with whom he may be compared even more fittingly. Tamo would have heartily approved of that reply which St. Francis of Assisi is said to have given to a monk who asked if he might be allowed to possess a psalter—

"Man can learn nothing but what he already knows. If to-day thou gettest a psalter, to morrow thou wilt want a breviary, and thou wilt end by sitting in thy chair like any prelate and saying, Hand me my breviary."

---

87 Cf. E. Underhill, Mysticism, p. 85.
88 Lloyd, Wheat among the Tares, p. 53,

Buddhist China

Bodhidharma
(Tamo)
from a rubbing from a Ming Dynasty stone tablet (dated 1624)
in the Shaolin Monastery, Honan.
(The original figure from which this is reduced is 4ft. 5 in. in height.)

No less readily would Tamo have welcomed a kindred spirit in St. Paul, who rejected "tablets of stone" in favour of "the fleshy tablets of the heart "; or in St. Augustine, who, in words which contain the essence of Tamo's own teaching, bade men look for truth in the depths of their own being: In te ipsum redi: in interiore homine habitat veritas. The same thought recurs in Richard of St. Victor's utterance: "If thou wishest to search out the deep things of God, search out the depths of thine own spirit.[89] "Similarly" spoke Hugo: "The way to ascend to God is to descend into oneself." Allowing for differences in terminology, this teaching harmonizes with the spirit that animates the contemplative school of Buddhism, as well as it harmonizes with the spirit of mystical Christianity[90]. "Sink into thyself and thou wilt find Him," says Eckhart. Find whom? Christ. "Sink into thyself and thou wilt find Him," says Bodhidharma. Find whom? Buddha.

Perhaps the "heart" theory of Tamo and his school is not quite so satisfactory as they imagined. It may be that a better knowledge of truth has been gained by looking outward at nature than by looking inward at one's own "heart "; or it may be that the most successful truthseeker combines both methods --methods which we Europeans may perhaps conveniently label as Platonic and Aristotelian. However this may be, it must be admitted that in China the results of Tamo's teachings have been both good and bad. On the one hand they are partially responsible for the decay of learning in the Chinese monasteries. Tamo's advice was taken too literally. Books were neglected, and monkish energy concentrated itself on ecstatic meditation. In many cases religious zeal died away for want of substantial nourishment, and there is reason to suspect that some of the monks who believed themselves to have attained the exalted state of mystical union were apt to confuse that state with the less honour able condition of physical somnolence[91]. On the other hand, the influence of Tamo and his successors undoubtedly tended to save Chinese Buddhism from the evils of priestcraft and "clericalism" and from a slavish worship of images and relics, dogmas, and sacred books. The great sutras of the Mahayana are, indeed, held in deep reverence by all Chinese Buddhists,

---

89 Cf. Dr W. Sanday's much-criticized theory that Jesus's "subliminal self" was the seat of his divinity or the medium through which he achieved oneness with the divine.

90 Cf. E. Underhill, Mysticism, pp. 56, 97, 103, 222-3.

91 Cf. E. Underhill, op, cit., p. 385.

Buddhist China

and images are to be found in all Buddhist temples including the gorgeous chapels attached to the great Ch'an monasteries; but these things are not regarded as ultimate objects of religious reverence except by those to whom spiritual religion is an unattainable experience. There are monks in China to-day who would not be sorry to see the temples cleared of every image that they contain; and there are many others who would plead for the retention of the images only for the sake of those simple-minded and unenlightened souls who cling to the material symbol because the truth that it symbolises is beyond their grasp.

The patriarch Tamo was succeeded by Hui-k'o (d. 593), Seng-ts'an (d. 606), Tao-hsin (d. 651), Hung-jen (d. 675), and Hui-neng (d. 713)[92]. Though the patriarchate is usually regarded as having come to an end with the death of Hui-neng, the sixth Chinese patriarch, this does not imply that there was any cataclysm in Buddhist fortunes in China at this time. Both before and after the eighth century of our era the Buddhists were, indeed, subjected to spasmodic and sometimes very severe persecutions at the hands of orthodox Confucianism, but the Chinese are an essentially tolerant people so far as religious beliefs, as such, are concerned, and most of the "persecutions" would scarcely be regarded as deserving of so disreputable a name if they had taken place in Western Europe instead of Eastern Asia.

Buddhist Subdivisions

The subdivision into sects which took place after the time of the sixth patriarch was not a consequence of any disruptive forces set in motion by Confucianism, but was due rather to the growth of what may be described as a sort of religious individualism within the pale of Buddhism itself, and to the fact that after the death of Hui-neng the leading Ch'an Buddhists separated into two branches the Northern and the Southern. The rivalry between the Wu Tsung the Five Sects that regarded Hui-neng and his predecessors as their common patriarchs was as a rule healthy and friendly, and it was not till comparatively recent times that a tendency towards reunion was brought about by the gradual decay of learning and of religious fervour in the monasteries.

---

92 The begging-bowl of Bodhidharma, which had been transmitted as token of investiture from patriarch to patriarch, is said to have been buried with Hui-neng.

The first and greatest of the Five Sects of the Ch'an school was and is the Lin-chi Tsung[93]. The writers of this school trace their descent from Hui-neng through Huai-jang, who was one of the first of that large company of distinguished monks who made their home on the Nan Yo or Southern Sacred Mountain, in the province of Hunan. Huai-jang is sometimes described as the Seventh Patriarch, and came to be regarded by his disciples as an incarnation of the great bodhisat Kuan-yin. He died in 744, and was succeeded by the patriarch Ma, commonly known as Tao-I (d. 788); by Huai-hai (d. 814); by Hsi-yim (d. about 850); and finally by I-hsuan (d. 867). It was from the name of I-hsuan's home (Lin-chi) that the sect derived the name by which it is known to Buddhist historians.

The remaining four sects w T ere the Hui-yang, the Fa-yen, the Yun-men, and the T'ao-tung all of which may be said to have come into existence (as separate sects) in the tenth century of the Christian era[94]. Of their patriarchs, full information is given us in the various compilations which occupy in Buddhist China a place similar to that of the Ada Sanctorum in Christendom.

Famous Religious Leaders

Emphasis is of course laid by the monkish chroniclers on the miracles and prodigies associated with their heroes, and personal peculiarities are lovingly depicted. Of Hui-chi (Hui-yang sect) we are told that from boyhood his heart had been set on a religious life. When his parents insisted upon his marriage, he knelt before them and implored them to allow him to enter the monkhood. He got his own way after he had deliberately broken two of his own fingers in token of his sincerity. Of Tao-I's personal appearance strange things are told. His secular name was Ma ("horse"), he walked like an ox, he had eyes like a tiger s, he had a tongue that reached beyond the tip of his nose, and a Buddhistic wheel (the "wheel of the law") was imprinted by nature on the soles of his feet. One of the most famous of the "ancestors" of the Ts'ao-tung sect was Hsi-ch'ien of the Rock, who lived as a recluse on the Nan Yo. He received titles of honour not only from the Emperor Te Tsung of the T'ang dynasty,

---

93 Like the other four sects, it belongs to the Southern branch. The Northern soon became extinct.

94 The ordinary Chinese terms for " Buddhist monk " are ho-shang and seng-jen. Nowadays the first of these is the term generally used by laymen and in ordinary conversation; the second is chiefly confined to books. At one time, however, when the principal Ch'an sects were the Lin-chi and the Ts'ao-tung, ho-shang was applied to Lin-chi monks and seng or seng-jen to Ts'ao-tuug monks.

in whose reign he died (790), but again from the third emperor of the late Manchu dynasty, who in 1734 conferred upon him the posthumous honorific title of Chih-hai ("Ocean of Wisdom").

It should be remembered that the Wu Tsung, or Five Sects, are all subdivisions of the Ch'an or Meditation school. The Ch'an school, as we have seen, is almost coterminous with the monastic Buddhism of the China of to-day; but other schools have flourished in the past, and some of them have not wholly ceased to exist even in this twentieth century. One of the most famous of these schools one which has had a great history in Japan as well as in China is the T'ien-t'ai (Japanese Tendai) school, which founds its dogmatic system on the well-known Saddharma-pundarika-sutra[95]. One of its chief Fathers was the venerable Hui-wen, of the Northern Ch'i dynasty, but by far the most famous was Chih-i, who made his home amid the beautiful scenery of the T'ien-t'ai mountains in north-eastern Chehkiang.

Another school was the Hua-yen Hsien-shou-chiao. Its favourite sutra was the Hua-yen-ching[96] a long work supposed to have been miraculously "discovered" by the patriarch Nagarjuna. The school originated with a very distinguished "imperial teacher" named Tu-shun, early in the Tang dynasty, who was succeeded in turn by Yun-hua and Hsien-shou. The last-named is regarded as the second founder of the school. His successor, Ch'eng-kuan, was a voluminous writer who received marks of distinction from seven emperors. He spent most of his life on the mountain of Wu-t'ai, and died in 838 at the age of one hundred.

Vinaya School

Yet another school of importance was the Nan-shan Lu. Nan-shan is the Chung-nan mountain, in the province of Shensi; and Lu is the Chinese word which stands for the Sanskrit "Vinaya." The Vinaya is that division of the Buddhist scriptures which treats of the moral codes of Buddhism and the disciplinary rules of the monk hood; it should be noted, however, that each of the great systems of Buddhism the Hinayana and the Mahayana has a Vinaya or Lu of its own. The most famous representative of the Chinese Mahayanist Lu school was a monk of the Chung-nan mountain named Tao Hsuan, who lived in the middle of the seventh

---

95 For English translation, see S.B.E., vol. xxi.

96 Avatamsaka-sutra, B.N. 87, 88; Har. i. vols. i.-iv. vii.-ix.

century. The strongholds of the school in later days were in the provinces of Kiangsu and Chehkiang. Chief among them were the monasteries of Ku-lin (Nanking), the Pao-hua mountain, and Chao-ch'ing, on the Western Lake. In the eighth century the Lu school established itself in Japan, where, under the name of the Ritsu-shu it took its place among the twelve Buddhist sects of that country. It was only by slow degrees that its influence and prestige, in both China and Japan, faded away before the rising sun of the Ch'an and Amidist schools. The rich monasteries of Puto-shan[97] were among the many which at a definite date in their history exchanged the Lu teachings for the Ch'an. The school seems to have come under the suspicion of unduly emphasizing the letter and neglecting the spirit of Buddhism, but it is doubtful whether the charge was a just one. It is true, however, that the Lu school laid stress on "right conduct," as distinct from the Ch'an school, which emphasized" right thinking "or" meditation "; and the Ch'an monks were perhaps not far wrong in arguing that "right conduct" may result only from a slavish obedience to a written code, and may have no root in the mind; whereas "right thinking "-the attainment of a correct mental attitude almost necessarily results in right action.

Amitabha

There is one school which deserves special attention, not only because it occupies a position of great prominence in the religious systems of both China and Japan, but also because it inculcates the form of Buddhism which appeals most strongly to the Buddhist layman. This is the Ching-t'u ("Pure Land") or Amidist school[98], which teaches salvation through faith in the god-Buddha Amitabha, and holds out the promise of a future life of unalloyed happiness in the Pure Land or Western Paradise, where Amitabha reigns in unending glory.

Strictly speaking, this school is quite separate from not to say antagonistic to the other great schools of Buddhist thought. A Chinese writer justly observes that believers in the Pure Land doctrines do not belong either to the Ch'an school or to the Lu.[99] But as a matter of fact we find nowadays that nearly every Ch'an monk is more or less of an Amidist;

---

[97] See chaps, xi.-xiii.

[98] The convenient terms Amidism and Amidist are taken from the Japanese form (Amida) of the name Amitabha.

[99] 修净土之业者非禅非律

and most of the Ch'an monasteries that is to say, a large proportion of the great monasteries now existing in China are perfectly tolerant of the Pure Land teachings. Many enlightened Chinese Buddhists will declare that the Ch'an and Ching-t'u teachings are not really inconsistent with one another, but that the Ch'an doctrines are to the educated Buddhist what the Amidist doctrines are to the ignorant. At the same time the fact must be admitted that the religion of the average Chinese layman has little in common with the religion of a highly-trained and perhaps mystically-minded Buddhist monk. The layman's creed in China as in other countries is a nebulous one. His religious conceptions are often crude, irrational, and superstitious; he is liable, to mistake symbol for objective truth; and he is apt to assume that faith is a sufficient guarantee of historic fact.

Amidist

The Pure Land, or Amidist, teachings have given rise to one phrase which may be said to sum up the hopes and beliefs of a very large part of Buddhist China a phrase which is constantly on the lips of monks and laymen alike, is inscribed on the tablets and walls of countless temples, and is carved on the rocks and cliffs of a hundred caverned mountains. This is Namo Omito-Fo, or simply Omito-Fo.

These words are nothing more than an invocation of the name of Amitabha, the most revered of the so-called Dhyani or "Meditation" Buddhas[100]. The following table will show the relations between these Buddhas and their bodhisats and their so-called "earthly" reflexes. The Buddhas, it will be seen, are represented as proceeding or emanating from a supreme being named Adibuddha; but the only Buddha with whom we shall have much concern in the pages that follow is Amitabha. If it were our task to study the Buddhism of Nepal or Tibet (Lamaism) or the doctrinal history of the Tantric or Mantra sects[101], we should be obliged to devote some attention to the complicated Buddhologies associated not only with the mysterious Adibuddha but also with the four Buddhas besides Amitabha whom Adibuddha is supposed to have brought forth by "meditation."

---

100 L. de la V. Poussin doubts whether the terms Dhyanibuddha and Dhyanibodhisattva are actually used in the Sanskrit texts, and whether Amitabha and the rest should not rather be described as " the five Buddhas" or " the five Jinas " (see E.R.E., i. 94).

101 Chinese Chen-yen (Japanese Shin-gon).

THE WHITE-DEER GROTTO, LU-SHAN, KIANGSI.

IMAGES OF MENCIUS AND TSĒNG-TZǓ AT THE WHITE-DEER GROTTO, KIANGSI.

ADIBUDDHA	Buddhas:	Bodhisattvas:	Earthly Buddhas
Central	Vairochana	Samantabhadra	Krakuchandra (Kakusandha)
East	Akshobhya	Vajrapapi	Kanakamuni (Kogagamana)
South	Ratnasambhava	Ratnapani	Kasyapa (Kassapa)
West	Amitabha	Padmapani or Avalokitesvara	Gotama Sakyamuni
North	Amoghasiddha	Visvapani	Maitreya (Metteya)

The Amidist branch of the Mahayanist Buddhology has elevated Amitabha to a position which, in a great part of the Buddhist world, is one of unchallenged supremacy. Theoretically, however, the historical Sakyamuni is mystically associated with the Buddha Amitabha through being his earthly embodiment, or rather reflex; and worshippers of Amitabha will not readily admit that Amidism inculcates any doctrine that is not at least implicit in the teachings of the Indian sage. They declare, indeed, that the Amida doctrines were actually delivered to the world by Sakyamuni Buddha himself in the evening of his life, and that they contain the quintessence of Buddhist truth. This view is still that of the Shinshu and Jodo sects of Japan, and it is shared by the Amidists of China, though Buddhist scholars in the East, as in the West, are well aware of the fact that the sutras in which Amidism is enshrined especially the larger and smaller Sukhavati and the Amitayurdhyana sutras were not the product of early Buddhism[102].

Amitabha

Of Amitabha we are told that countless ages ago he was a rich and powerful monarch. Filled with religious zeal and with profound love and compassion for his fellow-men, he gave up his throne, and became an ascetic under the name of Fa-tsang or Fa-hsing a word which corresponds

---

[102] These sutras which are often collectively described by Chinese Buddhists as the Ching-t'u San Ching, " The Three Sutras of the Pure Land" are known in Chinese as the Wu-liang-shou-ching, the Omito-ching, and the Kuan Wu-liang-shou-ching, English translations of the first and second from the Sanskrit and of the third from the Chinese may be found in S.B.E., vol. xlix. The extant Chinese translations of the three sutras belong to the third and fifth centuries of our era. (see B.N. 27, 198,, 200). The first Chinese translation of the Wu-iang-shou-ching seems to have been made in the second Christian century, but is lost (see B.N. 23 [5]). The popular Chinese version is that of Seng K'ai, whose labours are to be assigned to the middle of the third century.

to the Sanskrit Dharmakara, and signifies the Nature of True Religion or the Divine Essence. He attained to bodhisatship under the guidance of the Buddha of that distant age Shih-tzu-tsai-wang or (in Sanskrit) Lokesvararaja and in the presence of that Buddha (who is as mythical as Fa-tsang himself) he made a series of great prayer-vows or pranidhanas[103], whereby he under took to become a Buddha for the sake of the salvation of all beings, and to establish a heavenly kingdom of perfect blessedness in which all living creatures might enjoy an age-long existence in a state of supreme happiness, sinlessness, and wisdom. The vows of Fa-tsang are set out at full length in the Wu-liang-shou-ching[104]. These vows, which in the Sanskrit original are forty-six in number and in the Chinese version forty-eight, contain minute descriptions of the glories and wonders of the Paradise to which Fa-tsang undertook to welcome all creatures. The ordinary Chinese names for this region of ineffable blessedness and loveliness are Ching-t'u Pure Land, Hsi-T'ien Western heaven, and Chi-lo-shih-chieh, which corresponds to the Sanskrit Sukhavati, the Land of Supreme Bliss.

Buddhist Heavens

To save possible misconceptions, it should perhaps be explained that the supposed western position of Amitabha's heaven has no reference to mundane geography. Each of the Five Buddhas is understood to preside over one of the regions of the universe: Akshobhya, for example, rules in the East as Amitabha rules in the West. Each of the Buddhas has a "heaven" of his own, and all these "heavens" are supposed to be situated at an incalculable distance from the world of men. Mystical Buddhism even goes so far as to say that the Buddhas and their heavens are countless in number, and that each heaven is co-extensive with the universe. Strictly speaking, therefore, geographical terms should not be applied to. these Buddha-heavens, for they are outside space, just as the Buddhas are external to or independent of both space and time. To the mind of him who has attained a high degree of spiritual enlightenment, all the heavens are co-extensive, not only with the universe, but with one another, and all the Buddhas who rule in these countless heavens are sambhogakdya, or manifestations of the one ultimate truth.

---

103 Chinese yilan-tu.
104 For an English translation of the Sanskrit, see S.B.E.,vol. xlix. pt. ii. pp. 12-22.

Buddhist China

It is the eighteenth of the forty-eight "vows" that is largely responsible for the popular developments of Amidism, and especially for the doctrine that mere faith in Amitabha and repetitions of his name are sufficient to ensure a rebirth in the Western Heaven.

"When I become Buddha," says Fa-tsang, the future Amitabha, "let all living beings of the ten regions of the universe maintain a confident and joyful faith in me; let them concentrate their longings on a rebirth in my Paradise; and let them call upon my name, though it be only ten times or less: then, provided only that they have not been guilty of the five heinous sins, and have not slandered or vilified the true religion, the desire of such beings to be born in my Paradise will surely be fulfilled. If this be not so, may I never receive the perfect enlightenment of Buddhahood.[105]"

---

[105] 设我得佛十方众生至心信乐欲生我国乃至十念若不生者不取正觉唯除五逆诽谤正法

The Wu-ni or "five heinous sins" were originally these murder of a mother, of a father, of an arahant; shedding the blood of a Buddha; and causing schisms in the Buddhist Church. The Mahayanists invented a somewhat different classification, in which, however, the foregoing are included. The position of the final clause in the Chinese text suggests that it was a late addition. According to the Kuan Wu-liang-shou-ching, even he who has committed the five great sins will at last be saved and reborn in the Pure Land, though he deserve to suifer torments through a myriad ages." His lotus-flower, however (see p. 106), will not open till after an enormous lapse of time twelve greater kalpas.

AMITĀBHA BUDDHA.
(*For explanation of circles see pp.* 109-110.)

Buddhist China

Rebirth in Paradise

This vow, if we may believe the assurances of the Omito-ching, was more than fulfilled; for there we are told that it is not through personal merit that the Paradise of Amitabha may be attained but through trust in that Buddha's abounding might and pity and through faithful repetitions of his holy name. The Chinese commentators do not hesitate, indeed, to assert that no amount of virtue will ensure a rebirth in the Western Paradise if unaccompanied by invocations of the name of Amitabha[106]. The sutra itself informs us that the man who with steadfast faith and quiet mind calls upon that name for a period of only a week, or even for a single day, may face death with perfect serenity; for Amitabha, attended by a host of celestial bodhisats, will assuredly appear before his dying eyes, and will carry him away to a joyful rebirth in that Pure Land in which sorrow and sighing are no more[107].

Kuan-Yin

Of Amitabha's attendant bodhisats, by far the most conspicuous are Avalokitesvara (Chinese Kuan-yin) and Mahasthama (Chinese Ta-shih-chih)[108]. These are popularly represented as standing on either side of Amitabha, Avalokitesvara being on the left and Mahasthama on the right. These bodhisats are hardly inferior in glory and majesty to Amitabha

---

[106] 修万善福德而不持名者必无净土之往

Cf. the theory at one time held in Christendom (see, e.g., the thirteenth of the Thirty-nine Articles) that the virtues practised by those who do not put their faith in Christ are devoid of spiritual efficacy or are but " splendid vices." With regard to the origin of the Buddhist theory of salvation by faith, see above, pp. 60-65, 78. It is undoubtedly this doctrine which is answerable for the enormous popularity of Amidism in China and Japan; but it is nevertheless a doctrine which is repugnant to the spirit of early Buddhism as preached by akyamuni, who would have regarded it as highly objectionable from the moral standpoint. As Lord Ernest Hamilton observes in his Involution, 1912, pp. 157-167: " Any religion which guarantees immunity from the consequences of sin in return for an attitude of passive confidence is manifestly immoral. . . . Unfortunately, however, no religion is popular for long which is not proffered as a substitute for morals. Morals are irksome, and a mechanical dispensation from all sins of omission and commission is naturally attractive. It is always easier to sing a psalm than to be good." See also pp. 289-290 of the same work, and cf. Tyrrell's Christianity at the Cross-roads, 1910, pp. 72-3.

107 The vows made by the future Amitabha Buddha in the presence of the Buddha Lokesvararaja (a name which has the significant meaning of "Lord of the Universe") are not without a Christian or pseudo-Christian parallel. We are reminded of the apocryphal Transitus Sanctae Mariae, which relates how the Virgin offers up a prayer in Christ's presence that he will extend his help to all who call upon her name. Writing of this work, Prof. Yrjo Hirn observes that it was introduced from some Eastern country into the Roman Church during the fifth century of our era (The Sacred Shrine, 1912, p. 412).

108 Kuan-yin and Ta-shih-chih are the Japanese Kwannou and Seishi.

himself. Both are described with much luxuriance of language in the Kuan Wu-liang-shou – ching,[109] and both act as the protectors and guides of men in their perilous journey over the ocean of life and death. In China Ta-shih-chih (Mahasthama), the bodhisat of Great Power, takes a more prominent place in the sacred literature than he has secured in the religious affections of the people, for he has been overshadowed by the ever-increasing popularity of his brother-bodhisat. Kuan-yin (Avalokitesvara) probably receives a larger amount of willing reverence in China to-day than any other object of Buddhist worship not only on account of his association with the divine Amitabha, whose son, in a mystical sense, he is represented to be, but also on account of his own transcendent virtues, for he is regarded as the Lord of Love and Compassion, who is never weary of succouring those who are in danger or in pain[110].

There are various jnterpretations of the meaning of the word Avalokitesvare, the name is usually taken to signify "the Lord who looks down upon, or hears the cries of, the world.[111]" This meaning is supposed to be expressed in the Chinese Kuan-yin or Kuan-shih-yin. But in one important respect Kuan-yin differs from Avalokitesvara: for in popular Chinese and Japanese Buddhism Kuan-yin is not a male but a female bodhisat. She is the being who is known to Europeans in China and Japan as the "Goddess of Mercy." The change of sex has never been satisfactorily explained. That Christianity had anything to do with the matter is improbable; but it is hardly an exaggeration to say that in the eyes of multitudes of devout Buddhists Kuan-yin occupies a place that is not unworthy of comparison with that of the Virgin in Catholic Christendom. Kuan-yin is the patron-bodhisat of Puto-shan a fact which in itself is sufficient to account for the fame and popularity of that sacred island.[112]

The Pure Land

The language of the sutras is often highly mystical and not easily understood by the laity. For their benefit there exist large numbers of

---

109 See S.B.E., vol. xlix. (ii.) pp. 176, 181-189,

110 It is of interest to note that, like the God of the mystical writer of the Johannine Gospel, Amitabha both "draws" men to himself and " sends" his son Avalokitesvara to bring men to him.

111 For a full discussion of the name, see L. de la Vallee Poussin's exhaustive article in E.R.E., ii. 256 ff.

112 See chap. xi.

popular tracts and devotional handbooks which teach good Chinese Buddhists how they may best follow the path that leads to Amitabha and the Pure Land. Books of this or a similar kind (Taoist as well as Buddhist) are often printed and distributed at the expense of pious monks and laymen, and are usually as simple in doctrine as they are artless in style. Their moral tone and teachings are generally irreproachable. Many of them contain excellent discourses on such subjects as filial piety, brotherly love, charity, the evils of self-indulgence; and if we admit as we must-- that they often contain a good deal that is crude and unspiritual, we must bear in mind that they are intended for the edification, not of the learned, but of the simple-minded masses, who in China as elsewhere like to flavour their religion with the strong spices of superstition. To regard these popular tracts as authoritative statements of the creed of an enlightened Buddhist or Amidist would be as unfair as to suppose that the beliefs professed by a Spanish peasant or a mestizo of Ecuador, or the theological views entertained by the rank and file of the Salvation Army, are characteristic of Christianity at its highest spiritual level.

The tracts issued by the Pure-Land sects never fail to emphasize the advantages of repeating, with a faithful heart, the holy name of Amitabha. Those who follow other methods of religious advancement are likened to ants creeping slowly and arduously to the summit of a lofty mountain, whereas those who place their whole trust in Amitabha are said to be borne along easily, like a boat that sails down-stream with a favourable wind. The journey to the Pure-Land is often represented in more or less crude woodcuts, which show us shiploads of Amitabha's worshippers sailing over the "bitter sea" of human sorrow under the captainship of Kuan-yin[113], or portray the figures of Omito (Amitabha) and his two bodhisats, from whose aureoled heads shafts of light dart forth into the sombre places of the universe. In front of the three divine beings the Father Amitabha, the Son Avalokitesvara, the Spirit of Power Mahasthama are often pictured the sparkling waters of the sacred lake of the Pure Land, the surface of which is starred with lotus-flowers, each bearing in its calyx the spiritual body of one of those fortunate beings who by the grace of Amitabha or the guidance of Avalokitesvara have attained the felicity of a rebirth in the Western Paradise.

---

113 The ship was also used as a symhol in early Christianity. It indicated the Church, in which the faithful are safely carried over the sea of life.

THE SHIP OF SALVATION.
(From Chinese Woodcut.)

Buddhist China

There is much beautiful religious symbolism associated with the lotus a flower which may be said to occupy in the Buddhist imagination a place somewhat analogous to that occupied in Christian thought by the Cross. The canonical scriptures have preserved the striking words in which Sakyamuni compared himself with the lotus: "Just as a lotus, born in water, bred in water, overcomes water and is not defiled by water, even so I, born in the world and bred in the world, have now overcome the world." In Buddhist temples the images of the Buddhas and bodhisats are usually represented as sitting enthroned, or standing, on the open calyxes of lotuses; and the Mahayana sutras which serve as the foundation of Amidism make a symbolic use of the same beautiful flower in connexion with the passing of the souls of the blessed into the Pure Land of Amitabha. The theory (as set forth in the sutras and popularized in number less manuals of Amidist piety) is that when a believer in Amitabha is about to die, a multitude of divine beings will attend to soothe his last moments and protect his soul from the clutches of evil spirits; and as soon as he is dead he will be carried off instantaneously to heaven, where he will be reborn with a spiritual body within the calyx of one of the lotuses of the sacred lake.

One of the Japanese leaders (Honen) of the Pure-Land school taught that when a true believer in Amitabha is at the point of death his friends should put into his hand some parti-coloured threads, the other ends of which were to be fastened to one of the hands of an image or picture of Amitabha placed at the foot of his bed[114]. Thus the dying gaze of the faithful Amidist is directed towards the radiant figure of the lord Amitabha, just as the dying Catholic contemplates his crucified Saviour's image upheld before his failing eyes by the ministering priest. The Amidist practice has, of course, a symbolical value. As the physical body of the dying Amidist is united by silken bonds to a material image or portrait of his Lord, so, it is taught, will the spirit, when it is released from the flesh, be drawn by the divine Buddha into his glorious Paradise and into communion with himself.

---

114 For some remarks on this subject, and on Japanese Amidism in general, especially in its relations with fine art, see the Kokka (a Japanese art journal published in Tokyo), May 1912, pp. 243 ff.

Amidist Creed

Those who are happily destined to be reborn in the Pure Land do not necessarily enter immediately after death into the joys of their heavenly home. It is supposed that each of the "saved" is assigned to one or other of nine different classes. Those who throughout their earth-lives were always steadfast in faith and blameless in conduct are placed in the highest class, while the rest are assigned to the classes appropriate to the degree of their faith or merit. Faith in Amitabha is of itself sufficient, as we have seen, to ensure an eventual birth in his heaven, and without faith good works are of no avail; but the candidate who has virtue and good works to his credit, as well as a strong faith, will be placed in a higher class than one who has gained Paradise through faith alone. The virtues which receive the strongest emphasis in this connexion are of three kinds social, ceremonial, and religious; and the place of honour is given to filial piety[115]. He who is assigned to the highest class will enter into the joys of the Western Heaven immediately after death, for his lotus-flower will open out as soon as he has been reborn in the sacred lake, and he will therefore "see Buddha's form and body with every sign of perfection complete, and also the perfect forms and signs of all the bodhisats." He who belongs to one of the inferior classes will be carried no less speedily to the lake of lotuses, but his own lotus will not unfold immediately, and until it unfolds he will be excluded from the radiant light that streams from the glorious Amitabha. In the case of those who have been assigned to one of the lowest classes, the lotus will not open for immeasurable ages. The ninth class includes those who have committed the "five heinous sins" and other enormities, and who, if they had not saved themselves on their deathbeds by concentrating their last thoughts on the name of the Buddha Amitabha, would have had to expiate their evil deeds through ages of torment. Their lotuses will not open till after the lapse of "twelve greater kalpas" a period of time so vast as to be almost beyond the reach of thought. The state of those who lie imprisoned within the closed calyxes of their lotuses may be regarded as a kind of painless purgatory. They are in heaven and yet not of it, for they have no share in its delights, and are deprived of the joy of contemplating the glory of the lord Amitabha.

---

115 See the Wu-liang-shou-ching, S.B.E., vol. xlix. (ii.) p. 167.

Buddhist China

The Beatific Vision

The belief of the Amidist that the sinner's punishment will be a temporary exclusion from the presence of Buddha is strangely similar to that of Catholic Christendom that the real pain of hell consists in the carentia visionis Dei exclusion from the sight of God. According to Catholic doctrine, the greatest of all heavenly joys is the beatific vision optatissima beatitudo in Dei visione consistit; and "all theologians agree," writes a Catholic priest, "that whatever other torments there may be, the loss of God is immeasurably, transcendently worse than any other.[116]" But there is one enormous difference between the Christian theory and the Buddhist the de fide doctrine of the Catholic Church is that the punishments of hell are eternal; the Buddhist holds that there is no eternity in things evil, and that the whole universe will ultimately enter into Buddhahood. Perhaps it is not too rash to say that many devout Christian thinkers of the present time would subscribe to the Buddhistic doctrine on this subject much more readily than to the doctrine of eternal damnation which has been officially taught by the Christian Churches[117]. Indeed the Buddhistic view is not an unknown one in the Christian speculation of an earlier day: did not Scotus Erigena declare that evil has no substance, and is destined to disappear, and that all will ultimately be God? An Anglican theologian of to-day even finds traces of this belief in one of the Pauline Epistles[118], and his own views on the subject are hardly distinguishable from the universally-recognized tenets of Mahayana Buddhism[119].

Holy Name of Amitabha

The religious imagination has added various embellishments to the lotus symbolism of Mahayanist orthodoxy. It is said, for instance, that when any one becomes a disciple of Amitabha Buddha by invoking his

---

116 Rev. John Gerard, S.J.,,m The Hibbert Journal, Oct. 1906, p. 125.
This is the punishment inflicted upon infants who die unbaptized (see above, p. 63).
117 G. Lowes Dickinson, in his Religion and Immortality, 1911, p. 47, says: I am aware, of course, that many modern people calling them selves Christians do not accept the doctrine of Hell; but it has been an essential doctrine of Christian theology at least from the time of Augustine."
118 Romans chap. viii.
119 See Dr. W. R. Inge's Christian Mysticism, ed. 1912, pp. 68-9, 328-9. In this hope," says Dean Inge, meaning the hope of eternal salvation, ff we may include all creation." See especially the fine passage beginning, (< The human spirit beats against the bars of space and time," and ending, " an earnest of a final victory over the grave."

name, a lotus-plant representing that person makes its appearance in the sacred lake. If during his earthly career he is devout, virtuous, and zealous in his religious and social duties, his lotus will thrive; if he is irreligious, vicious, or negligent, it will languish or shrivel up. It is also said that when the worshipper of Amitabha is about to die Kuan-yin will appear before him holding the dying man's lotus in his hand. The spirit, when it leaves the body, will immediately be placed by Kuan-yin in the heart of the lotus, which will then be carried back to the waters of the Pure Land. At the appointed time the closed flower will re-open on the surface of the sacred lake, and the happy spirit will awake to find itself enthroned in Paradise.

The excessive emphasis laid on the efficacy of mere repetitions of the name of Amitabha has led to various foolish fancies. It may be noticed, for example, that many of the crude woodcuts relating to the Western Heaven and its Buddha and bodhisats are starred with little circles. These do not serve a merely decorative purpose. They are supposed to be used as a means of recording the number of times that the possessor of the picture has invoked Amitabha's name. When he completes a hundred (or a thousand) invocations he takes a brush-pen, dips it in red ink, and fills in one of the circles. When all the circles are filled in he begins the process over again by using ink of a different colour. Having made the most of the circles on one sheet or tract, he puts it away in a safe place and starts work on another. If he perseveres in these proceedings for a few years, his sheets of inked circles will reach the thickness of a book, and the total number of invocations which they will represent may amount to millions. He must carefully preserve all his circled sheets until his last illness deprives him of the hope of making any further additions to their number. When he is at the point of death he should cause them to be ceremonially committed to the flames: they will then become his spiritual passport to the Western Heaven, and he will receive full credit for each invocation uttered and recorded during his life on earth.

This childish faith in the efficacy of a mechanical repetition of a sacred name has many parallels in other countries and in other religions. The Bengali Vaishnavas, for example, believe that the mere utterance of the name of Krishna is a religious act of great merit, even though such utterance is unaccompanied by any feeling of religious devotion. A European observer has defended the worshippers of Krishna against hostile critics of this practice by remarking that the mechanical repetition of the holy name is based on sound principles, inasmuch as the practice was originally prompted by a devotional intention, "which intention is virtually continued so long as the act is in performance.[120]"

In the case of Amidism it is quite true that a genuine, and steadfast faitb in Amitabha is enjoined upon all who call upon his name. The enlightened Amidist holds that the invocation of Amitabha is efficacious because the man who with a pure and faithful heart calls upon that holy name will thereby awaken the Buddha that is within the depths of his own being. The sense of egoism and of individuality will fade away, and he will become conscious of essential oneness with the Dharmakaya the Buddha that is at the heart of the universe. It must be admitted, however, that the more ignorant Amidists believe -and are allowed, if not encouraged, by their spiritual teachers to believe that the mere utterance of the name of Amitabha has a quasi-magical efficacy proper to itself, and that such efficacy is not necessarily dependent on the existence of a robust faith in the person by whom the name is uttered. In other words, the spoken or written name of Amitabha (as is the case with many other names and phrases) is regarded as a peculiarly potent .charm. Nomen est numen has been considered a sound maxim in most of the great religious systems of East and West[121]. Its validity was unquestioned by the ancient Egyptians, whose magical use of the holy name of Osiris is known to us through the Book of the Dead; it was accepted by the followers of the Gnostic Basilides, and the formula retains a remnant of vitality in some of the darker corners of Christendom to-day.

We need not be surprised, therefore, to find word-spells still occupying a somewhat important place in the machinery of Buddhist priestcraft in China. In Taoism, be it mentioned in passing, spells and charms occupy a far more conspicuous position than they do in Buddhism; and even in certain popular adaptations of Confucianism they are not unknown.

Fortunately for the ethical welfare of its votaries, Buddhism seldom forgets, in spite of its occasional leanings towards magic, its more austere functions as a teacher of sound morals. Devotional manuals of even the simplest and most popular description do not suffer from any lack of wise

---

120 See Growse's Mathura, p. 197, cited in Hastings, E.R.E., ii. 493. Growse (himself a Roman Catholic) quotes a Catholic manual in which it is explained that (C it is not necessary that the intention should be actual throughout; . . . only a virtual intention is required that is to say, an intention which has been actual and is supposed to continue, although, through inadvertence or distraction, we may have lost sight of it."

121 Gf. Minucius Felix: " Nee nomen Deo quaeras; Deus nomen est."

saws and moral apothegms, some taken from the recognized scriptures, others from the poems, sermons, and essays of monkish philosophers. Some times exhortations to good conduct are accompanied by quaint diagrams such as the following –

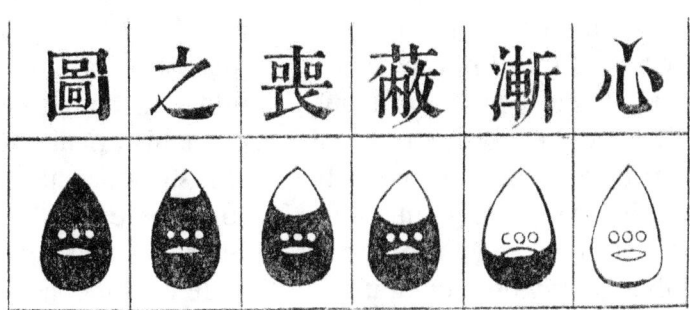

This is a pictorial illustration of the fate that overwhelms the "heart" or character of a man who gives way to evil impulses. Reading the diagram from right to left, we see that the heart of the child is pure and guileless. As he grows older the heart becomes gradually darker, and at last it is wholly black. These are the retrograde stages in the life of the man who was born with a good endowment of character, or "karma," but failed to maintain its pristine purity or to develop its higher potentialities. There are corresponding diagrams in which the "heart" shows a progressive improvement from blackness to whiteness. These stand for cases in which the inherited karma was thoroughly bad; and indicate how the possessor of such a karma, after a long struggle against the sinful tendencies of his nature, may finally emerge victorious over evil and ready for an immediate rebirth in the Pure Land of Amitabha.

Time and Space

An English writer on Buddhism refers to the fondness of the Buddhists for associating sacred persons and events with incalculable periods of time and immeasurable regions of space. They love, he says, "to deal with immense numbers, in a meaningless fashion." But the criticism is a mistaken one, for the frequent and rather tiresome references to immense numbers are very far from meaningless. They are intended to convey to the unphilosophic mind some conceptions of truths which are independent of the limitations of space and time. Aristotle, in a famous passage, said that poetry was a more philosophical and a higher thing than history[122], because poetry tends to express the universal, whereas history deals with the particular. Somewhat similar in kind so the Mahayanist doctors would say are the relations between the Hinayana and the Mahayana forms of Buddhism. The latter is higher and more philosophical than the former because, under the forms of religious or mystical imagery, it expresses the universal, whereas the Hinayana cannot set itself free from the domination of the historical fact. The Mahayanist would not, perhaps, admit in so many words that his form of Buddhism is unhistorical, but he would affirm, nevertheless, that it is independent of history because it transcends it[123]. The Chin-kuang-ming sutra says it would be easier to count every drop of water in the ocean, or every grain of matter that composes a vast mountain, than to reckon the duration of the life of Buddha. That is to say, Buddha's life does not belong to the time-series: Buddha is the "I am" who is above time.

Buddhism Independent of History

There are some interesting passages bearing on this subject in a Japanese Buddhist Catechism which has recently been translated into English[124]. The pupil is warned by the catechist not to lay too much stress on mere matters of historical fact, inasmuch as these have no religious significance. The Buddha Amida (Amitabha) made a great vow that he would prepare a way for all living beings to attain the perfection of Buddhahood. This vow was fulfilled when he made the "White Way" that leads from the world of men to the so-called Western Heaven, of which he is the ever-compassionate Lord. When was this great work performed? Some say ten ages ago, some say in the eternities of the past.

---

122 Poetics, ix. 3.

123 This feature of the Mahayana is of interest to Western students in view of the efforts of a large and growing body of Christian scholars to secure a similar independence of historical fact for their own religion. This tendency does not show itself in Catholic c Modernism " only: it is also very prominent in recent developments of Anglican scholarship. (Cf., for example, the works of the Rev. J. M. Thompson, more especially Through Facts to Faith, 1912.) Dr Shirley Case, in his recent book on The Historicity of Jesus, emphasizes the need "to break the entangling alliance between religion and history in order to give the spirit liberty."

124 A Catechism of the Shin Sect, trans, by A. K. Reischauer in Transactions of the Asiatic Society of Japan, 1912 (see vol. xxxviii. pt. v. pp. 362-7).

Reginald Fleming Johnston

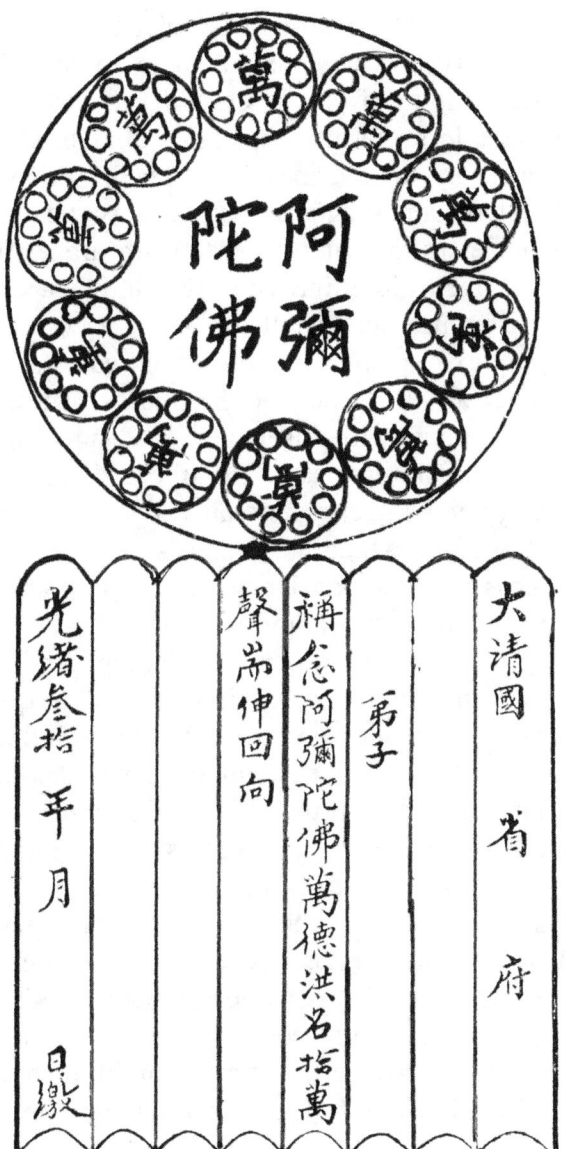

FORM FOR RECORDING UTTERANCES OF THE
NAME OF AMITĀBHA.
(*For explanation of circles see pp.* 109-110.)

Buddhist China

"But it does not matter," says our Buddhist Catechism, "whether we say ten kalpas or eternity, for the essence of the universe is not subject to space and time. Still it is the free and eternal truth which belongs to the timeless and measure less eternity that after all has value for a world which is conditioned by space and time. There fore the Amida who attained perfection ten kalpas ago is the same as the one who attained Buddha-hood in the eternities of the past. Both are explained in terms suited to meet the degree of intelligence to which they are revealed, and in reality there is no difference between them."

We need not perplex ourselves, continues our catechist, with questions as to the time or place at which the Buddha (that is, Amitabha) performed the great works associated with his name. The important thing is that Buddha's body, as the scriptures say, "fills the ends of the universe. It is revealed to all living beings everywhere and always in a manner suited to meet the needs of the life to which it appears."

It is hardly necessary to emphasize another standpoint from which the Buddhist practice of associating religious truths with vast periods of time and immeasurable space may be defended. Geology and astronomy were not long ago regarded in Europe as "terrible Muses" to quote Tennyson's expression because they made havoc of current religious notions and taught truths which (before the development of new apologetic methods) were seen to be inconsistent with the theory of scriptural inspiration. The Buddhist, on the other hand, finds nothing to shock or disturb his religious faith in modern discoveries concerning the immensities of stellar space, the antiquity of man, or the age of the globe. Not only does he accept with perfect equanimity all that science has to teach him on these and other subjects, but he sees in these new discoveries many striking confirmations of the teachings of his own sacred books. Even the doctrine of evolution, which is working so remarkable a transformation in the treatment of many branches of scientific knowledge, is in perfect harmony with Buddhist thought[125].

---

[125] The late Dr Moule (a missionary bishop in China) observes that in Buddhism cc creation is unknown or frankly denied. As a substitute we find emanation, permutation, evolution under the persistent influence of the chain of causation." It is as a reproachful critic that the bishop makes this observation; but is there not, after all, something to be said for the Buddhist position even as thus crudely stated?

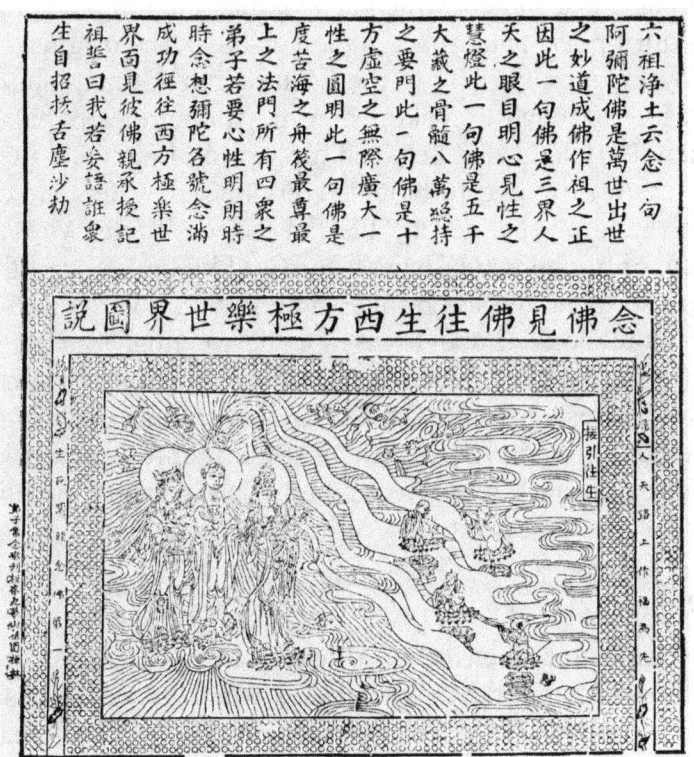

THE WESTERN HEAVEN.
(*From Chinese Woodcut.*)
[*See p.* 103.]

Buddhist China

The White Way

The White Way of Amitabha, to which reference was made on a foregoing page, is a subject which has kindled the religious imagination of many Buddhist poets and artists in the Far East. The origin of the allegory is traced by Japanese writers to the Chinese monk Shan-tao, of the T'ang dynasty, who did much to make the Amidist doctrines popular among his countrymen. He taught that between the world of men and the Paradise of Amitabha there flow two turbulent rivers one of water, the other of fire. The two rivers are separated by the Pai-tao, or White Way an extremely narrow path or bridge which must be crossed by the souls of the dead. The dangers are so great and the bridge so narrow that without divine help no wayfaring soul could hope to escape destruction. But at the western extremity of the bridge, which touches the shining coasts of heaven, stand the radiant figures of Amitabha and his two great bodhisats, by whose gracious guidance and cheering counsel the faithful pilgrim is enabled to defy the perils of the White Way and to reach in safety the blissful shores where his divine Saviours stand waiting to receive him[126].

Nirvana

At first sight the doctrine of a quasi-material Paradise seems wholly irreconcilable with that theory of Nirvana which is usually associated with orthodox Buddhism. If, indeed, we accept the belief of many Western critics of Buddhism that the goal of Buddhist ambition is non-existence, and that Nirvana is practically equivalent to, or terminates in, annihilation, then it is only by means of a somewhat violent exegesis that the two doctrines can be harmonized. But this belief is not accurate. According to canonical Buddhism, Nirvana is a state of blissful tranquillity attainable in this life (not necessarily terminable in this life), and is conditioned by a passing away of all egoistic lusts and cravings. Buddhism taught that it was only through the persistence of these lusts and cravings that the reincarnations of human karma could take place, and it necessarily followed that "rebirths" were at an end for the man who had attained Nirvana. On his death his false and impermanent ego would be

---

[126] The conception of a road or bridge which must be crossed by the souls of the dead is to be met with in many parts of the world and in association with many faiths (see Hastings, E.R.JE., ii. 852-4).

disintegrated or dissolved, for the reason that this "ego" is compounded of shifting unrealities which only the ignorant and unenlightened mistake for permanent substance. In a sense, then, it is true to say that the Buddhist who has attained Nirvana cannot look forward to a continuation of his conscious individuality after death. But this does not mean that Nirvana is another name for blank Nothingness, or that the extinction of the phenomenal ego is equivalent to the annihilation of the real or transcendental self[127].

We shall understand the matter better, perhaps, if we compare the "nihilism" of certain Buddhist philosophers in their treatment of the Nirvana problem with the via negativa of some of the Gnostic and Christian mystics in their theorizings concerning the nature of the Deity. Clement of Alexandria, for example, can tell us what God is not; he cannot tell us what God is, because God transcends all that exists[128]. The Pseudo-Dionysius, too, speaks of "the absolute No-thing which is above all existence "; Basilides says that no assertion can be made about God, because he is nothing that can be named; and much the same doctrines are to be found in Minucius Felix, Justin Martyr, Origen, Maximus the Confessor, and John of Damascus. If Nirvana is "nothing," it is only so in a sense similar to that in which Scotus Erigena says of God that he is "predicateless Being, above all categories, and therefore not improperly called Nothing" [129]; and the Buddhist would see no startling novelty in that assertion of the same Christian philosopher that "the things which are not, are far better than those which are.[130]" In Christian theology such views as these are traceable to Neoplatonism; and we find them affecting the thought of all who came within the range of Neoplatonic influence, not excepting St. Augustine. In Buddhism, however, they are associated with

---

127 Prof. Yoshio Noda, himself a Japanese Buddhist, describes Nirvana (from the psychological point of view) as "the consciousness that supervenes on the negation of self. It is thus the absorption of the individual into the Absolute... In the state of Nirvana there is no separated self, no life and death, consequently no desire, no sorrow, no fear. It is the consciousness of absolute peace, of absolute bliss, of absolute truth. It is salvation from the misery of the world, deliverance from suffering, enlightenment, and blessedness. This was the most profound philosophical thought ever presented to the Japanese mind" (The Quest, Oct. 1911, pp. 67-8).

128 Dr W. R. Inge, in Christian Mysticism, ed. 1912, p. 87, remarks that Clement " apparently objects to saying that God is above Being, but he strips him of all attributes and qualities till nothing is left but a nameless point; and this, too, he would eliminate, for a point is a numerical unit, and God is above the idea of the Monad,"

129 A. S. Pringle-Pattison. The word used by Duns Scotus is nihilum.

130 A flippant waywardness may perhaps lead some of us to call to mind that fantastic Chinese emperor who never died because he never lived.

very early developments in its own dogmatic system, and need be traced to no source extraneous to Indian philosophy[131].

Symbols and Parables

It is hardly necessary to say that definitions by negatives were not likely to make a very strong or lasting appeal to the religious emotions. A Nirvana which admittedly transcended the possibilities of positive description might conceivably bring a certain amount of cold satisfaction to a philosophic mind, but it could not be expected to arouse devotional exaltation or religious enthusiasm in the hearts of the lay masses[132]. This truth was fully recognized by the Mahayanist teachers, who allowed and encouraged the more ignorant and simple-minded members of their flock to picture Nirvana to themselves in the form of a Paradise in which the individual soul is represented as continuing to exist in a state of perpetual, or at least age-long, blessedness under the loving rule of the celestial Buddha Amitabha and his bodhisats. But the enlightened Amidist (especially if he be a monk of the Ch'an, or Meditation, school) no more believes in the literal truth of the tales of Sukhavati's lotus-pond, and in the personal and separate existences of its divine lords, than the educated Christian of today believes in the real existence of the winged cherubim, the golden crowns and white thrones, the jewelled streets and glassy seas, that characterize the "bric-a-brac rococo heaven," as George Tyrrell called it, of hymnal and Apocalypse. "These," says the Christian priest, "are symbols of divine truth." "Those," says the Buddhist monk, "are parables of Buddhahood."

---

131 In the mystical concept of God,, as well as in the Buddhist concept of Nirvana^ it is precisely the inexhaustible positivity which bursts through every conceptual form and turns every determination into an impossibility" (Hoffdiug, quoted by James Ward, Realm of Ends, 1911, p. 35).

132 Those who complain of the emptiness of the conception may be reminded of Bergson, Creative Evolution pp. 290-314 (Mitchell's trans. 1911). Cf. Faust, pt. ii. Act i. (Latham) But on, we'll plumb the Deep, whate'er befall, For in the Nought I trust to find the All."

Reginald Fleming Johnston

VI. Pilgrimages And The Sacred Hills Of Buddhism

It was lately remarked by a writer on China that the charm of this country, for the jaded visitor from the West, largely consists in the impression which it gives him that he has been carried magically backwards into the European Middle Ages. If this be China's principal title to the homage of mankind, she seems to be reconciling herself with a light heart to its speedy forfeiture. Already "Old China" is retreating to various remote fastnesses far off the beaten tracks of commerce and travel; while that section of young China which is at present in somewhat bewildered and precarious possession of the country's strategic centres seems to be fully determined of one thing only that whatever other faults may disfigure its future proceedings, medievalism shall not be one of them.

It may be doubted, after all, whether there was more than a superficial resemblance between the China of pre-reform days and the Europe of the Middle Ages. The civilizations of East and West had developed on different lines, and social conditions were in many important respects profoundly dissimilar. On the whole, there is strong reason to believe that until the inauguration of the modern scientific and industrial era in Europe, the civilization, culture, and wealth of China were on a higher and grander scale than anything that the West could show; but the difference was in kind as well as in degree. Such is the impression we gain from a perusal of the chronicles of Marco Polo and other early travellers, and even from the works of some of the pioneer Catholic missionaries, most of whom express admiration as well as wonder at the outstanding features of Chinese civilization, with the necessary exception of the deplorable errors of the people in the matter of religious belief.

Chinese Civilization

The traveller who finds much to charm him in what he regards as the medievalism of China is perhaps only giving unconscious testimony to feelings common to many a harassed victim of "the weariness, the fever, and the fret" which are, unfortunately, part of the price payable for the material advantages of twentieth-century civilization. "The heir of all the ages"sometimes gets a little weary under the load of his birth right, and if

Buddhist China

a kind destiny guides his pilgrim-steps to the Far East, he is perhaps sometimes tempted to ask whether it is true, after all, that fifty years of Europe are in all respects to be preferred to a cycle of Cathay.

But such questions as these will soon be asked no more. The Cathay which the English poet had in his mind is already rivalling the West in its headlong haste and desire for change. The time is not far off when China's foreign guest will point to this or that quaint feature of the national life and exclaim with enthusiasm: "What a picturesque relic is this of the grave and courteous China of the good old days!" Will his Chinese host receive this remark with anything but chilling disapproval? "The object of your misdirected admiration," he may observe, "is indeed a hideous survival from that grotesque and barbarous age which was happily brought to a close by our glorious Revolution."

It would be difficult to specify which of the characteristics of Old China is likely to be so tenacious of life as to be still in a position, a century hence, to excite either sympathetic interest or disdainful censure. It is a matter of common observation, however, that religious observances and superstitions, all the world over, possess a wonderful vitality which enables them, under the protection of various disguises, to carry on a more or less maimed existence for ages after they have been formally discarded. This being so, it is fairly safe to prophesy that the old customs and institutions of the Chinese which will survive the longest will be those which possess some religious significance. Among such customs is one which is of interest as forming a link not only with the China of a very remote age, but also with the Europe of the Dark and Middle Ages, and even with the Roman Catholic countries of to-day.

Pilgrimages in Christendom

The cult of saints and martyrs in the West is paralleled by the cult of canonized heroes, bodhisattvas, and incarnate divinities in the East. In nearly all lands which have reached a moderately high level of religious development we find that a favourite mode of imploring the favour of spiritual beings or of paying reverence to the popular ideals of virtue and holiness has been to lay offerings of prayer or sacrifice before the images or sepulchres of the sanctified dead. Thus the performance of pilgrimages is a practice which is associated with the religious history of nearly every civilized or semi-civilized country of which we have authentic record.

Perhaps it might surprise some of the devout Catholic pilgrims of today, and still more those of a few centuries ago, if they were told that in journeying to their favourite shrine of St. Anne d'Auray, or St. James of Compostella, to the Holy House at Loretto in Ancona, to the apostolic tombs at Rome, to the grave of St. Martin of Tours, to Cruach Phadraig in the west of Ireland, to La Salette in Dauphine, or to the grotto of Our Lady of Lourdes, they were obeying the same imperious religious instinct as that which sent the ancient Egyptians to the shrines of Sekhet at Bubastis, Isis at Busiris, Apis at Memphis, and Ammon at Thebes. Greece, we know, had her pilgrimages to the temples of Apollo at Delphi and Zeus at Dodona; and, indeed, the famous periodical gatherings at the Olympic, Pythian, Nemean and Isthmian games are believed to have been, in origin, gatherings of religious pilgrims. There was an annual Semitic pilgrimage to the temple of Ashtoreth at Hierapolis. Rome, too, had its pilgrimages in Pagan times as well as in Christian. Even in the so-called New World the invaders from Europe found that pilgrimages took place to the shrine of Quetzalcoatl in Mexico and to that of the Sun at Cuzco in Peru. The pilgrimage to Mecca, as every one knows, is a religious duty incumbent upon all true Mohammedans; but Mecca (which, indeed, was a holy place before the rise of Mohammedanism) is not unique in Islam, for pilgrims also go in their thousands to worship at Meshhed Ali in Nejef and at the tomb of the Prophet at Medina. The Bahaist has already commenced to make pilgrimages to Akka and Tabriz, though his religion only sprang into existence in the nineteenth century. In India, the classic land of pilgrimages, nearly every racial and social group has sacred places of its own. The list of Hindu pilgrimages alone, in that nursery of religions, is far from exhausted when we have taken note of the Pauch-kosi and the five ghats of Benares, the temple of Vishnu at Badarinath, and the much-maligned shrine of Jagannatha (Juggernaut) in Orissa[133]. Even enlightened and modernized Japan still annually sends forth untold numbers of pilgrims to the shrines of Ise, to the reputed grave of Jimmu Tenno, to the deified peaks of Fuji and Ontake, and to that holy hill of Koya, near Nara, which enshrines the relics of the revered Buddhist saint Kobo.

---

133 It has been proved that there is no truth in the hideous stories of the mangling of pilgrims under the " Car of Juggernaut. "

Buddhist China

Chinese Pilgrimages

China, then, is not alone in being a land in which pilgrimages have flourished in the past and continue to enjoy a great if gradually diminishing popularity to-day. But pilgrimages in China possess certain features of their own which make them well worthy of special study, and certainly no student of Chinese life can hope to arrive at a sympathetic understanding of existing religious conditions in China unless he is prepared to become if only imaginatively a member of one of those merit-making (and merry-making) bands of pilgrims who annually traverse the plains of China on their way to the Sacred Hills and the wonder-working shrines of pusas and "immortals."

When the Reformers in sixteenth-century Europe condemned the cult of saints as super stitious or idolatrous, pilgrimages naturally fell into disrepute among the peoples that accepted Protestant principles, and it is now only the Catholic countries in which we may still witness scenes comparable with the religious pilgrimages of Eastern lands. It is a curious fact that though the Puritan-Protestants discouraged pilgrimages on principle, it was none the less a brave little band of Puritans that made the most momentous of all pilgrimages recorded in history. But it was not to visit an old shrine that the Pilgrim Fathers crossed the wide Atlantic: it was to found a new one.

The Canterbury Tales

In the far-off "ages of faith" the pilgrims of Europe were of many classes. Conspicuous among them was the sandalled palmer, whom most of us now regard only through the filmy haze of romance. We think of him, perhaps, as a travel-worn wanderer who appeared from time to time before the raised drawbridge of some moated castle, bringing tidings to its lonely lady of her lord's heroic deeds and piteous death upon the crimson plains of Palestine. The crusaders themselves, indeed, were pilgrims as well as soldiers. Perhaps this type of pilgrim was inclined to be more truculent and masterful than the patient disciple of Christ should be; but such characteristics were hardly to be wondered at in men whose lot was cast in a bellicose world, and in whom religious devotion was tempered by martial ambition. We of British race have had palm-bearing wanderers among our ancestors, and sword-bearing crusaders too, as many coats-armorial in our village-churches and manor-houses still remain to testify. But if pilgrimages to the Holy Sepulchre, whether warlike or peaceful, were beyond either the hope or the ambition of the masses of our people, there were always multitudes of pilgrimages in which even the poor could take part without having to leave their native shores. Pilgrim-shrines existed in large numbers all over England and southern Scotland: no fewer than thirty-eight of them were to be found in a single English shire[134]. That Englishmen entered upon such pilgrimages with all the zest of their fellow-Christians on the Continent there is no reason to doubt; and the fact that such undertakings were a source of delight (not always of an exclusively spiritual kind) to those who took part in them will not be disputed by any one who has imbibed the spirit of the Canterbury Tales.

The main source of the popularity and vitality of ordinary religious pilgrimages in all parts of the world seems to be this that they are among the few mundane activities in which keen physical and mental enjoyment may co-exist with an exhilarating sense of religious fulfilment. Very early in life we all make the rather dismal discovery that duty does not always coincide with pleasure, and that the things which are alleged to be good for us are seldom the things we like best. But he who assumes the scrip and staff of the conscientious pilgrim has no qualms about any possible conflict between the pleasant and the good. Provided only that he possesses enough worldliness to make him heartily responsive to beautiful sights and sounds and the joys that accompany a relaxation from the routine of daily toil or business, and enough spirituality to make him appreciative of the religious significance of his pilgrimage, he will find himself in the fortunate position of being able to gratify soul, mind, and body all at the same time. Travel has been aptly described as "a perfect epitome of life," because it presents to us an infinite fluidity of circumstances and demands from us an equal flexibility of character[135]. If applicable to travel in general, these words are pre-eminently true of the religious pilgrimage.

---

[134] This was Norfolk. See Sidney Heath's Pilgrim Life in the Middle Ages.

[135] See The Spectator (13th July 1912),

Buddhist China

ROCK-CARVINGS AT LUNG-MÊN, HONAN.

Reginald Fleming Johnston

Religious Fanaticism

No doubt there were many abuses connected with pilgrimages, abuses which in Christendom sometimes assumed so serious a character that princes and bishops were occasionally obliged, in the interests of public and private morality, to recommend the intending pilgrim to stay at home and to "expend the sum thou hast gathered for the journey on the support of the poor." Even saints (unconscious, perhaps, of the reverence with which their own mortal remains might be regarded by the pilgrims of a later age) have been known to express disapproval of pilgrimages. One of these was St. Gregory of Nyssa, who in the fourth century wrote a letter de euntibus Hierosolyma, in which he expressed himself on the subject with no uncertain voice. In both East and West, more over, there have been cases in which pilgrimages of a painful and excessively arduous kind were undertaken in consequence of a vow, or by way of penance, or in accordance with the gloomy tenets of a semi-savage code of religious ethics. Thus in both Europe and Asia we hear of self-inflicted agonies caused by spiked shirts, iron chains and girdles, terrible lacerations of the body, deliberate self-torture of almost every imaginable kind. In many well-authenticated cases in the East we read of pilgrimages that ended in the wilful self-destruction of hapless and ignorant pilgrim-devotees. There are she-shen-yai, or Suicide Cliffs, at the summits of some of the holy mountains of China; and the name given to these precipices is significant, not of a grotesque fancy in nomenclature, but of a grim tragical reality. Yet there is nothing in the theory of pilgrimages to countenance a loose morality or a morbid fanaticism. Manifestations of religious frenzy are not peculiar to pilgrims. Far oftener, indeed, they accompany the psychological eccentricities of the solitary mystic and the cave-dwelling hermit just as it is these, too, who have been most fiercely assailed by the devils of human passion.

From many points of view the Protestant reformers of Christendom did right in suppressing pilgrimages in north-western Europe. Yet it must be admitted that the change involved losses as well as gains. Moreover, in this as in many other matters, the zeal of the reformers led them into the delusion that human nature was soft clay, and that they alone were the potters who had the power and the right to mould it into new shapes. Pilgrimages might be suppressed, but the pilgrim-instinct, if we may call it so, survives to this day, though it has become secular rather than religious in its aims, and tends to identify itself in many cases with the "globe-trotting" instinct. It is perhaps the Positivists, in their reverent visits to the places associated with the lives of the "saints of humanity" (as distinct from the saints of the Catholic Church), who are the best representatives of the pilgrims of medieval Europe. Most of us, indeed, are pilgrims still, though instead of seeking the tomb of a saint we now direct our pilgrim-steps towards shrines of another kind the most popular of all, it is to be feared, being the shrine that is consecrated to that nomen daemonis Mammon.

In Chaucer's age the most popular months for pilgrimages were April and May the period of the year that has been always greeted with exuberant delight by the poets of England. "Then longen folk to goon on pilgrimages"-not necessarily, indeed, because the lamp of piety then burned more brightly in their souls than at other times, though doubtless this was often the case too, but rather because, as our poet so well divined, Nature then "pricked their hearts" with a longing for the open air and all the sweetness of an English spring; because April with its fragrant showers, and the west wind with its warm breath, had driven away the last signs of the torpor and gloom of an English winter; because "tender fowles maken melodye" to welcome the birth of summer, and had a glad song for the welcoming of man, too, if only man would come out under the blue sky to hear it.

Pilgrim-Seasons

In the Far East, as in fourteenth-century England, there are "pilgrim-seasons." In Japan the blossoming of the plum and cherry in spring and the tinting of the maple-leaf in autumn are signals that send young and old out to the hills and woodlands, and it is at these seasons that the roads to the popular shrines of Shinto and Buddhism are worn smooth by pilgrim-feet. In China, where the diversities of climate are greater, and the competing shrines far more numerous and widely-scattered, the seasons for pilgrimages vary with local climatic conditions. It is fitting that the sacred peaks of the lofty mountains of north and west should be the pilgrim's goal during the scorching summer, and that the shrines and temples in the tropical and sub-tropical southern provinces should receive their meed of homage during the winter.

Reginald Fleming Johnston

Confucian and Buddhist Shrines

No attempt can be made in these pages to enumerate and describe all the great pilgrim-centres of China, for we should have to deal with the sacred places not of one religion only, but of three. The places of pilgrimage recognized by the devotees of the heterogeneous system of Taoism are so numerous that a mere catalogue of them would fill several pages. Conspicuous among them are the Wu Yo, or Five Sacred Hills, the sanctity of which is indeed of pre-Taoist date but has come to be associated with Taoist develop ments. Of Confucianists, as such, it can hardly be said that they are in the habit of travelling in the guise of religious pilgrims, because the cult of the canonized Confucius, as distinct from Confucianism as a rule of life and code of moral law, is not a cult which requires or expects the religious co-operation of the masses of the people. The Confucian worship is (or was) a part of the State ritual, and was conducted by the emperor and his delegates in their official or priestly capacity. Yet there are certain holy places in China which, as a matter of fact, are visited by thousands of professing Confucianists every year, and which will doubtless continue to be visited by Chinese and foreigners of every creed long after the Confucian system has ceased to occupy in China a position of semi-religious pre-eminence. The most important of these places are to be found within a radius of a few miles, in a south-western corner of the province of Shantung. They consist of the grave of the famous Duke of Chou, whose saintliness was such as to haunt Confucius according to a well-known anecdote even in his dreams; the temple and tomb of Mencius, and the grave of Mencius's mother the Chinese model of what a good mother should be; the splendid temple to Confucius himself, within the walls of his own venerable city of Ch'u-fou, which to this day is chiefly populated by men of his own clan and surname, and within which resides the ducal representative of the seventy-sixth generation of his direct descendants; and, lastly, the great sage's own grave, situated in one of the most beautiful and impressive cemeteries in the world. In addition to the sacred places of Taoism and Confucianism, China possesses innumerable shrines of Buddhism, and it is with these, or rather with a few of the most famous and important of them, that we shall be mainly occupied in the later chapters of this book.

Buddhist China

Struggles of Early Buddhism

There are various theories held by the Chinese as to the date at which Buddhism entered their country. The truth of the matter probably is that it had to be introduced on several different occasions before it succeeded in gaining a firm foothold. As we have seen, there is some reason to believe that the religion first reached China in the third century B.C., possibly as a result of the missions sent out from India by Asoka, but that it speedily disappeared under the discouraging influence of the book-burning and wall-building emperor Ch'in Shih-huang. The next attempt of Buddhism to enter China seems to have taken place in the year 2 B.C. In that year a Chinese embassy was sent to the Yueh-chih, or Indo-Scythians. The king of the Yueh-chih, whose Buddhism must have been of a heterogeneous type, is said to have ordered his son, the prince-royal, to instruct the Chinese envoys in the Buddhist scriptures, in order that on their return to China these envoys might act as missionaries of the "true religion." But Chinese Buddhists do not attach much importance to these stories. According to the popular account, the beginnings of the continuous history of Buddhism in China are associated with the reign of the Emperor Ming Ti, who, having been visited in a vision or dream by a "Man of gold," sent envoys to Central Asia in the sixty-sixth year of our era to look for him. This resulted in the arrival of two Buddhist missionaries Kasyapa-Matanga and Gobharana (in Chinese, Mo-t'eng and Chu Fa-lan) who were accommodated at the capital in a building which subsequently became famous as the Monastery of the White Horse.

Although these monks or missionaries made a modest beginning of the prodigious task of translating the Buddhist scriptures into the Chinese language, it is not to be supposed that the progress of the religion was uninterrupted from that time forward. It was not till about the fourth century of our era that Buddhism began to emerge from obscurity and to occupy a conspicuous place in the religious life of the Chinese people.

Confucianism has always been more or less hostile to, or severely critical of, the whole Buddhist system; more especially has it been the declared enemy of the Buddhistic institution of monasticism, which with a good deal of reason it regards as inconsistent with a sound social ethic. Most of the persecutions undergone by Buddhism, therefore, have been initiated by Confucian state craft. But there is reason to believe that the first enemies against whom Buddhism had to strive in China were not

Confucians, but the priests of Taoism, who, as the generally recognized guardians of occult secrets, and as adepts in demonology and sorcery, were jealous of the appearance of a foreign doctrine which would or might prove a dangerous rival.

Defeat of the Taoists

The contests between Buddhism and Taoism are commemorated in stories which often remind us of the legends relating to the early struggles in Europe between paganism and Christianity. The two Eastern religions seem to have competed for the royal favour in China just as St. Patrick (to take one example) is said to have competed with the Druids in Ireland for the favour of King Loigaire, each of the contesting parties striving to vanquish its rival by giving evidence of a superior skill in the working of miracles. A well-known Buddhist legend tells us how certain priests of the Five Sacred Hills submitted a memorial to the throne shortly after the arrival of Mo-t'eng and Chu Fa-lan in the first century of our era. In this memorial the Taoist priests recorded their solemn protest against the friendly attitude assumed by the emperor towards the religion of the "Western barbarians" and reproached him for his neglect of the native wisdom of China. We are willing, they said, that our teachings and those of the Buddhists should be put to the proof. Take the books of the Buddhists and our own holy writings and set them afire. If theirs are consumed, let the barbarians be banished; if ours are burned, we are prepared to suffer death. This suggestion seems to have appealed to the emperor's sense of justice. Elaborate preparations were made for a public competition in wizardry between the rival priesthoods, and for testing the truth or falsity of their respective teachings by submitting their sacred books to the ordeal of fire.

Buddhist China

COLOSSAL FIGURE AT LUNG-MÊN, HONAN.

COLOSSAL ROCK-CUT FIGURES AT LUNG-MÊN, HONAN.
(The *small* figures are life-size.)

The Taoist priests, we are told, were ordinarily in possession of various supernormal or spiritualistic faculties which gave them control over the forces of nature and enabled them to ride through the air on dragons made of straw. They arrived on the scene of the competition full of confidence in themselves and full of contempt for their Buddhist rivals; but when the time came for a public demonstration of their skill they were horrified to find that all their magical powers had mysteriously deserted them. Complete failure attended all their efforts to produce what modern spiritists would term "phenomena "; and no sooner were their holy writings placed on the pyre than the flames attacked them with irreverent fury. One book only was saved: this was the Tao-te-ching, which was snatched from the fire by one of the priests. The turn of the Buddhists came next. Without hesitation they took their images of Buddha and their volumes of sutras and thrust them into the midst of the flames. There, in full view of the emperor and his court, they remained absolutely uninjured, for the flames were miraculously transformed into petals of water-lilies, by which all the books and images were enfolded and supported. The chronicler concludes by telling us that of the vanquished and discredited Taoists some committed suicide by hanging and drowning themselves, while others shaved their heads which means that they entered the Buddhist monkhood[136].

It is needless to speculate as to whether there is any basis of fact in this story. Its chief interest for us lies in its reference to the position of the Taoists as priests of the Five Sacred Hills. Mountain-worship, indeed, had existed in China many centuries possibly thousands of years before Taoism came into existence, or at least before it had evolved itself out of its primeval nebula. From one of the first pages of Chinese history, dealing with events ascribed to the third millennium B.C., we learn how the Emperor Shun made a solemn pilgrimage to the sacred hills of the four quarters^ of his empire; and it is clearly implied that in doing this he was carrying out state-ceremonies which were part of the religious inheritance of his race.

---

136 Another account says that the Taoists fell dead in the presence of the assembled company. There are several versions of the story of the contest between the Taoists and Buddhists. That followed in the text is taken from a commentator's notes to a Ming dynasty edition of The Sutra of Forty-two Sections the work which was translated by the pioneer-missionaries Mo-t f eng and Chu Fa-Ian (B.N. 678, Har. xxiv. vol. v. pp. 1-2; see also B.N. 1471, 1472).

Buddhist China

The Taoists were the first to associate them selves and their traditions with the Wu Yo, or Five Sacred Hills, but the Buddhists were not disposed to allow their rivals to monopolize mountains in general. Buddhism had itself originated in a land where mountain-worship was deeply-rooted, and it has always tended directly or indirectly to foster in its adherents a strong love of wild nature. It was not through mere imitation of Taoism that the Buddhists began to establish themselves on mountain-heights, but rather in obedience to a strong instinct to place the sanctuaries of Buddha high up amid the solitudes of crag and forest and lonely ravine, far out of reach of sights and sounds hurtful to the serenity of souls that had abjured the vanities of the world and the flesh. Some of the hermitages which they built amid the romantic scenery of the most beautiful mountains in China grew into great and famous monasteries, and in the days when Buddhism in China was still in what may be called its constructive and productive period (which closed about a thousand years ago) such monasteries were thronged with learned scholars, translators, and religious philosophers. So long as Buddhism remained a power in India there was uninterrupted intercourse of a most friendly and inspiring kind between the great religious houses of the two countries. Chinese pilgrims spent years of their lives in visiting the holy land of their faith and in collecting and collating palm-leaf manuscripts of the sacred sutras. Natives of India, too, were in the habit of paying long visits to the seats of Buddhist learning in China, and many of these Indian pilgrims, having become honoured residents in the great Chinese monasteries, collaborated with native monks in the arduous work of translation and exposition.

The Four Famous Hills

Among the great mountain strongholds of the Buddhist faith in China four emerged into a position of relative prominence, especially as objects of pilgrimage. These are known as the Ssu ta-ming shan "The Four Famous Hills.[137]" They are Wu-t'ai-shan in the northern province of Shansi; Omei-shan in the western province of Ssuch uan; Chiu-hua-shan in the central province of Anhui; and Puto-shan off the east coast of the province of Chehkiang. Of Omei-shan we shall have little to say in these pages, for it has already been fully described for English readers[138]. The

---

137 Lion and Dragon in Northern China, p. 394.
138 See A. Little, Mount Omi and Beyond, the present writer, From

position of Wu-t'ai is somewhat exceptional, for this mountain has to a great extent become a seat of Mongol Lamaism. It is mainly to the shrines of the remaining two, Chiu-hua and Puto, that the reader's attention will be directed in the following chapters.

At first sight it seems difficult to understand why the four mountains just named were singled out for exceptional distinction, especially when we remember that there were other groups of mountain-monasteries which were no less celebrated as centres of Buddhist light and learning. The abbots of the monasteries of the Four Famous Hills have no control, customary or statutory, over the abbots of other Buddhist establishments, nor does their position carry with it any dignity to which other abbots may not aspire. Only a restricted number of monasteries in China possess the right of granting ordination, but the monasteries of the Four Hills are not exclusively favoured in this respect. Some establishments, again, are distinguished as having been the centre of some important movement in Buddhist history, or as having sheltered a monk or group of monks who founded a new sect or school; but these are to be found on many mountains other than the privileged Four.

The Four Elements

Thus we are obliged to conclude that the rank or precedence accorded by common consent to the Famous Hills belongs to the mountains themselves, irrespective of the fame of the numerous religious houses perched on their slopes. Though the Buddhists did not require to go to the Taoists to he taught a love of mountains, it seems likely enough that it was in imitation of the Taoist or pre-Taoist classification of Four (afterwards Five) Sacred Mountains that the Buddhists resolved to create a kind of nobility or aristocratic pre-eminence for certain favourite mountains of their own. The history of the Wu Yo goes back for thousands of years indeed four of the five peaks were regarded with religious veneration at a period anterior to the earliest days of which we have written record. The four famous hills of Buddhism can lay claim to no such antiquity. Two of the number Wu-t'ai and Omei are associated by history and legend with the beginnings of Buddhism in China; but the other two Chiu-hua and Puto did not come into prominence until Buddhist prosperity in China had

---

Peking to Mandalay, and Miss E. Kendall, A Wayfarer in China.

already reached and passed its climax. Of the sacred isle of Puto we hear little until we reach the closing years of the T'ang dynasty, and its Buddhist associations cannot be proved to be much more than a thousand years old. Chiu-hua has had a longer monastic history than Puto, but it was not included in the category of "Famous" Buddhist mountains until a date that was subsequent even to that of the inclusion of Puto,

But the two questions are still unanswered as to why the Buddhistic writers of the Sung dynasty should have finally decided upon four as the proper number of "Famous Hills," and why the four selected for elevation to this peerage of mountains should have been Wu-t'ai, Omei, Puto, and Chiu-hua. With regard to the first question, it seems clear that the number was chosen in order to establish what might be called four corner-stones of the Buddhist faith in China and to bring them into mystical association with the four cosmogonical "elements" which, according to the ancient Hindu philosophy adopted by Buddhism, are concerned in the alternating processes of construction and dissolution through which the whole phenomenal universe is continually passing. These four so-called "elements" were wind or air, water, fire, and earth[139]. It is unnecessary here to go into the interesting question of the origin of the system of cosmogony of which this "great element" or mahdbhuta theory forms a part. Its antiquity is indicated by the fact that it was adopted, with or without modification, by some of the earliest Greek speculators in physics.

That the intention was to connect the Four Hills of Buddhism with the Four Elements is no mere guess; for it is explicitly stated by Chinese writers on the subject of these mountains that Wu-t'ai is associated with the element Air, Omei with Fire, Puto with Water, and Chiu-hua with Earth. These pairs were not selected at random. Wu-t'ai stands appropriately for the element Air, which in this connexion is represented in the Chinese language by a character commonly used to denote Wind. Omei is situated in the warm region of Southern Ssuch uan: what more fitting "element" could be chosen for it than Fire? Puto is entirely surrounded by the sea: it is obviously the region of the element Water. Chiu-hua is sacred to a bodhisat or saint whose works of mercy are

---

139 Feng, Huo, Shui, Ti. According to another Chinese classification of the "elements" they were five in number, and consisted of metal, water, fire, vegetable matter, and earth (Chin, Shui, Huo, Mu, T'u). These are the Wu hsing, or "five elements," mentioned in the Historical Classic (Shu Ching). They occupied a prominent place in the semi-mystical system of the Taoists of the Han dynasty, and were the subject of much theorizing on the part of the orthodox Chinese philosophy of the Sung period.

associated with the Buddhist "hells." These regions are supposed by the ignorant to be situated somewhere under the earth, and are known to the Chinese by a word (ti-yu) which signifies "earth-prison." It is clear that the element correctly associated with Chiu-hua must be ti-Earth.

As to the second question why these hills, rather than any others, were honoured with the distinctive epithet of "Famous" it may be said at once that their mere altitude had very little to do with the matter. Wu-t'ai and Omei, indeed, are among the loftiest hills in China, if we rule out the vast ranges of the extreme west, which geographically belong to Tibet and Turkestan; but Chiu-hua is of no exceptional height, and Puto barely reaches even the modest elevation of a thousand feet. The matter was simply determined by a desire to place a physical pillar of Buddhism at each of the four points of the compass. It is certain that the Wu Yo were chosen as sacred mountains on account of their positions in the north, south, east, west, and central regions of the China of classical or pre-classical antiquity. Similarly, it was considered fitting that the four mountain-pillars of Buddhism should occupy positions which would justify their assuming the duties of wardens and protectors of religous interests in each of the four quarters of the empire. Wu-t'ai, therefore, was selected as the northern mountain, Omei as the western, Puto as the eastern, and Chiu-hua as the southern. It is true that Chiu-hua is in the centre rather than in the south of the China that we know to-day. It is to be remembered, however, that nearly all the territory on the right bank of the Yangtse lay to the south of the so-called "orthodox" states of the China of the Chou dynasty; and the pedantic spirit of literary and historical conservatism would prevent the Sung scholars from admitting that the southern expansion of China in the intervening centuries could render obsolete the geographical and political demarcations of the classical epoch.

Another reason, and a very important one, for the promotion of our four mountains to the exclusive rank of "Famous" was that all four had already become celebrated in Buddhistic lore through their legendary association with four of those great Bodhisats (or Pusas, to use the ordinary Chinese term) who play so important a part in the mythological and symbolic system of the Mahayana. The four in question are Wen-shu, P u-hsien, Ti-tsang, and Kuan-yin; and these divine beings are the spiritual patrons of Wu-t'ai, Omei, Chiu-hua, and Puto respectively.

Buddhist China

The Eight Mountains

We have now seen that certain of the numerous hills sacred to Buddhism in China have been selected for promotion to a position of special honour. But there is another category of Buddhist mountains which is worthy of notice, if only because it includes the names of certain monastic centres which are also visited by multitudes of pilgrims, and which, on account of their historical and religious importance, would necessarily occupy a conspicuous place in any comprehensive account of Buddhism in China. The mountains that come within this category are eight in number and are known as the Pa-hsiao-ming shan "Eight Small Famous Hills "to distinguish them from the pre-eminent Four. They are T'ient'ai, in Chehkiang; Yunt'ai and Tamao, in Kiangsu; Chitsu, in Yunnan; Wu-chih, in Kuangtung (Hainan island); Ch'iyun, in Anhui; Wutang, in Hupei; and Wu-i (Bohea Hills), in Fuhkien. Some of these (Tamao and Wutang, for example) are celebrated in the annals of Taoism no less than in those of Buddhism. The most famous from the Buddhist point of view are T ient ai, Wutang, and Wu-i; but all are annually visited by numerous bands of worshippers.

Among other holy mountains and monasteries which occupy a prominent place in the Buddhistic history of China may be mentioned Chiao-shan Chin-shan and Pao-hua, in Kiangsu; Lofou, in Kuangtang; Lu-shan, in Kiangsi; Yu-wang and T ien-mu, in Chehkiang; Ku-shan in Fuhkien; Chung-nan, in Shensi; the Nan-Yo, in Hunan; Miao-feng, Shang-fang, and other mountains, in Western Chihli; and the monasteries of Shaolin, on the Shao-shih mountain in Honan, Chao-ch'ing and others on the Western Lake near Hangchow, and Ling-yen, to the north-west of T'ai-shan, in Shantung.

When it is realized that the shan-chih, or mountain-chronicles of China, would alone con stitute a library of thousands of volumes, it will be understood that the subject is not one that can receive exhaustive treatment in the narrow limits of a single book. In devoting special attention, in later chapters, to two of the Four Famous Hills, we shall be only touching the fringe of a subject which is well worthy of far closer attention than it has hitherto received from students of the religious and artistic sides of Chinese culture.

Reginald Fleming Johnston

VII. "The Pilgrim's Guide"

The Chinese pilgrim to the holy mountains does not, as a rule, tread the pilgrim-path in solitude unless he is fulfilling a, special vow. Pilgrims form themselves into bands of comrades, who tramp together day by day, stop at the same inns, keep a common purse, and discharge the religious duties of the pilgrimage under the guidance of a selected leader. Many such groups are composed of subscribers to a pilgrim-fund, from which a certain sum is drawn each year and allocated to a restricted number of subscribers selected by lot; others are composed of fellow-villagers, personal friends, or members of the same trading guild, who unite their forces with a view to mutual convenience and protection.

These remarks, however, are chiefly applicable to lay-pilgrims. We must also take into account the numerous pilgrims who are ordained members of the Buddhist monkhood. Such persons are able to travel from mountain to mountain with greater comfort and security than laymen, for their chieh-tieh, or certificates of ordination which they always carry with them on such occasions entitle them to food and lodging at the various monasteries that lie along their route. Monks, too, are better able than laymen to benefit by the accumulated experience of the past, for many travelled monks have furnished their own monasteries with detailed information as to the best means of journeying from one shrine to another.

Buddhism in Practice

In the Middle Ages in Europe there existed a class of literature specially designed to provide Christian pilgrims with information of both a sacred and a secular character concerning the routes they were to follow and the shrines at which they were to bend the knee and open the purse. If there were no Murray's or Baedekers in those days, there were numerous Itineraria which seem to have been equally well adapted to the needs of their time. One such book, based on a French bishop's journey to the Holy Land, was written by Adamnan, abbot of Iona, as early as the seventh century; and this was followed by innumerable treatises and pamphlets dealing more or less exhaustively with the favourite loci sanctorum martyrum.

Buddhist China

The Buddhists of China, like the Christians of Europe, have their Pilgrims Handbooks. One of these is a little modern work named Ch'ao Ssu Ta-ming Shan Lu-yin "The Pilgrim's Guide to the Four Famous Hills" which is printed and issued by the monks of the monastery of Yung-ch'uan, on Ku-shan[140]. This little compilation (which deals with many sanctuaries besides those of the Four Hills) is primarily intended for the use of monkish travellers, but Chinese lay-pilgrims and at least one English pilgrim as well have found it useful and interesting.

The greater portion of the book consists of a description of routes, and with that we need not concern ourselves here; but the preliminary part, which contains maxims and instructions relating to matters of religion and morals and monastic etiquette, will perhaps be found to throw a welcome glimmer of light on the Chinese theory of pilgrimages and on the present state of popular Buddhism.

The short preface urges the pilgrim, in general terms, to cultivate reverent and decorous habits of thought and conduct while engaged in the serious business of visiting the holy mountain-shrines of Buddha. From his mind all feelings of vexation, hatred, and ill-will must be eradicated. Gentleness and compassion and humility of spirit must be his guiding principles. When he arrives at a shrine of Buddha let him bow his head and in due reverence worship the Three Holy Ones the Buddha, the Law of Buddha, and the Company of the Saints[141]. Let him extirpate all thoughts of worldly ambition and personal gain; let him wholly cease from eovetousness and selfish anger.

---

140 See p. 148. This mountain overlooks the city of Foochow.

141 In early Buddhism the Three Holy or Blessed Ones are the Buddha, the Law preached by the Buddha,, and the Order,, or company, of those who have entered upon the "eight-fold path" that leads to Nirvana. These are the " Three Refuges" of the ordained monk Buddha,, Dhamma (Sanskrit Dharma), and Sangha. In the Mahayana system the Three Blessed Ones are f the same with a difference " namely: (1) The whole company of Buddhas; (2) the Sons of the Buddhas the bodhisattvas and all men of good-will who aim at the salvation of the world and the final attainment of Buddhahood; (3) the Dharmakaya, or Body of the Law, which con tains the essence of all the wisdom of all the Buddhas (see above, p. 77).

ROCK-CUT COLOSSAL FIGURE OF A BODHISAT
AT LUNG-MÊN, HONAN.

Buddhist China

The preface is followed by a page contain ing four precepts: Hold written characters in respect; Regard all living things with love and pity; Keep your mind free from evil thoughts; Let your mind be directed unswervingly towards Buddha. By observing these precepts you will enjoy good health, spiritual and physical; you will enjoy a prosperous and respected old age; you will not be contaminated by the foulness of the world; and heaven will be your final reward.

Buddhist Teachings

The first of the four precepts is Confucian rather than Buddhistic. The prevalence of this characteristically Chinese notion as to the sanctity of written characters is well known. It is considered wrong to misuse any paper that bears written or printed ideographs. These are the symbols which conserve the great thoughts and teachings of the wise, and they are therefore to be held sacred. The second injunction is thoroughly Buddhistic. Love and kindness must be shown to all beings that have life not men only, but all kinds of animals. This is not, as is sometimes supposed, because the bodies of the lower animals may contain transmigrated human souls. The doctrine that all living things should be regarded with absolutely pure and unselfish feelings of love and compassion is deeply rooted in Buddhist ethics. The chief claim that the great bodhisats are supposed to have upon the adoration and gratitude of men is based on the boundless charity and pity extended by them towards all things that live.

The third precept requires no elucidation- The "heaven" referred to in the fourth is literally "the western region" (hsi fang) of the universe, in which the Mahayana Buddhists have placed the Paradise of Amitabha Buddha. In popular Chinese Buddhism it is chiefly through the good offices of the "gracious and compassionate" Kuan-yin (T'zu-pei-Kuan-shih-yin Pusa) that this heaven may be reached.

Next follows a little poem of four lines, which may be prosaically rendered thus: "Better is it to live the lowly life of a monk than to return again and again to mundane vanities and illusions. The true disciple of Buddha has delivered himself from all sensuous fetters; he who has entered the monkhood no longer allows his mind to be occupied with the countless vain cares of worldly life."

These lines perhaps require some expansion or explanation. It is better to pursue the contem plative life, says the Buddhist, than to condemn yourself to future human lives of woe (through metempsychosis) by neglecting the quest of truth and giving yourself up to worldly pleasures and ambitions, The root of all evil lies in delusion and ignorance. Until we extinguish the desires that accompany or result from ignorance, we shall continue to be bound to the wheel of phenomenal existence. The perfect Enlightenment to which the Buddhist aspires implies the complete removal of all delusion concerning the apparent differentia tion of objective existences and the annihilation of the appearances that veil reality. The monk will not allow his intellectual and moral energies to be dissipated in futile strivings and longings. He knows that the things of this world are impermanent and unreal, and that the prizes so earnestly sought after by the ignorant and deluded masses of mankind are nothing, after all, but mists and shadows.

In the next pages of the book emphasis is laid on the dignity of the religious life, and monks are warned that those who cannot live up to the high ideals which they profess should withdraw from the monkhood. The enlighten ment towards which Buddha pointed the way is not attainable with equal facility by all. There are some who devote their energies throughout life to its attainment and are not successful; there are some who, after a life-long struggle, do at last succeed; and there are some who seem to make no effort at all, and yet the prize is theirs. Sakyamuni[142] taught the good law for forty-nine years; all that his followers can do is to follow faithfully in his steps as far as they are able, though they have not been privileged, as Kasyapa and Ananda were, to see the Master face to face.

Etiquette for Pilgrims

Next comes a short model dialogue for the guidance of pilgrim-monks when they arrive at a strange monastery. Having reached the reception-room, the visitor, we are told, should deposit his bundle outside the door, go three paces into the room, and seat himself decorously on half the seat of a chair. It may be necessary to explain that in a Chinese guest room the chairs are so arranged that host and guests may seat themselves in

---

142 Sakyamuni (Chinese Shih-chia Fo) is one of the titles of Gotama the Buddha "the Sakya Sage."

accordance with the recognized rules of etiquette. The humblest seats are those nearest the door. By going only three paces into the room, and then seating himself, the visitor is therefore acting with due modesty. The further injunction that he is to content himself with half the seat of a chair is quite in accordance with Chinese propriety. A young man in the presence of an elderly one, or a subordinate official in the presence of his superior, must (unless the meeting is quite informal) sit bolt upright on a corner of his chair in an attitude of respectful attention[143].

Host and Guest

The "Guide" goes on to inform the pilgrim that when the chih-k o enters the room he must stand up and make a ceremonious bow. The chih-k o is a member of the monastic fraternity whose special duty it is to receive guests and offer them the hospitality of the establishment. After the usual greetings the chih-k o and his guest will sit down, and the dialogue that ensues will be somewhat as follows[144].

Chih-k'o: May I ask where you have come from?
Visitor: I have come from A--- .
Chih-k'o: May I ask where is your honourable monastery?
Visitor: My humble place of residence is the monastery of B----.
Chih-k'o: Have you received the robe and bowl? [The outward signs of monkhood are the robe and begging-bowl.]
Visitor: I am fully ordained.
Chih-k'o: What sect do you belong to?
Visitor: I belong to the --- sect.
Chih-k'o: May I enquire what my reverend brother's name is?
Visitor: My humble name is ----. [Buddhists receive a fa-ming, or "name in religion," when they ch'u-chia that is, when they leave the world and enter a monastery. Thenceforward their family and personal names are ignored.]
Chih-k'o: May I enquire what is the name of your reverend father-in-religion?
Visitor: The name of my father-in-religion is ----.

---

[143] Mores mutantur. The Chinese are rapidly growing less punctilious in these small matters.

[144] The guest would be made to take a higher seat than that modestly occupied by him at first; while the chih-Jc o himself would take one of the humblest seats. This manoeuvre^ and also the serving of the usual cups of tea, would be taken for granted by Chinese readers.

Reginald Fleming Johnston

Chih-k'o: May I venture to ask what your honourable business is in this place, or whither you intend to proceed?

Visitor: (If he proposes to remain where he is.)--My intention is not to go elsewhere. I have purposely come here with the desire of devoting myself to the study of the lofty rules and principles of this monastery. (If he intends to go elsewhere.} I propose to go on to ---. May I ask you to endorse my certificate for me? [Monks on pilgrimage receive certificates from, or have their own papers sealed by, the different monasteries which they visit, as proof that they have carried out their task[145].]

Chih-k'o: Certainly. Have you been here before?

Visitor: This is my first visit.

Chih-k'o: Please bring your papers.

The two then rise, and the visitor follows his host to an upper reception-room, which is also a chapel and contains sacred images. Here the visitor is presented to two or three of the heads of the various monastic departments, though he does not address them until he has knelt in prayer before Buddha. When his papers have been sealed or endorsed and the time has come for him to depart, he takes ceremonious leave of his hosts, taking care to adapt himself to circumstances as they arise. Perhaps he may be presented to the abbot. In this case his demeanour should be scrupulously modest and reverential.

Warnings to Pilgrims

The next section of our "Pilgrim's Guide" consists of "Ten important subjects for reflection while visiting the holy mountains." These ten subjects are discussed in a series of miniature sermons, each of which closes with the phrase tz u nien wei yao "it behoves you to ponder on these things." The general sense of the sermons is as follows:

Firstly, the pilgrim is told that a journey to the sacred hills will not only foster habits of reverent study and research, but will also enable him to acquire a useful knowledge of the world. You, the pilgrim, will meet with varied experiences, some pleasant and others disagreeable or vexatious. Should you meet with unexpected hardships, do not be discouraged. Regard your troubles as dreams and illusions, as shadows or echoes, as things of no substance. It should be your endeavour to find

---

145 A similar practice is in vogue in India^ where the priests in charge of places of pilgrimage issue sealed certificates to the Sadhus or wandering Hindu ascetics.

some experienced person to act as your guide and teacher. If it is not your good fortune to come across any such person, then put your faith in the holy pusas of the mountains; and when you burn incense at their shrines let your supplication be this that their spiritual powers may be so put forth on your behalf that through them you may at last attain the goal of spiritual wisdom.

Secondly, you must cultivate steadiness and sincerity of moral purpose: then will the unseen powers be moved to grant you their spiritual guidance and protection. If, for the sake of avoiding a lonely journey, two or three travel in company, they must watch over one another in sickness, guard one another from robbery, and be one another's support in the hour of danger and during the night watches. But in choosing his associates the pilgrim must seek only those who are of upright and religious nature. On a long pilgrimage one is sure to fall in with false friends and true. Select as your companions only men of good character, and, having made your selection, be yourself a loyal friend. By this means you and your fellow-pilgrims will be honoured comrades in religion, and you will address one another with seemly respect and treat one another with courtesy. It sometimes happens that a band of pilgrims will give a loose rein to the basest propensities of lawless natures. When they arrive at a monastery which cannot give them lodging-room they will forcibly establish themselves on the premises, and when they come to a temple which is unable to offer them hospitality they will defiantly help themselves to supplies of food and drink. Conduct like this is altogether to be condemned: it reveals a disposition that is quite contrary to the spirit of religion. Be careful never to acquire such bad habits as these, which will certainly ruin your reputation. But when you meet any one of noble and exalted character you should honour him with all the marks of respect that you would show to your religious instructor; and when you come across people who are crippled and in misery you should do all in your power to relieve them.

Thirdly, you should begin by acquiring full information concerning your route, and when you have done this you may go on your way with a trusting heart. You should make up your mind definitely about the places to be visited, and map out your journey in accordance with the position of the different mountains. If you neglect to make preliminary arrangements of this kind, and simply follow others in an aimless way, you will find yourself continually wasting time by retracing your own footsteps, and thus you will become bewildered and embarrassed. Not only will you fail to carry out your original intentions regarding your pilgrimage, but you will also show yourself to be a person of irresolute character. If while on the road you hear of some monastery which is inhabited by men of distinguished virtue and wisdom, you should make careful enquiries as to whether the report is true or false. If you find it to be true, go thither. If you perceive while lodging in a monastery that the rules of the monkhood are observed with great strictness and fidelity, be particularly careful in your own observance of such rules, always remembering that you are on a religious pilgrimage and should therefore be specially zealous in your obedience to religious law. If, on the other hand, you find that the monastic regulations are but laxly observed, you should carefully abstain from any expressions of reproach or criticism.

Follow Good, Eschew Evil

Fourthly, when on pilgrimage it is not fitting to count the time spent in travelling: look on the road as your home for the time being. Cherishing a frank joyousness in your heart, pursue day by day your wanderer's path. Keep your thoughts directed towards the way of truth, and fling aside all ideas of fame or personal profit. In making up your mind when to halt and when to proceed, when to take long stages and when to take short ones, you should be guided by circumstances. If you are in the company of a truly wise and noble companion, regulate your own stages in accordance with his, so that you may be always near him. Cultivate humility and patience, and make firm resolutions to carry out your pilgrimage in spite of difficulties. Do not be too particular in what you eat and drink, and do not reject the fare that is placed before you on the plea that it is tasteless. If hardships beset you, do not run away from them: reflect that they have come to you only because the sins committed by you in a former life must be expiated by you in this one. Make it your business at all costs to follow the good and eschew evil.

Buddhist China

LU-SHAN, KIANGSI.

MOUNTAIN AND STREAM, SOUTHERN ANHUI.

Fifthly, it should be remembered that the proper object of the pilgrim's quest is truth; he must not expect to find his path an easy one. In this world of ours we cannot hope that heaven will make Buddhas of us for the asking. It is not till the plum-tree has endured the icy rigours of winter that its blossoming time will come. It is not till the pilgrim has won his way with zeal and courage through all the pains and woes of human life that he can hope to attain the object of his quest. Ponder earnestly the teachings of the wise. When you have the good fortune to meet a sage, treat him with the same respect that a child is taught to pay to his schoolmasters or his elders. Neglect no opportunity of cultivating wisdom and virtue. Sometimes you will meet wise men whose language is different from yours, or who speak a strange dialect, so that it is difficult for you to derive full benefit from their discourse. In that case you should take notes of what they say, so that you may ponder their words at leisure.

Sixthly, it should be remembered that there are two classes of pilgrims laymen and monks. Lay-pilgrims, if they are provided with money, can find lodgings for themselves without difficulty; but Buddhist and Taoist monks are scantily furnished with the wherewithal to meet the expenses of travel, and they, therefore, must claim their privilege of free board and lodging at the monasteries along their route. But when a monk asks for hospitality at the door of a strange monastery he should do so as a lowly suppliant and in a spirit of humility. If his request is granted, he should be grateful. If, however, his diploma fails to command the expected hospitality, let him instantly quell any rising anger or ill-will against those who turn him from their door. If he has been overtaken by darkness or caught in the rain, or if he is wearied with a long day's tramp, let him make a courteous appeal to their pity and charity. If they resolutely refuse to receive him, then-still without any show of impatience he should ask to be directed elsewhere. He must refrain from uttering a word of reproach, for not only would that stir up feelings of resentment in those whom he addressed, but it would also be injurious to his own character, and hinder him from maintaining that serenity of mind which is necessary to the attainment of true wisdom.

Buddhist China

Forbearance and Patience

Seventhly, in the course of your pilgrimage you will come to places which are the resort of people from every quarter. Sometimes you will find that old customs have undergone great changes, and that there is no longer any one to give hospitable reception to far-travelled monks. In these circumstances you should conduct yourself in accordance with local conditions, and beware of showing resentment against the people of the district on the ground of their non-observance of religious usages. Sometimes you will pass through decayed villages, or among people who are themselves so sunk in poverty that they can spare nothing for strangers; or you will meet with people who are parsimonious or avaricious, and who will supply you with no means of support whatever. In such cases you must refrain from referring to such people as ungenerous or uncharitable. If there is really nothing else for you to do, you may go on your way as a mendicant, carrying your begging-bowl in your hand. There is a saying that it takes the offerings of a thousand families to fill a single begging-bowl, yet a solitary mendicant will not starve even on a journey of three thousand miles. To beg one's food is to act in accordance with the rules laid down by the blessed Buddha himself; no one, therefore, need feel shame in relying upon charity. The word pi-ch'iu when applied to a Buddhist monk has an outer and an inner significance [146]: the mendicant begs for food that he may nourish his body; he begs for instruction in the law of Buddha that he may nourish his character. Let the good example of others be an incentive to yourself. When you are receiving alms, ask your own conscience how you yourself would treat a pilgrim-stranger at your gates: perhaps you will have cause for shame. When you accept the charity of others, fail not to register a vow that when occasion arises you will treat others as considerately as others are now treating you.

Be Content With Little

Eighthly, the pilgrim must carefully observe the thirty-seventh secondary commandment of the Fan-wang-ching, which strictly admonishes the Buddhist monk not to make journeys into dangerous

---

146 The Chinese pi-ch';iu represents the Sanskrit bhikshu, or Pali bhikkhu, and literally means " beggar/ but is technically applied to a religious mendicant. For the more ordinary Chinese terms for Buddhist monk.

places or to incur unnecessary risks[147]. He should make enquiries as to whether the places he proposes to visit are in a state of prosperity or decay, and whether the roads are open to travellers. Only when the answers to such enquiries are satisfactory may he proceed on his way. He must remind himself, moreover, that temples and monasteries were built for the purpose of paying worship to Buddha and the unseen powers, not with the object of providing for the wants of people like himself; and that the provisions stored in such establishments were in tended to be used primarily for sacrificial purposes and secondarily for the support of the resident monks, and were not meant to be at the disposal of chance comers. If you are offered hospitality, take gratefully the quarters and the food that your hosts may provide for you. Do not grumble if you are cramped for want of space or if the food and drink are not of superior quality. If you show anger or discontent, how can you expect to escape the charge of being covetous and ill-tempered? You should train yourself to be happy and satisfied with your lot. The contented man will be cheerful even if he has to sleep on the bare ground. There was a time when your lord Buddha himself was supplied with nothing better than the coarse fodder of horses [148]: remind yourself that at least you fare better than your Master did.

Ninthly, remember that every temple and every monastery, wherever situated, is in itself equivalent to a holy mountain. It is for this reason that its principal gate is known as shan-men -- Gate of the Hill[149]. The temples and monasteries which offer hospitality to the pilgrim must all, therefore, be regarded by him with equal reverence and their inmates treated with equal respect. He must not make invidious comparisons between them. Moreover, he must be careful to adapt himself to the different customs in vogue in the different monasteries which he visits. If he arrives at the hour of morning or evening service, or at the time of the burning of incense, or

---

147 The Chinese Fan-wang-ching (Brahmajala-sutra), which is No. 1087 in B.N., is riot to be confused with the Brahmajala Suttanta mentioned in S.B.E., xx. 376, and xxxvi. pp. xxiii.-xxv., and translated by Rhys Davids in his Dialogues of the Buddha. The Chinese version has been translated into French, and annotated, by Dr J. J. M. DeGroot, in his Le Code du Mahdydna en Chine. The " thirty-seventh secondary commandment " will be found on pp. 69-71 of De Groot's work.

148 For the canonical story referred to here, see Beal's Lectures on Buddhist Literature in China, 1882, p. 52.

149 In spite of the popularity of pilgrimages in China, it is freely admitted by both Buddhists and Taoists that a man can worship the divine powers quite as well by staying at home as by going on a long journey. Many a little Taoist temple, unknown to fame, bears above its gateway an inscription to this effect: f Why do you wander far from home and seek a distant shrine? Here, close to your own doors, is T ai-shan! " In this and many similar sayings (Buddhist as well as Taoist) a reference is understood to the theory mentioned in the text that every temple or monastery is, or is equivalent to a Sacred Hill.

Buddhist China

when the monks are going out to labour in the fields or when they are about to go into the refectory, let him strictly conform to the rules of the fraternity. He should also show himself willing to join the brethren in the performance of their prescribed duties, and must on no account excuse himself from doing so on the false plea that he is wearied with travel and must needs seek rest.

Avoid Covetousness

Tenthly, and lastly, on his way to the holy mountains the pilgrim must keep a careful watch over his moral conduct. He must rigorously keep the commandments, and must not abandon him self to self-indulgence of any kind[150]. He should not allow his mind to be occupied except by pure and honourable thoughts, and he must not be led astray by carnal enticements. Amid all the beautiful scenes that meet his gaze let it be his first object to be master of himself. Let him also avoid all reckless covetousness; whether his desires be set on books and scrolls or on gold and jade and precious stones. Such objects as these are all liable to corrupt the character of those who long for them overmuch. Worldly-minded men may value such things: to the pilgrim they should be of no account. To covet the material possessions of others will assuredly bring discredit on the pilgrim who yields to temptation, and his deeds may even be injurious to other pilgrims who in future happen to traverse the same road. Where fore let the pilgrim rigidly abstain from making free with the property of another, irrespective of whether the coveted object be a thing of real value or only a worthless trifle.

Hospitality in China

It will have been observed that some of the warnings and suggestions contained in these little sermons are evidently intended for the edification of pilgrims of a humble and unlettered class. That this is so is clear not only from the matter, but also from the manner of the discourses; for their style is simple and unpretentious and quite devoid of the classicisms and artifices which appeal to the literary instincts of the average Chinese

---

150 Both lay and monastic Buddhists are bound by " commandments," but those imposed on the monks are much stricter and more numerous than those enjoined on laymen.

scholar. The remarks on the subject of mendicancy, in the seventh sermon, perhaps require a word of comment. As a matter of fact, the orthodox

Buddhist practice of mendicancy is not carried out in China to any appreciable extent. It is only when their lot is cast among a lay population of devout Buddhists that Buddhist monks can hope to support themselves out of the voluntary daily offerings of the faithful; and lay China is not, and never has been, so enthusiastically Buddhist as the people of Burma, Ceylon, and Siam. To witness a procession of yellow-robed monks wending their way, begging-bowls in hand, through a Burmese village or through the streets of a city like Mandalay, is an experience that may fall to the lot of any Western visitor to south-eastern Asia; but he will be disappointed if he expects to see anything of the same kind in China. The Chinese monastic communities are supported by their endowments and by the offerings brought to the monasteries at festival-seasons and on special occasions of private urgency by pilgrims and other visitors and worshippers. Buddhist monks in China often, indeed, go into the towns and villages with subscription-books for the purpose of collecting money for such objects as the rebuilding or restoration of a temple or monastic building; but a monk who tried to procure his daily food by carrying a begging-bowl from door to door would probably suffer from chronic hunger, and might even meet with a good deal of abuse. He would be more likely to get his bowl filled and would run less risk of insult by throwing off the monkish garb altogether and making his appeal to the charitable in the guise of an ordinary lay beggar. It is true, however, that religious pilgrims, whether Buddhist or Taoist, need have little fear of suffering from lack of food or shelter. The Chinese are a hospitable and kind-hearted people; and they will rarely allow a stranger to turn away hungry from their doors.

Buddhist China

VIII. Ti-Tsang Pusa

The mountain of Chiu-hua, one of the principal objects of pilgrimage in Buddhist China, consists of a range of pinnacled hills which lie at a distance of a score of miles from the south bank of the Yangtse in the province of Anhui. Its patron divinity is the compassionate Ti-tsang, the pusa or bodhisat whose gracious function it is to fling open the gates and lighten the gloom of hell and rescue tortured souls from the pitiless grasp of the lictors of Yenlo-wang (Yama-raja), the king of devils.

The Vow of Ti-Tsang

Mahayana literature contains several sutras which tell us about Ti-tsang and his works[151]. The Sanskrit name of this bodhisat is Kshitigarbha, meaning Earth-Womb or Earth-Treasury, of which the Chinese words Ti-tsang are a trans lation. The name is explained thus. According to one of the cosmological theories of the Tantric Buddhists[152], the Earth is 180,000 yojanas thick- say, six million miles. The deepest or lowest of the various earth-layers is the Diamond-earth (Chinese chin-kang-ti], which is absolutely unyield ing and unbreakable. Even so, it is said, is the inflexibility of the virtue and courage which fill the heart of Ti-tsang; for he has uttered a vow before the throne of the eternal God (the glorified Buddha) that he will devote himself to the salva tion of suffering mankind, and that he will not be deterred for a single instant from his self-imposed task until, after the lapse of aeons, he has brought all living beings safely to the haven of Buddha-hood. Having uttered his vow, nothing can make Ti-tsang swerve from his purpose. Just as the earth rests immovably on its adamantine foundation, so will mankind find its surest support in the diamond-like firmness of the will of the unconquerable Ti-tsang[153]. The hosts of evil spirits cannot daunt him, and from sorrow and danger and pain he will not shrink. He will take on himself the burden of the woes of

---

151 See B.N. G4, 05, 981, 997, 1003, 1457, and several other sutras (Har. iii. vol. vii., etc.). Chinese editions of the Ti-tsarig sutras are frequently published at the monasteries of Pai-sui and Ch'i-yuan, on Chiu-hua, and also at the Yung-ch'uan monastery of Ku-shan, near Foochow.

152 As expounded, for instance, in the Chin-kuang-minq-chinq (see B.N. 126, 127).

153 Yen-ming Ti-tsang Ching.

all who trust him, and he will never regard his work as finished so long as a single soul languishes in sorrow or in pain.

It is with reference to his position as nourisher and consoler and rock of refuge that Ti-tsang is sometimes known as the Earth-spirit (ti-shen), the world-supporting spirit (ch'ih-ti-shen), and the Diamond or Adamantine spirit (Chin-kang chien-ku-shen). He bears the name of Earth partly because his sympathy and compassion are all-embracing, and partly because his will to afford help and the means of salvation to struggling souls is unchangeable and indomitable. But there is also an allusion to his special function as opener of the gates of hell: for the Chinese name for "hell" is ti-yu, which literally means earth-prison. Ti-tsang is generally represented as carrying a staff or crozier in one hand and a miraculous jewel in the other. When he touches the doors of hell with his staff they are burst asunder; when he passes the gloomy portals and holds forth his radiant jewel the darkness of hell is dispelled by rays of celestial light.[154] According to another account of the articles carried by Ti-tsang, he is the bearer of the gleaming pearl which by the reflection of its light cracks and bursts the iron walls of hell, and of the golden crozier with which he causes the dark halls of death to shake and tremble.

It is not to be supposed that the educated Buddhist really believes that the hells in which erring human souls are tormented are situated in the bowels of the earth. Indeed, when we consider how the Oriental mind understands the use of symbolism, and what stress is laid by Buddhist metaphysics on the impermanence and non-reality of all that pertains to the phenomenal world, we may doubt whether Buddhists ever held such crudely materialistic views of the unseen world as those which till recent years were current in Europe[155]. In any case it is well to emphasize the point that the Buddhist "hells" are comparable not with the eternal Hell of which Christianity teaches, but rather with Purgatory. Everlasting or eternal punishment is not, and never was, taught by Buddhism. Salvation is eventually to be attained by all living beings, even by the very devils themselves.

---

[154] 手中金锡振开地狱之门掌上明珠光摄大千之界

[155] "The Roman Catholic Church," as Dean Inge tells us, "still teaches not only that the purgatorial fire is material, but that it is situated in the middle of the earth " (Personal Idealism and Mysticism, p. 150). The Dean is careful to add that educated Romanists no longer believe this.

Buddhist China

JIZŌ.
(TI-TSANG PUSA.)

The Treasure House of Ti-Tsang

The second part of the name Ti-tsang means a storehouse or treasury. This, too, is symbolically descriptive of the pusa, whose love and compassion are an inexhaustible treasure which is for ever poured forth for the benefit of souls in sorrow. The treasure-house of Ti-tsang is open to the whole world, and its riches are distributed freely among all who seek them. Not the most forlorn and abject wretch in the profoundest and most hideous of the hells need be without hope of sharing in the bounteous gifts of Ti-tsang[156].

This gracious pusa appears as a speaker in several of the Mahayana sutras; but it will be readily understood from what has been said in an earlier chapter that the Buddhists make no attempt to identify the original Ti-tsang (as distinct from his subsequent "incarnations") with any historical personage. For the true Ti-tsang, as for the true Amitabha, Kuan-yin, P u-hsien, or Wen-shu, we may search historical records in vain. The great bodhisats are independent of history and unconditioned by space and time. Just as Buddhahood can be realized only by him who has himself become Buddha, so Ti-tsang is truly knowable only by the man who has first sought and found his own unfettered Self an achievement which will be followed by the additional discovery that Ti-tsang and all his fellow-pusas are but as star-flashes from the aureole of Buddha, and that Buddha and the unfettered Self are One.

But a creed that is to meet the religious and emotional needs of the unlearned multitude as well as those of the philosopher and the mystic is obliged not only to soar starwards, but also to keep in touch with homely earth. Deity, if it would be recognized as such, must undergo a partial humanization; the sublimest ideals must be interpreted in terms of human thought and knowledge the divine, in short, must become incarnate.

Ti-Tsang Sutra

It will perhaps help us to understand how the problem is dealt with by the Mahayanists if we briefly examine one of the numerous sutras in which the doctrine of the bodhisats is instructively handled. The sutra which deals with the Vow of Ti-tsang -a vow which, as we shall see, is

---
156 Cf. the Catholic theory of the Treasure of the Church

practically the same as that taken by every bodhisat and by the glorious Amitabha Buddha himself in the days of his bodhisatship may be regarded as typical of its class. This work[157] has existed in a Chinese form since the last years of the seventh century of our era, but its Sanskrit original is of much greater antiquity.

The sutra opens with a description of a great assembly of pusas and other supernatural beings in the paradise known in Chinese as Taoli and in Sanskrit as Trayastrimsa the heaven of the Brahmanic god Indra. Over this vast crowd of divinities presides the Buddha himself, who, it must be observed, is the same and yet not the same as the historic founder of the Buddhist religion[158]. He is the same, because in attaining Buddhahood Gotama reached the highest state which can be reached by any being, human or divine; yet not the same, because he has transcended the category of human personality.

Redemption of Mankind

The description of the opening scene is obviously intended to attune the reader's imagination to the keynote of a celestial melody. He is warned at once that the events to be related are on a far grander and vaster scale than is possible or conceivable within the narrow bounds of mundane life. The unimaginable immensity of the number of spiritual beings who assemble from all the "worlds" of gods, angels, men, and demons to do honour to Buddha is brought home to us by Buddha's opening speech and the answer thereto. Buddha turns to the great pusa Wen-shu (Manjusri), and asks him whether he can count the number of these beings. Wen-shu replies that even with the aid of supernatural power he would be unable to do so, though he were to devote to this sole task a thousand aeons. We should be wrong if we were to regard this merely as an example of Oriental grandiloquence. It is an attempt to make us realize the utter futility of all efforts to measure the infinite, and an indication that we have been lifted into a region in which mundane standards and qualifications are inadequate and inapplicable. This point is emphasized by the fact that the confession of incapability is put into the mouth of Wen-shu. If even he the wisest of all the pusas is unable to answer Buddha's question, it would

---

157 The Ti-tsang p'u-sa-pen-yuan-ching.

158 He is represented as having visited this "heaven" for the purpose of preaching the Law to his mother Maya, who had been re-born there after her life on earth. There are sutras dealing with this subject (see B.N. 153 and 382.)

be obviously impossible for any one else to do so. Buddha himself, of whom it is said that there is nothing he does not know, nothing he does not hear, nothing he does not see[159] admits that the infinite cannot be brought within the scope of any intellectual process. He goes on to explain that these countless myriads of spirits are the beings who through immeasurable ages of past and future time have been or will be brought to salvation by the power of Ti-tsang; and, in response to a request from Wen-shu, Buddha tells the story of Ti-tsang's Vow and its incalculable results.

Ages ago, in a remote kalpa or aeon, the future pusa was born as a member of a certain noble family, and became a devoted disciple of the Buddha[160]. Filled with religious enthusiasm and with intense pity for his suffering fellowmen, he swore a solemn oath, which was duly registered by the Buddha, that he would consecrate his whole life and all his future lives for incalculable ages --to the work of the redemption of sinful and miserable man kind. Never would he desist from his task such was his vow until, having brought all men safely across the river of life and death, he had landed them on the shores of Nirvana, and seen them pass into eternal beatitude.

Story of the Brahman Girl

Aeons passed away, and the successive re-incarnations of the pusa were all marked by incessant acts of untiring altruism and unswerv ing devotion to the welfare of man. At last, in a later kalpa (still immeasurably remote from the present age), he was reborn as a Brahman girl. This maiden was virtuous, religious, and of exceptionally good repute among both gods and men; her mother, on the contrary, was an impious heretic and a scoffer, to whom holy things were of no account. After an evil life the elder woman died unrepentant, as a result of which she was condemned to the torments of the Avichi hell[161]. The girl, whose knowledge of the laws of yin-kuo (cause and effect) assured her that her mother must have been reborn in hell, devoted herself more heartily than

---

159 This is quoted in a Chinese commentary on the Ti-tsang sutra.

160 That is to say, the Buddha of that kalpa since succeeded by many other Buddha s, of whom Gotama was the last. The next Buddha is to be Maitreya, who is still a bodhisat, dwelling in the Tushita heaven, awaiting the day when he shall be born again on earth and become Buddha.

161 The Chinese name of this, the last of the "eight hot hells" is Wu-chien, which signifies a place of uninterrupted torment.

ever to good works and religion, in the hope that she might thereby ease her mother's pain. One day she was kneeling in a sanctuary praying to Buddha and weeping bitter tears because she knew not what sufferings her mother was undergoing or how she could relieve them. Suddenly she heard a voice. "Dry your tears, poor weeping saint," it said; "I will reveal to you the place whither your mother has been taken." The unseen Buddha for it was he then bade the girl return home and ponder his name silently and faithfully, after which the secret of her mother's abode would assuredly be revealed to her. She did as she was bidden, and after spending a day and a night in an ecstasy of meditation she suddenly found herself transported to the edge of a wildly-raging ocean in which wallowed vast numbers of hideous marine animals. Above them skimmed and flapped uncanny beasts with wings. Into the turbulent waters were flung the living bodies of shrieking men and women, whose writhing limbs were greedily wrenched asunder by the pitiless jaws and talons of the wrangling monsters. Yakshas (hell-demons), too, there were, of uncouth shapes yakshas many-armed, many-eyed, double-headed, and multiped, and with teeth that protruded from the mouth with edges like sharp swords. When the miserable human sufferers struggled desperately to wrench themselves free and to reach the neighbouring shores, back they were driven by the yakshas to the crimsoned waters and the insatiable teeth and claws. The sight was insupportable, and the Brahman girl felt terrified and sick at heart until, having offered silent prayer to Buddha, she acquired new fortitude through her faith in him. After a little while she was approached by a "devil-king," who asked her what she was doing at the entrance to hell; for this ocean, he remarked, was one of the three great waters which have to be crossed by the souls of dead sinners on their way to their place of punishment. "This one," he observed, "is not nearly so dreadful as the second one; and the second is not nearly as bad as the third." The girl explains that her object in coming to the confines of hell is that she may find her mother. "My mother died a short time ago," she says, "and I am in doubt as to where her soul has gone." In answer to the devil-king's questions she then gives him full details as to her mother's name and earthly residence; whereupon he clasps his hands respectfully and assures her that all is well, and that she may go home in comfort. "Your mother," he says, "is already in heaven. Sinner as she was, she has been saved by the virtue and filial piety of her saintly daughter. You have rescued your mother from the worst of the hells, and now she is at peace in Paradise." With these cheering words the devil departed, and the Brahman girl fell into a trance, from which she awoke amid the familiar surroundings of her own home. Full of gratitude to Buddha, she hurried off to the sanctuary in which she had received his promise, and there she renewed the oath made in a former age that she would become a saviour of mankind, and consecrate all her activities to the rescue of suffering sinners from the pains and sorrows incident to both life and death. More especially would she strive to assuage the miseries of those who were being tormented in the underworld, nor would she consider her vow fulfilled until every soul in hell had become a partaker in the ineffable bliss of heaven.

The next part of the sutra describes how throughout unimaginable ages and in countless worlds Ti-tsang in his successive reincarnations has been steadily carrying out his benevolent purpose. In the presence of all the divine beings who have assembled in the Taoli paradise he now receives the blessing of Buddha, to whom he has made a report of the work already performed.

The Mother of Buddha

The first speaker in the next scene is the Lady Maya, the "Holy Mother (Sheng Mu), who begs Ti-tsang to expound the nature of the punishments meted out to the wicked. Maya is the traditional name of the earthly parent of Gotama Buddha, and according to a Mahayanist theory she is "the eternal Mother of all the Buddhas.[162]" In accordance with her request, Ti-tsang proceeds to enumerate and describe the different kinds of sins which can only be expiated in the Avlchi hell. Into these detailed descriptions, which are similar to those in numerous sutras and sermon-books, we need not enter. It is interesting to note that the list of sins is headed by the gravest moral offence known to Chinese ethics lack of filial piety. Among those which follow are sacrilege, contempt for holy things, and irreverence towards the books of the Buddhist scriptures.

After a short dialogue between Buddha and Ti-tsang on the subject of the working of the inexorable law of karma (moral character in action and its results), Buddha gives a further account, in answer to a question put by

---

162 摩耶夫人永为千佛之母 Here again we have a hint of the mystical truth that all the Buddhas are one.

a pusa named Ting-tzu-tsai (the "Self-Existent"), of some of the acts of self-sacrifice performed by Ti-tsang in certain of his former incarnations. Once, for example, he was born as king of a country which was noted for the wickedness of its inhabitants, and through love and pity for his misguided subjects he swore that he would refuse to accept the rewards due to his own virtue so long as a single man in his kingdom remained entangled in the meshes of vice or worldly delusion. In another age he was born as a girl, and was known by the name of Bright-eyes[163]. This damsel's characteristic virtue was filial piety, and the story told of her is similar in essentials to that of the Brahman girl.

For the benefit of the Four Heavenly Kings[164] Buddha now explains the doctrine of retribution, and enumerates the punishments that follow the different classes of misdeeds. The important Buddhist commandment "Thou shalt not take life" is given special prominence in this chapter. To deprive any being of life, says our Chinese commentator on this passage, is one of the gravest of sins, from two points of view. In the first place, all men and animals instinctively cling to life, and are therefore bound to respect life in others. In the second place and this is a far graver consideration all living beings, even the lowest insects, are sharers in the Buddha-nature; to commit needless and wanton slaughter, therefore, is to incur the guilt of killing a Buddha. The commentator gives several little anecdotes to illustrate the text. For example, he tells us that once upon a time there was a wealthy noble who had an only son. The son married a wife. Seven days after the wedding he climbed a tree to pluck blossoms to make a garland for his bride, but he fell from a branch and was killed. The noble, overcome with grief, visited Buddha and besought him to explain what he had done to deserve so severe a calamity as the loss of his only son. "Long ago," said Buddha, "there was a boy who went out with a bow and arrows to shoot birds. Three men were with him and gave him encouragement. That boy was no other than your own son in a former incarnation; and you yourself and your wife and your son's bride were the three who encouraged him in his cruel sport."

---

163 Kuang-mu.
164 Ssu ta t'ien-wang.

Reginald Fleming Johnston

P'u-Hsien Pusa

The next speaker is P'u-hsien pusa[165], at whose request Ti-tsang gives an account of the various hells which he has visited for the purpose of saving souls. When this is concluded Buddha arises and exhorts all pusas and spiritual beings to protect and keep holy this sutra concerning the Vow of Ti-tsang, so that through the sanctity and spiritual efficacy of its words all men may reach the heaven of Nirvana. As he speaks, all the myriad worlds comprising the whole universe are illuminated by a radiant light which emanates from his transfigured person. He goes on to describe the results of a true and devout faith in Ti-tsang. Devotion to this pusa will infallibly bring peace and happiness to those in pain, sick ness, or sorrow, and will be a sure protection to all who are in danger or are disturbed by evil spirits[166].

After a religious dialogue between Ti-tsang and an "elder" named Ta Pien ("Great Argument") concerning death and judgment and rebirth, we come to the most dramatic event described in the sutra the arrival of Yenlo-wang (Yama), the king of hell, with a vast crowd of "great devil-kings" and "small devil-kings." Yenlo kneels before Buddha and explains that he and his diabolical company have been enabled to pay this visit to the Taoli heaven through the spiritual might of Buddha himself and that of the pusa Ti-tsang, and that they have come to implore the World-honoured One to remove their doubts and perplexities concerning the nature of Ti-tsang's great work of redemption and rescue, especially with reference to those backsliding souls to whom the helping hand of the saviour Ti-tsang has already been extended, but who have again fallen into evil ways and have incurred fresh punishment. Buddha proceeds to preach a sermon on this subject, in which he says that men are often of a froward and untamable nature, which causes them to fall into sin as often as they are helped out of it. The patience and compassion of Ti-tsang, however, are limitless, and he does not turn away from those who are in need of his

---

165 The patron divinity of Omei-shan.

166 Reverence to Ti-tsang may be shown in many ways. One of them consists, we are told, in making copies of this sutra. The copying or reprinting of any portion of the Buddhist scriptures is always re garded by Chinese Buddhists as an act of great religious merit. This is why we constantly find at the end of monastery-editions of the sacred books a list of the names of all who subscribed towards the cost of printing. Such names usually include those of monks,, nuns, and lay-believers. It sometimes happens, as we shall see, that a monk or hermit uses his own blood in making copies of the scriptures or in drawing portraits of his favourite pusa.

help even though they have wandered again and again from the safe path to which he has led them.

"Evil Poison"

One of the principal devils, whose unpromising name is O-tu ("Evil Poison"), is the next protagonist in the heavenly drama. His speech throws light on the ideas of Chinese Buddhists concerning the devil-nature.

"Lord," he says, "we demons are countless in number. Each of us has his own duty assigned to him; we are engaged either in helping men or in harming them, in accordance with the fate that they have brought upon themselves. We ask for leave to wander through the world of men, where there is so much evil, so little good. When we come to a house whether it be a city mansion or a farmer's cottage in which we find a single man or a single woman engaged in doing good, be it on ever so small a scale, or showing reverence for the Buddhas and holy things, though it be only by the offer of an altar-ornament, or the burning of a little incense, or the laying of a single flower before Buddha's throne, or the devout recital of one verse of a hymn of praise when we come to the house of such a one as this, we demons will hold such man or woman in highest honour. Let but the holy Buddhas, past, present, and to come, vouchsafe to grant the permission we crave, and it will then be our privilege to act as guardian-spirits of the homes of all righteous men and^women and to prevent disaster, sickness, and misfortune from approaching their doors."
To this remarkable speech Buddha makes a gracious reply, commending "Evil Poison" and his fellow-demons for their laudable desire to range themselves on the side of virtue.

"You and your companions, and Yenlo himself," says Buddha, "are empowered to guard and watch over good men and good women; and I will command the lord Indra, the mighty guardian of devas, to become your divine patron."

AT THE SOUTHERN BASE OF CHIU-HUA.
(*Peaks covered with mist.*)

A MOUNTAIN STREAM, CHIU-HUA.

With regard to this reference to the god Indra, it may be observed that the Brahman deities, when allowed to figure in Buddhist mythology, are always kept in their proper place of subordination. A "god" like Indra has earned his divine position by good karma, but the accumulated merit which sent him to heaven will in time be exhausted, and he will revert to a condition perhaps inferior to that of men. The "gods" are treated with comparatively slight respect by Buddhism, because they, like men, are still subject to the law of change. They are inferior not only to a Buddha, but to any one who has advanced so far along the road to Buddhahood that he is henceforth in no danger of retrogression. According to the Buddhist theory, moreover, the state of Buddhahood is never reached direct from any of the "heavens" of the Brahman system. The "god" who aims at Buddhahood must be born again as man in order that he may arrive at bodhisatship, which is the final stage short of Buddhahood.

The Lord of Fate

The next speaker is a demon who bears the imposing name of Chu-ming ("Lord of Fate"). "My lot," he says, addressing Buddha, "is to control the destiny of all men in respect of both their lives and their deaths." His own earnest desire, he explains, is that happiness shall be the lot of all mankind: men's failure to attain happiness is not due to him, or to any other power or influence outside them selves, but is attributable entirely to their own lack of righteousness and their own errors. The greater part of his speech is concerned with the religious and ceremonial observances which, he says, are rightly associated with the two extremes of human life. He tells us that the spirits and demons hostile to man are apt to show special activity at the time of birth and in the hour of death. They assail the woman in childbirth, because it is their malignant desire to injure or destroy her offspring; they assail the dying, because they desire to gain posses sion of the discarnate soul and make it their plaything in hell. It is therefore of great importance that men should be provided with proper safeguards when they enter and when they make their exits from the stage of life. A woman in childbirth, we are told, must on no account be fed on a flesh diet or given any food which has involved the slaughter of a living animal. This injunction is not merely a reiteration of the Buddhist commandment against killing, but is based on sympathetic magic. If the woman spares the lives of other beings, so will her own offspring live and prosper; if she causes the destruction of other lives, so will the fruit of her own womb pine and die. Again, when a man draws near to death, and sickness or old age clouds his judgment and numbs his faculties, the evil spirits who are waiting for his soul will appear before his dying eyes in deceitful and seductive shapes, diverting his mind from thoughts of the Buddhas. Let him defeat the devils by reading the scriptures and calling upon the names of the holy ones. Unless his life has been so bad that nothing can save him from the pains of hell, the baffled devils will assuredly leave him unharmed. Chu-ming himself under takes to further the good cause which Ti-tsang has at heart by doing his best to rescue sinners from the grasp of devils less benevolent than himself. Sakyamuni listens graciously to Chu-ming's speech, and utters some words of encouragement; then, turning to Ti-tsang, he delivers the prophecy that this demon, owing to his tender and merciful dealings with men, will, in time to come, lose his demonhood, and at a certain period in the remote future (one hundred and seventy kalpas hence) will become a Buddha.

Use of Images

The next section of the sutra consists of an enumeration by Ti-tsang of the names of various Buddhas of past ages and a description of the blessed lot of those who put their trust in them. The next, of greater interest, eulogizes the men and women who are charitable and sympathetic, and who devote themselves to the relief of the sick, the crippled, and the aged. Thereafter we have a section which contains a speech from a powerful earth-spirit who joins the throng of spiritual beings who have assembled to do honour to the name of Ti-tsang. A passage on the merit of making and paying reverence to images and pictures of the pusa is of interest, as it gives our commentator, the monk Ching-lien, an opportunity of emphasizing the truth that no sanctity attaches to images and pictures as such, and that their sole use was to stimulate the religious imagination and to engender feelings of veneration for the spiritual reality of which they are an imperfect expression. Images of the Buddhas may be of gold or silver or copper or iron, and they may be exposed to public reverence in a shrine made of clay or stone or bamboo or timber so says the text. But let us remember, says the commentator, that the truth which these outward shows are intended to shadow forth has no local habitation, nor can it be said to belong to north, south, east, or west that is to say, it has no spatial relations. The image serves its purpose if it helps to bring the human spirit into communion with the divine, but it is rightly to be regarded as a means and not as an end.

This view of images is undoubtedly that of educated Buddhists in China though the uneducated and superstitious multitude, to whose minds nothing is conceivable as having real existence unless it is cognizable by the bodily senses, and who do not understand the uses of symbolism, are of course prone to become mere worshippers of stone and clay, in Canton or Peking as in Moscow or Rome.

Faith in Ti-Tsang

The sutra next introduces us to one of the greatest of the pusas, Kuan-yin the glorious being who, as we have seen, is one of the three divinities who preside over the so-called Western Paradise, and who, like Ti-tsang, is a guide and saviour of mankind. In this sutra Kuan-yin is only brought in to give Buddha an opportunity of showering further praises on Ti-tsang, who is here described as the supporter and comforter of the poor, the hungry, the sick, the oppressed, the dying, and the dreamer of evil dreams. The believer in Ti-tsang may ascend dangerous mountains, traverse trackless forests, cross deep rivers and seas, travel on robber-haunted roads he need only repeat with faith the name of Ti-tsang, and he will be surrounded and protected by the ghostly guardians of the soil[167], who all reverence that pusa's name. Travelling or resting, waking or sleeping, the believer will always be attended by an invisible bodyguard; even wild beasts and poisonous reptiles will be powerless to do him harm. Not if he spoke for a hundred thousand kalpas, says Sakyamuni, could he exhaust the manifold blessings that result from a good man's faith in Ti-tsang. Finally, Sakyamuni stretches forth his arm and touches the pusa's head.

"Oh Ti-tsang, Ti-tsang," he says, "your spiritual might is beyond the reach of thought. So too are your loving pity, your knowledge, and your wisdom. If all the Buddhas were to spend innumerable ages in declaring the glory of your works, they would not be able to say all that is your due."

---

167 Tu-ti kuei shen.

He then encourages Ti-tsang to continue his benevolent task of saving those who are still in the "burning house" of sin and delusion and watching over them so that they may fall into misery no more. Finally he declares that owing to Ti-tsang's transcendent virtue as redeemer, salvation will be extended not merely to those who have lived good lives, but also to those who have sown only a minute number of good seeds, those whose personal merit is as small as a hair, or a speck of dust, or a grain of sand, or a drop of water. In the very jaws of hell Ti-tsang will come to their help and set them free.

Ti-tsang now kneels before the throne of Buddha and, clasping his hands, solemnly repeats his promise to devote himself to the salvation of mankind. A speech in praise of Ti-tsang by a fellow-pusa named Hsu-k'ung-tsang is followed by a final address by Sakyamuni, who enumerates twenty-eight different kinds of blessings which will be conferred upon those who choose Ti-tsang for their patron and saviour. The last of the twenty-eight is the attainment of Buddhahood.

The closing scene shows Sakyamuni and Ti-tsang receiving the homage of the whole vast assembly of pusas and other spiritual beings by whom the Taoli heaven is thronged. Celestial hands bring offerings of heavenly raiment and jewels, and showers of sweet-scented blossoms fall at the feet of the Lord Buddha and the great pusa.

Filial Piety

To one of the modern editions of this sutra[168] is appended a note to the effect that the printing-blocks "have been reverently carved by the ordained monk Ching-hsi and his two brothers," and that they have carried out this work of piety in the prayerful hope that their mother, Wu Shih, might enjoy a long, happy, and prosperous life. Inscriptions of this kind are very frequently to be found in the reprints of Buddhist tracts and books. It is hardly necessary to say that Buddhism lays almost as much stress on filial piety as does Confucianism itself. Were it otherwise, indeed, Buddhism would never have struck a deep root into Chinese soil. In the case of the Ti-tsang sutra an inscription of the kind referred to is specially appropriate, inasmuch as this work is regarded as occupying a place in Buddhist literature similar to that occupied in Confucian literature by the

---

168 The reference is to the edition published at Ku-shan in 1886.

Buddhist China

Hsiao Ching, or Classic of Filial Piety. Indeed the commentator Ch ing-lien, describes it as "The Gospel of Filial Piety as expounded by our Lord Buddha.[169]" The sutra has earned this high distinction owing to the many passages in which the cardinal Chinese virtue is emphasized and illustrated, though in other respects it is hardly deserving of special praise. It may be regarded, however, as a typical example of a large and influential subdivision of Chinese Buddhistic literature, and our summary of its contents will justify us in dispensing with an examination of many similar sutras dealing with those great pusas Wen-shu, P u-hsien, and Kuan-yin who, with Ti-tsang, are religiously associated with our Four Famous Mountains.

Yama

Next to nothing about the cult of Ti-tsang (whose very name will be strange to many Western readers) is to be found in European books on Chinese Buddhism; and the little that exists is by no means free from error. It has been supposed, for instance, that he is "the ruler of hell," and a student of Buddhism has even hazarded the suggestion that he is rightly to be identified with Yama the Chinese Yenlo. That these conjectures are erroneous the reader of the foregoing pages is now aware. It is not difficult to see how the mistake has arisen. It was vaguely understood that prayers are addressed to Ti-tsang on behalf of those who are supposed to be suffering the pains of hell, and it was known that the ruler, or one of the rulers, of hell is a being named Yenlo: therefore (so it was assumed) Ti-tsang and Yenlo are one and the same. We now know, however, that Ti-tsang is a blessed pusa, a glorious saviour-deity, who visits hell only on errands of love and mercy; whereas Yenlo, king and judge among devils, is himself one of the damned. It is true that a popular title of Ti-tsang is Yu-ming-chiao-chu Lord and Teacher, or Pope, of the Underworld and that another of his titles is Yu-tu-wang King of the Dark City; but these names do not signify that Ti-tsang actually holds the position of hell's king or judge. They mean that he is the master and guide of those who look to him for salvation from its torments the conqueror, rather than the ruler, of hell.

---

169 Wo Fo so shuo chih Hsiao Ching.

JIZŌ.
(Ti-tsang Pusa.)

Buddhist China

Yenlo is the Chinese name for the Vedic and Brahmanical and Iranian hero or deity Yama. In India and Persia he was identified with several different divinities and forces of nature. A predominating belief was that he was the son of the god Vivasat and appeared on earth as the "first man." After his death he became ruler over the souls of dead men. His twin-sister Yami, the "first woman," similarly became ruler over the souls of dead women[170].

In the epic of the Mahabharata, Yama figures as a "king of hell," and it is in this capacity that he has been recognized by popular Buddhism in China. The story of how he came to be ruler of the damned is told thus: Ages ago Yenlo was an ordinary human monarch and ruled over the kingdom of Vaisali, in Northern India. Once when at war with the king of a neighbouring state he was in danger of suffering defeat in a great battle, and swore a mighty oath that if the powers of the underworld would come to his help and give him the victory, he and his followers would agree to be reborn in hell. Thereupon eighteen generals suddenly made their appearance at the head of a million warriors, all of whom fought on his side with terrific rage and ferocity. The battle was soon won, and the king marched victoriously through the territory of his defeated neighbour. But the oath was not forgotten, for the king in his next incarnation was born as principal king of hell. The eighteen generals became the eighteen minor kings, and their million warriors were also reborn in hell as demon-lictors.

Evil Not Eternal

Yenlo as king of hell possesses a grand palace, and multitudes of servile devils are always at his beck and call; but his life is not unmixedly happy. Three times every twenty-four hours his majesty is seized by a band of devils and laid flat on a scorching frying-pan. His mouth is then forced open with an iron hook, and a stream of molten copper is poured down his throat. After this he is set at liberty and allowed to amuse himself with the female devils of his court until the time comes for the punishment to be repeated.

Yenlo is sometimes described as a shuang-wang, or "double-king." This is really a Chinese translation of the Sanskrit Yama, which means "twin." According to one interpretation, the word shuang ("double") has

---

[170] According to a Brahmanic belief, Yama was one of the numerous forms of the god Agni, and Yami was the Earth.

reference to the king's alternating experiences in hell, the torture of the boiling copper being always succeeded by the exhilarating companionship of the demon-ladies. But, according to another view, the word implies that Yenlo possesses two personalities male and female. In Indian legend, as we have seen, the two are known as Yama and Yami, who as brother and sister hold joint rule over the denizens of hell. This literal interpretation of the term shuang has not commended itself to Chinese Buddhists, by whom the existence of Yami is usually ignored.

Buddhist Demonology

According to the Buddhists, Yenlo has been one of hell's chief kings for countless past ages, and a king of hell he must remain for a long time to come. But neither he nor any other inhabitant of that dismal region is regarded as eternally damned. It is important that we should remember that the doctrine of everlasting or eternal punishment is not inculcated by Buddhism, and would, indeed, be utterly repugnant to the Buddhist theory of spiritual evolution. Every living being will sooner or later attain the bliss of Buddhahood, and from this rule the souls in hell are not excepted. This being so, we not be surprised to find that in Buddhism there is no recognition of the existence of a spirit of unmitigated evil. There is no Satan: the innumerable hells of darkness and pain are thronged by the spirits of men and women languishing in utter misery, but among these tortured hosts there is not a single soul that will not at last purge itself from all sin and foulness and win its way to the light.

To the believing Buddhist, then, the task undertaken by the compassionate Ti-tsang is not a vain or hopeless one. In bursting the gates of hell by the touch of his staff, and in dispelling hell's darkness with the radiance of his wondrous jewel, he is but hastening an inevitable consummation the triumph of good and the annihilation of all evil. Thus it is, as we have seen in our sutra, that the very king of hell and his devils join the saints of heaven in offering praise and honour to Ti-tsang[171]. So far are Yenlo and his fellow-devils from regarding Ti-tsang as their enemy that they themselves volunteer to hasten the final defeat of evil by

---

171 Every one is familiar with the saying about Satan's sick-bed repentance: "when the devil was ill the devil a monk would be," etc. It is curious to note that a very similar observation has been made of Yenlo, who in the midst of his torments in hell is said to have sworn an oath that when he is released from punishment and born again as a man he will enter the monkhood. But the Buddhist fancy, unlike that of the Christian satirist, assumes that the devil will not go back on his word.

shielding all virtuous men and women from moral or physical injury. This implies not only that the very fiends are engaged in working their upward way towards the light, but also that only the wicked are in any danger of falling even temporarily into the hands of demons. Like the Lady in Milton's Comus, the truly virtuous and pure-minded man or woman will pass unharmed through the serried ranks of evil spirits. That the religious imagination of the West should conceive of "the Devil" as characterized by utter malevolence towards mankind and defiant hatred towards God is a natural accompaniment of the pessimistic conception that Lucifer and the rest of the "fallen angels" and other denizens of hell are irremediably damned to an eternity of hopeless woe; but this gloomy theory (which Christianity seems to have inherited from Judaism) has no counterpart in the more merciful demonology of the Buddhists, who realize that the existence of an eternal hell would be the eternal proof of an irreversible victory if only a partial one of evil over good.

We are not concerned in these pages with the various changes and adaptations which Buddhism has undergone in Japan; but it is interesting to note that among the many Buddhist divinities whose cult has taken firm root in that country Ti-tsang holds one of the highest places in popular affection and reverence. His Japanese name is Jizo, a word which merely represents the Japanese sounds of the two Chinese characters which in China are pronounced Ti-tsang. In essentials there is no difference between the Chinese and the Japanese conceptions of the functions and attributes of the pusa, but in Japan he has been endowed with one most pleasing characteristic which is in that country the chief source of his popularity. He is pre-eminently the protector, comforter, and loving friend of dead children[172]. Perhaps religious reverie has seldom evolved a more pleasing fancy than this that the stern vanquisher of hell, the bearer of the world's burdens, the steadfast hero whose duty it is to strive with hosts of demons and to face the ghastliest terrors of the underworld, is at the same

---

[172] A charming account of the Jizo cult may be found in Lafcadio Hearn's Glimpses of Unfamiliar Japan, i. 34 ff. (London: 1905). He describes a certain sculptured image of Jiz5 as a dream in white stone of the playfellow of dead children,, like a beautiful young boy, with gracious eyelids half-closed, and face made heavenly by such a smile as only Buddhist art could have imagined the smile of infinite loving-ness and supremest gentleness." For the portraits of Jizo in this book I am indebted to a Japanese Buddhist scholar, Mr Tachibana.

time the gentlest and most lovable of spiritual beings, the tender playmate of little children[173].

A Chinese monk describes Ti-tsang thus: He is the guide and counsellor of men during the ages that must elapse between the passing away of the last Buddha (Sakyamuni) and the coming of the next (Maitreya). He is the ship of mercy that conveys mankind across the perilous seas of pain and sorrow; the torch that illumines the dark ways of our earthly life; the path that leads direct to heaven: the gate that opens upon the Way of the Buddha. Another commentator observes that ordinary well-meaning men think first of securing their own salvation, and then consider the advisability of saving others; but Ti-tsang puts the welfare of every creature in the universe before his own. Another writes thus

"The great teacher Ti-tsang countless ages ago uttered a most solemn vow that he would take upon himself the sins and burdens of all creatures in all the six states of existence,[174] and that he would teach and exhort men to hold fast to the true religion so as to promote the development of all virtue. Patiently he endures anguish and toil, for he is greatly compassionate and greatly pitiful.[175]"

Ti-tsang's chief claims to religious reverence are his love for mankind, his willingness to bear the burdens of all sufferers, and his victorious descents into hell for the purpose of releasing tormented souls. In view of the fact that these functions or qualities have parallels in the myths and doctrines of several religious systems outside China, the Western reader will naturally ask whether there is here any evidence of indebtedness to Christianity[176]. The general problem of a possible contact between the two

---

173 I should like to draw my reader's attention to a striking passage in Mr A. C. Benson's semi-allegorical picture of the world beyond the grave in his Child of the Dawn, pp. 205-6. The Lord of the Tower of Pain, "the most tried and trusted of all the servants of God," who had to endure "all the pain of countless worlds," proved to be the most beautiful and gracious sight of all that I saw in my pilgrimage."

174 发弘誓愿荷负罪苦六道众生
175 Quoted in Ti-tsang Pen-yuan-ching K'o-chu.
176 Christ's descent into hell was not an article of the Christian faith at the time of the composition of the earliest form of the so-called Apostles Creed. The descendit ad inferos does not appear in the Creed till after the middle of the fourth century, though the doctrine itself seems to have been traditional in the Church at a much earlier period. It is quite possible that the tradition was of independent growth and owed nothing to any non-Christian source. The theories as to the motive of the descent into hell have been numerous. In the " Faith of St. Jerome" (discovered in 1903) we have the words "crucified, buried, descended into hell, trod down the sting of death, rose again the third day." The more usual theory (taken from the First Epistle of St. Peter and a few other texts) is that Christ's descent was for the purpose of preaching to the spirits in prison " words which may have formed the basis of what has been called " one of the most beautiful of legends, that of the deliverance of Adam's spirit from the nether world by the Christ." Dr T. K. Cheyne in Encycl. Brit. (llth ed.), i. 170. He points

great religious systems of East and West has already been considered, and we found reason for suspecting that neither Christianity nor Buddhism directly borrowed from the other, but that to a certain limited extent both availed themselves of common stores of religious material common not only to Christian and Buddhist creed-makers, but also to the builders of other religious systems. It is very possible, moreover, that some of the numerous legends about the descent of saviours and heroes into the nether world sprang up quite independently of one another. Such legends are to be found in the religious and literary traditions of peoples as widely separated as the Greeks, the Finns, the West Africans, the American Indians, the South Sea Islanders and the Japanese. Coming nearer to the regions from which both Christianity and the Mahayana seem to have drawn some of their doctrinal material, we find that the Mandaeans made their Hibil Ziwa the hero of a descensus ad inferos, and that a similar belief was associated with Mithraism. Mithras was regarded as a divine friend of man, a saviour from death and hell, and like both the Chinese Ti-tsang and the Greek Hermes –or Guide of Souls.

Buddhism and Hinduism

But it is to India and Hinduism that we must look for the undoubted origin of the beliefs which associate Ti-tsang with the world of the dead. Of Krishna we learn that one of his greatest feats was his descent into hell, where he over threw Yama and rescued some of the souls of the condemned sufferers; and somewhat similar stories are told about Ravana in the epic of the Ramayana, about Yuddhishthira in the Mahabharata, and also about the divine Vishnu. Such stories as these were probably embedded in Indian religious tradition long before they made their appearance in literary form, and it is scarcely possible to say precisely at what period they came to be accepted by Buddhism. We may remember, however, that the very deep influence which Hinduism has had on the development of Chinese Buddhism is due to the fact that during the whole period of the missionary activity of Indian Buddhists in China, Buddhism in India was slowly and surely losing its characteristic features and becoming absorbed into the general system of Indian religious thought, which assimilated all that it found congenial in both Buddhism and

---

out that the earliest form of the legend is a Christian interpolation in a Jewish text, and adds that "we may compare a partly parallel passage where the agent is Michael."

Brahmanism. The result of the assimilating process was the religion we now know as Hinduism; but before that process was complete it would have puzzled many a Chinese Buddhist and many a native of India too to say where Buddhism ended and Hinduism began; and there is no doubt that a great deal of Hinduism entered China under the auspices of a Buddhism which had already lost much of its own self-consciousness.

Mahayana Mysticism

While studying the beliefs relating to the various divine or semi-divine personages who occupy prominent positions in the Mahayana mythology, we cannot fail to be struck by the frequent repetitions of the same ideas in slightly different forms. We shall often find that all or nearly all the qualities and functions ascribed to this or that pusa are identical with those ascribed to others, and the Western mind will be very apt to grow impatient at the apparently needless multiplication of divine personalities all possessing the same or very similar characteristics. Practically all that has been said of Ti-tsang, for example, might be transferred without material alteration to Kuan-yin; even in his errands of mercy to tortured souls in hell Ti-tsang can lay claim to no originality, for Kuan-yin is credited with exploits of precisely the same kind[177]. The vows taken by the saviour-bodhisats are all very much the same, and most of the Mahayana sutras describing the deeds and virtues of the pusas might easily be applied, with the alteration of very little besides names, to the celebration of each of the great pusas in turn. We should be wrong, however, if we were to conclude that these facts prove a lack of originality in the religious imagination of the Buddhist writers. No serious attempt is made by them to disguise the resemblances between one pusa and another: on the contrary, such resemblances often seem to be given almost unnecessary emphasis, as though the writers wished to compel the least thoughtful reader or worshipper to comprehend something of the unity that underlies all external manifestations of religious energy.

It is the belief of the Mahayana mystics that all the Buddhas and bodhisats are ultimately an undifferentiated One, which constitutes the only Reality. He who holds this belief may worship Ti-tsang at the sacred hill of Chiu-hua or elsewhere, but in doing so he will know that through

---

177 Vajrapani (see the BodhIcharyavatara of Santi-Deva) is also supposed to visit hell on errands of mercy.

Buddhist China

Ti-tsang he is paying reverence to Kuan-yin and Wen-shu and P'u-hsien and all the myriad Buddhas and pusas in all the myriad worlds that comprise the universe. Similarly, at Wut'ai he will praise the holy name of Wen-shu, at Omei that of P'u-hsien, at Puto that of Kuan-yin; but he will know that the real object of his worship has been in all cases the same. These conceptions are beyond the reach of the majority of the throng of worshippers who year by year ascend the steep pilgrim-path of the beautiful mountain of Chiu-hua. The object of their quest is Ti-tsang and Ti-tsang only, for to them he is no phantom, no mere abstraction, but a powerful deity who can and will be a guide and protector to suffering humanity, especially in the dark ways of death. Yet some of the pilgrims know that it is not in images of clay or bronze that they can hope to find the real Ti-tsang, and they, while performing all the outward rites that are expected of them, will look for Ti-tsang not in garnished temple or in curtained shrine, but rather in the secret places of their own hearts. Each human being is himself the bearer of the staff that will break open the gates of hell, and the possessor of the jewel that will illumine the darkness through which his own soul is groping. So long as he is sunk in sensuous delusion, or in sin, or in selfishness, or is led astray by the false glare of worldly wealth and honours, he will be encompassed by all the dangers that beset a blind man who is wandering guideless in a strange land; but deep in his inmost nature (ti) there is stored (tsang) a treasure which, if he will only clear away the dust and rubbish under which it lies concealed, will assuredly prove to be everlastingly precious and incorruptible. Similarly, the only hell that man need fear is the hell that he creates for himself out of his own evil thoughts and deeds. Purity of thought is Ti-tsang's jewel, strength of character is his staff, and these are the weapons against which the gates of hell shall not prevail.

Reginald Fleming Johnston

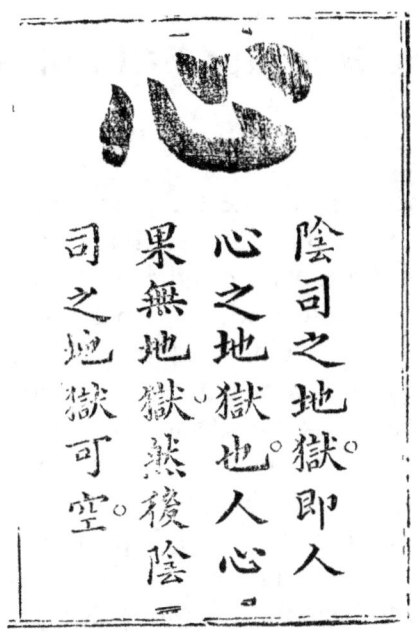

"The hell that is ruled by the judges of the dead is no other than the hell that is within your own heart. If there be no hell within your heart, the judges of the dead will have no hell for you hereafter."

[From the *Yü-li-chih-pao*.]

The large character at the top stands for Heart or Mind.

IX. The Prince-Hermit Of Chiu-Hua And His Successors

At the commencement of the foregoing chapter it was mentioned that Ti-tsang was the patron divinity of Chiu-hua-shan, but nothing has yet been said to indicate any connection between the pusa and the mountain. The story which associates the two is soon told.

About the middle of the eighth century of our era a certain foreigner named Chin Ch'iao-chio [178], a native of a country named Hsin-lo (according to the modern Pekingese sounds), came to China by sea and landed on the coast of Kiangsu. He was a man of wealth and consequence in his own country, for he was a prince of the royal house and a near relative of the king; but riches and high position had no attraction for Ch'iao-chio, whose temperament was deeply religious, and who longed for nothing better than to become a life-long disciple of Buddha. It was in the guise of a humble Buddhist monk that in or about the year 741 he set out from his native land, his only object being to wander among the holy mountains of central China until he should have the good fortune to find among them some home of peace in which to spend the tranquil life of a contemplative recluse. His choice was soon made. No sooner had he espied the cloud-piercing heights of Chiu-hua than he felt impelled to explore its deepest and loneliest recesses, and thither he made a path for himself through the brambles and brushwood and tangled creepers. In this secluded region the princely hermit dwelt contentedly, isolated from human companionship, and dependent for subsistence on the wild herbs of the hillside. But though separated from mankind, he was not neglected by beings of another order; spiritual beings were his companions and protectors, and we are told that once when he was bitten by a venomous animal his wound was tended by a fairylike creature who caused a miraculous stream of healing waters to issue from a rock.

By degrees the fame of the recluse spread far and wide among the people of the neighbour ing plains. In the year 756 a man named Chu-ko Chieh and a party of friends from the district city visited him in his

---

178 Ch'iao-chio, which may be translated "Lofty Enlightenment" was his fa-ming, or name in religion; Chin was what we should call his surname.

mountain retreat, and found him sitting meditatively in the stone hut which he had built for himself. Looking into his cooking-pot they found nothing but a handful of what appeared to be white clay and boiled millet his only fare. Touched at this evidence of Ch'iao-chio's frugality, Chu-ko and his friends threw themselves at his feet, imploring him with tears to treat himself more generously and promising to provide him with a better place to live in and an endowment of land. They were as good as their word. Later on, some of his admirers, of whom one was a man named Sheng Yu, built for him a beautiful monastic dwelling, in which he spent the rest of his life surrounded by a few devoted disciples, among whom were a few of his own country men who followed him into voluntary exile.

The Hermit's Death

He died in 794, at the great age of ninety-nine, having lived at Chiu-hua for more than half a century. The spirits of the streams and peaks joined his disciples in mourning his loss, for we are told that at the hour of his death there was heard a crashing of rocks and a sound of moan ing in the hills. But it was not till after his death that the monks and hermits of Chiu-hua discovered the real secret of their revered master's identity. Three years after his decease the coffin was opened in order that the remains might be deposited in the tomb that had been specially prepared to receive them: and lo! the dead monk's body showed no trace of decay, and his complexion was that of a living man. A strange thing happened, however, when the body was lifted up: for the bones gave forth a sound like the rattling of golden chains. Remembering a passage in their sacred books which tells how the relics of a pusa may be known by the fact that when touched or lifted they give forth the sound of rattling chains, the monks realized for the first time that their master was indeed divine[179]; and when they reflected on the boundless love and tenderness of his nature they felt assured that he could have been no other than an incarnation of the loving and pitiful pusa Ti-tsang. This belief was confirmed by the miracle which took place after the body of the saint had been laid in its new tomb; for out of the ground came forth a tongue of fire which curled

---

179 There seems to have been a somewhat similar superstition with regard to the bodies of Christian saints. We are told, for example, that after the sacred bones of Pascal Baylon had been enshrined, "a noise and a clatter could be heard from within the relic shrine every time the Host was raised above the altar, as if the bones had knocked against the walls of the chest" (Yrjo Hirn's The Sacred Shrine, 1912, p. 121).

itself upwards and remained for a long time suspended over the grave like a flaming aureole.

Kingdom of Hsin-Lo

Miracles apart, there is no reason to doubt that Chin Ch'ao-chio was a real person, that he was a native of a country called Hsin-lo, and that he spent many years of his life as a hermit on Chiu-hua-shan. But where was the kingdom of Hsin-lo? It has always been assumed by the few European travellers and missionaries who have mentioned the saint of Hsin-lo that he was a prince of Siam. This assumption is erroneous, though the mistake on the part of Europeans may be readily excused when we find that it has also been made by native scholars. An examination of the historical records of Chiu-hua and a scrutiny of various stone tablets preserved in the mountain-

monasteries reveal the fact that the prince's home is sometimes described as Hsin-lo and sometimes as Hsien-lo. Hsien-lo is the ordinary Chinese name for Siam; Hsin-lo is the almost forgotten name of a certain kingdom of south-eastern Korea, which became extinct in the tenth century of the Christian era. A perusal of the inscriptions and records makes it clear that the recluse of Chiu-hua was not a native of Siam but a native of the Korean kingdom of Hsin-lo or (to adopt the native pronunciation of the Chinese characters) Sil-la. The confusion obviously arose from the careless ness or ignorance of some Chinese monks of the Ming and Ching dynasties who, having never heard of the long extinct kingdom in south eastern Korea, assumed that the word Hsin-lo was merely an erroneous or old-fashioned variant of Hsien-lo[180].

That no prince from Siam could have travelled to China in the eighth century is sufficiently obvious from the fact that it was not till a much later period that the southern section of the Tai race succeeded in establishing a kingdom on what we now know as the Gulf of Siam. The great southward movement of the race was mainly the result of certain important political events in China, which did not take place till the thirteenth century, and it is hardly correct to speak of a kingdom of Siam until about a hundred years later. A Tai prince of the eighth century would probably have entered China through Yunnan, which was at that time

---

180 The matter is sensibly discussed, and a correct conclusion come to, in the Chiu-hua-shan-chih, x. Zff.

under the control of various sections of the Tai race. A clue to our princely wanderer's real place of origin is to be found in his own surname, which is given in all the records as Chin or Kin. Now if we turn to the scanty annals of the old Korean kingdom of Sil-la, we find that this was indeed the name (pronounced Keum in Korean) of the line of kings who occupied the throne at the very time when Chin Ch'ao-chio is said to have come to Chiu-hua-shan. Further, it may be observed that the monastic records of other parts of Central China contain ample evidence that there was frequent intercourse between the Buddhists of Korea and those of China; and the recluse of Chiu-hua was by no means the first or the last native of Sil-la to take up his residence in a Chinese monastery.

Korean Kingdoms

The beginnings of the kingdom of Sil-la are ascribed to the first century B.C. It was one of the three ancient Korean states, the others being Pai-chi, or Paik-chyoi, and Kao-chu-li, or Ko-ku-ryo[181]. The royal house of Chin was of ancient lineage, for we hear of a king of that time as early as the year 262 Keum-mi-chhu. Coming down to the year 668 we find that by this time Sil-la had become the most powerful state in the Korean peninsula, for Paik-chyoi had been extinguished after its submission to China, and Ko-ku-ryo had recognized Sil-la as its suzerain. The Chin or Keum family was still (or again) in possession of the throne in the seventh and eighth centuries. Chin Li-hung or Hyo-syo-oang reigned from 692 to 701, and his brother Syong-tok-oang from 702 to 736. If our hermit were really a king's son, it is possible that one of these monarchs was his father. In 737 a son of Syong-tok-wang named Hyo-syong-wang ascended the throne, but only reigned four years. The last year of his reign (741) was the very year in which Chin Ch'iao-chio is said to have started on his lifelong exile. The kingdom of Sil-la continued to exist, with varying fortune, till the year 935, when the fifty-sixth king gave in his submission to the monarch of a united Korea.

From the time of Chin Ti-tsang (as our royal recluse is often named) to the present time the records of Chiu-hua-shan are continuous; but of the previous history of the mountain we have only scanty information. The Taoist adepts of two thousand and more years ago seem to have regarded

---

181 Pai-chi and Kao-chu-li represent the modern Pekingese sounds.

it as a spur of the Huang mountain, which lies to the south, and which, with its thirty-six haunted peaks and its hot springs, has always had a great reputation as the home of Taoist "immortals." The shadowy Emperor Huang-ti (2698 B.C.) is said to have travelled thither in the company of a wizard named Fou-ch'iu, his purpose being the same as that which moved him to visit Omei-shan and other mountains the mastery of the secret of longevity. This was a pursuit in which, if the Chinese dates of those remote ages are to be trusted, he met with very creditable success, for he reigned for a hundred years, and then (according to some authorities) went to heaven without dying.

Wizards and Buddhist Monks

Among other distinguished Taoists who visited Chiu-hua is Tou Po-yu, who lived about 100 B.C. He became magistrate of the neighbouring district city, and set himself to govern the people in accordance with the precepts of Lao-tzu. On one occasion he went a-fishing and caught a white dragon, which he promptly released. The dragon's gratitude was such that Tou became endowed with magic powers, and at the end of his long life the white dragon came and carried him off to Paradise. His two daughters also attained immortality by transforming themselves into a pair of wild ducks and flying after their father.

Still more famous was Ko Hung, who lived in the fourth century of our era. He was in the habit of wandering from mountain to mountain in order to pry into nature's secrets and to collect the ingredients of the elixir of life; but he found time to write, under the name of Pao P'-tzu a curious and fascinating book about Taoist marvels, and he also composed biographies of the hsien-jen, or mountain rishi.

Yet another Taoist expert who visited Chiu-hua in his rambles was Chang Kuo-lao, of the seventh and eighth centuries. He was himself a noted hsien-jen, and he is classed among the select company of the Pa Hsien or Eight Rishi, who are very familiar figures in Chinese art and legend[182].

The first Buddhist monk who lived at Chiu-hua is said to have been one Pei Tu, a pilgrim from, and native of, India. He reached the mountain

---

182 There is a hill in the Weihaiwei territory (at present under British rule) which, according to the local folklore, was cut in half by Chang Kuo-lao. One half was carried off to Manchuria for some mysterious reason, the other half remains in situ, and is still known as pan-pi-shan, the " cut-in-half hill."

in the year 401 of our era and erected a small hermitage. Our authorities differ as to the name and situation of this building. Some say the founder styled it the Chiu-hua-ssu, and that it subsequently gave its name to the mountain. Others say he chose the name because it was already that of the mountain. It is also said that in the year 780 the Throne officially recognized the existence of this monastery and changed its name to Hua-ch'eng-ssu. On the other hand, the weight of authority supports the view that the Hua-ch'eng-ssu was no other than the monastery which was built for Chin Ti-tsang by Sheng Yu and his friends; and it is certainly the case that the saint's name has always been associated with this monastery, which to this day (after many demolitions and restorations) remains the principal religious house on the mountain and the centre of the cult of Ti-tsang. It is by no means impossible, however, that Sheng Yu's monastery was built on the site of an older hermitage which, three and a half centuries earlier, had been the home of the monk Pei Tu. Thus both stories may contain truth, and we shall perhaps be not far wrong if we conclude that though the Buddhistic history of Chiu-hua goes back to the year 401, the mountain owes its sanctity mainly to the fact that an incarnate pusa chose it as his dwelling-place about the middle of the eighth century.

The Poet and the Hermit

As to the name of the mountain, the best authorities agree that the old name was Chiu-tzu-shan, which may possibly be taken to mean the "Mountain of the Nine Philosophers," and per haps contained a reference to the row of peaks which crown the summit of the range and give it a fantastic appearance when viewed against the sky-line from the plain below. The alteration of the name to Chiu-hua "Nine Flowers" is ascribed to the great T'ang dynasty poet Li Po (eighth century) who seems to have paid his first visit to the mountain not long before the arrival of the stranger from Hsin-lo. The poem in which the name Chiu-hua appears for the first time is said to have been written by Li Po when he caught sight of the peaks from his boat on the Yangtse River and likened them to the upturned petals of the lotus[183].

---

[183] It should be mentioned that the authenticity of the poem is not beyond dispute, and it is excluded from some editions of the poet's works. It will be found in the Chiu-hua-shan-chih, viii. 2.

Buddhist China

CHARM USED AT CHIU-HUA WHEN OFFERING PRAYERS
FOR OFFSPRING.

There is a tradition to the effect that the great poet and the Korean recluse met on Chiu-hua and had many a long talk and ramble together. A Chinese essayist has dwelt on this story with much delight, and quotes a proverb to the effect that "a meeting between Chuang and Meng would be a sight worth looking at." Chuang and Meng were the philosophers Chuang-tzu and Mencius, of the third and fourth centuries B.C. An Englishman, in a similar mood, might picture to himself a meeting between Shakespeare and Rare Ben at the "Mermaid." We know too little of Chin Ti-tsang to justify any positive statements as to his intellectual or conversational capacity; but Li Po is universally admitted to have been one of the wittiest and most brilliant men of letters that China has ever produced, and a mountain ramble in his company must have been an exhilarating experience even for a saintly recluse. Li Po himself had no pretentions to sainthood, though one of the names by which he is best known to his idolizing countrymen is that given him by a brother-bard the "Banished Angel.[184]" Another of the titles genially bestowed upon him by his admirers was the "Inspired Drunkard": for Li Po, like many a poet before and since his time, loved to see the "beaded bubbles winking at the brim." When he was a little boy, it is said, he had a dream that from the tip of his brush-pen there burst forth sweet-scented flowers[185]. No one who is qualified to judge of Li Po's poetry will deny that the dream came true and that the flowers are immortal.

Chin Ti-tsang himself is said to have wielded the pen of both poet and essayist with very creditable results[186]. A little poem by the recluse is preserved in the annals of Chiu-hua. It consists of an eight-line stanza, and is addressed to a boy who had long been his faithful servant and companion, on the eve of the boy's return to the busy world of the plains. In English prose the gracefulness of the original is lost, but its general sense may be expressed thus:

"Lonely and still is the life of the recluse, and your heart longs for home. Bid farewell, my boy, to this cloudland hermitage, and then leave the heights of Chiu-hua for ever. Your delight has been in the games and

---

184 This is Professor H. A. Giles's translation of the Chinese words tse hsien.

185 The same story is told of the fifth-century poet Chiang Yen.

186 This fact is in itself sufficient to dispose of the theory that he was a Siamese. It is highly improbable that a Siamese who came to China as an adult could have learned the difficult literary language of that country so thoroughly as to be able to compose essays and verses that were worthy of commendation by native scholars; whereas a Korean of high birth would have been taught classical Chinese in his childhood, and would probably speak the language with perfect fluency.

Buddhist China

toys of childhood, and you have loved to build golden castles in the yellow sands. But now, when you fill the water-jar in the stream you no longer try to catch the moon's reflection, and when you wash the bowl in the pond you care no more to play with the floating bubbles[187]. Go now, and dry those fast-flowing tears. The old monk will have the mists and clouds for companions when you are gone."

Pilgrim-Routes

There are several pilgrim-routes to Chiu-hua, but the nearest port on the Yangtse from which it can be reached is Ta-t'ung, in the prefecture of Ch'ih-chou. A small stream, broad and shallow, comes down to Ta-t'ung from the mountain and is navigable for small craft for several miles. After leaving our boat at a point near the hamlet of Ch'ien-chia-lung we find ourselves on a path that winds through undulating country, well cultivated and populous. The monastery of Lo-shan ("Happiness and Virtue") is the first Buddhist building on our route. Opposite the main gate way and on the left side of the pilgrim's path will be seen an image of Ti-tsang. Beyond the village of Kuo-ming-kai there are several Buddhist temples, and also a notable ancestral temple belonging to the Chang family.

The traveller who leaves Ta-t'ung in the morning may find it convenient to stop for the night at the village of Miao-ch'ien-chen, near the base of the mountain, about eleven miles from Ch'ien-chia-lung, but a better lodging might be found in one of the monasteries on the mountain itself. Miao-ch'ien-chen is a market village with a good three-arch stone bridge. It practically forms one village with the place called Shan-ken ("Mountain-base").

The Tea of Chiu-Hua

The pilgrim-season lasts from September to November, which is a pleasant time for travelling in the Yangtse valley. Those who visit the mountain as students of Buddhism, or with the view of forming a correct idea of how the popular forms of Buddhistic belief find expression, should certainly choose the pilgrim-season for their journey, though they may sometimes find the inns and temples inconveniently crowded. The country

---

187 The meaning is that the boy is growing out of childhood and is no longer content with childish amusements. He is thinking of his far-off home; and the moonlight on the waters and the hubhles in the pond have ceased to interest him.

itself is attractive at all seasons, for southern Anhui is rich in trees, plants, and flowers. Azaleas and rhododendrons are among the chief glories of the spring, and the beautiful tints of the candle-tree and maple are the pride of the autumn. Chiu-hua itself was once densely forested, and its valleys, as well as its southern slopes, are still well wooded. Among the trees to be found on mountain or plain, or on both, are the evergreen oak, the chestnut, the camphor, and coniferse of many varieties. The graceful bamboo, which has been so constant a source of inspiration to artists and poets in China, is very common; rice is grown in terraced fields; and the tea plant flourishes in many a valley. The monks them selves cultivate a special kind of tea which, accord ing to tradition, was brought from Hsin-lo by Chin Ti-tsang. They put it up in rectangular tin canisters bearing the name of the mountain, and large quantities of it are disposed of annually to the pilgrims, who take it home as a highly-prized trophy of their visit to the holy mountain. It should be mentioned that the cultivation of tea (which used to be regarded as a magic herb and as one of the necessary ingredients of the Taoist's elixir of life) is a favourite employment of the Buddhist monks in many parts of central China besides Chiu-hua.

The first temple beyond the village of Shan-ken is called the original First Gate of Heaven[188]. In the small village of Lao T'ien is a large ancestral temple of the Wu clan. Farther on we pass the Wu-hsiang-ssu Hsia-yuan, or Branch of the Wu-hsiang Monastery. It is usual for large monasteries to have branch establishments at the base of the mountain or in the neighbouring plains, with a view partly to the supervision of business matters connected with the monastic revenues and partly to the entertainment and guidance of pilgrims bound for the mountain. Hsia-yuan, or Lower Temple, is the term applied to such subordinate houses.

The well-made pilgrim's path, which winds all the way up the mountain-side, passes by so many monasteries and hermitages that a list of their strange-sounding names would be wearisome to the Western reader. Let us confine our attention, then, to those which present some feature of special interest. It must be regretfully admitted that there are no really ancient buildings on Chiu-hua, as all the monasteries were destroyed by the T-ai-p'ing rebels during their devastating march through central China in the terrible years 1850 to 1864. Nearly all the monastic buildings now to be seen on this mountain have been built since 1865, and

---

188 Ku T'ou Tien-men.

though the old names of the monasteries were preserved, and the ruins made use of as far as possible in the process of restoration, there is no doubt that the architectural and artistic glories of the mountain have been sadly dimmed. Some of the old stone tablets, with their inscriptions, remain intact, but these offer but slender compensation for the many buildings and articles of value and beauty which were totally destroyed by the ruffianly armies of Hung Hsiu-ch'uan. The name which that furious iconoclast selected for the new era which he hoped to inaugurate was T'ai-p'ing T'ien Kuo "The Heavenly Kingdom of Perfect Peace." But, alas! the only peace which he succeeded in establishing among his sorely-stricken countrymen was the peace of a desert.

A temple which is well situated close by a bridged stream and bears the name of the "Temple of the Great Bridge," or the "First Gateway of Contemplation,[189]" may be said to mark the beginning of the real ascent of the mountain. The first religious house of importance at which we arrive is the monastery of "Sweet Dew.[190]" It was founded in 1667, at the suggestion of a nature-loving pilgrim, by a monk named Tung-An. In the eighteenth century it secured the right of conferring ordination a privilege which can properly be exercised only by those houses which have received an official diploma. After its destruction by the T'ai-p'ings in 1861 a monk named Fa-yuan built a little hermitage on the old site, but the monastery was not rebuilt till 1895. It owed its restoration to the unremitting exertions of a monk named Ta-Hang, who in 1898 went to Peking to enlist the imperial sympathy in his work not without some success.

"Half Way to the Sky"

Above the "Sweet Dew Monastery" is a rock known as the "Rock of the Tranquil-Mind,[191]" which is said to have been a favourite resting-place of the poet-monks of Chiu-hua. One of these poets Shen-Ying of the T'ang dynasty lived in a temple which we now reach, and which is named after a Dragon's Pool in the vicinity[192]. The next temple is the Shen-hsiu-an, with a pavilion named Pan-hsiao-t'ing "Half way to the sky." Here

---

189 Ta-ch'iao-an or Ti-i-ch'an-men.

190 Kan-lu-ssu.

191 Ting-Hsin-shih.

192 Lung-ch'ih-ch'an-lin.

there is a shrine to the spirit of the mountain (shan-shen) with an interesting modern inscription by one Chou Pin, a Confucian scholar, who was liberal-minded enough to take a deep interest in the Buddhistic lore of Chiu-hua, and was co-editor of the latest edition of the annals of the mountain.

"In days of old," he tells us in this inscription, "the gods of the land and grain had names, while those of the hills and streams had no names. Thus Kou-lung tilled the soil and Chu and Ch'i sowed the crops[193]. But they performed their work through the medium of men's labour, hence it was from men that they derived their names. But streams flowed and hills reared their crests before the first appear ance of men in the world: therefore, though there were always spiritual beings in the hills and streams, these were nameless spirits."

Confucian Hostility

He then goes on to discuss the rivalry and hostility that have characterized the relations between Buddhists and Confucians, and tells a story of an eccentric monk who disgusted the Confucian scholars of the district by hanging up a pair of scrolls in his temple bearing an inscription to the effect that the tutelary deity of the locality was no other than the famous T'ang dynasty states man, essayist, and poet, Han Yu[194]. As Han Yu had been a determined opponent of Buddhism and a strenuous supporter of Confucianism, the monk's action was regarded as highly improper. Complaints were made to the authorities, with the result that the scrolls were destroyed and the monk flogged.

---

193 Kou-lung, according to legend, was the son of a mythical ruler, Kung-Kung, and came to be associated in sacrifice and worship with the god of the soil," Hou T'u, with whom he is commonly, but not correctly, identified. Chu is supposed to have been the son of the Emperor Lieh-Shan or Shen-nung (2838 B.C.), and under the Hsia (2205-1766 B.C.) and earlier dynasties was associated in sacrifice and worship with the " god of the crops," or Ku-shen. Ch'i was the son of the Emperor Kao-hsin (2436 B.C.), and has been similiarly associated with the "god of the crops" since the rise of the Shang dynasty, (1766-1122 B.C.). As the Shang dynasty superseded the Hsia, so did Chi take the place of Chu. The emperors of the Chou dynasty, which succeeded the Shang, traced their descent to Chi, who consequently maintained his religious position under the Chou rulers. He is generally known as Hou Chi, Ruler of Crops, though this name should apparently belong by right only to the deity with whom Ch'i is sacrificially associated. In ordinary language, as in the minds of the people generally, Kou-lung, Chu, and Chi are actually identified with the gods of soil and grain. The passage in the text is an example of this identification. The matter is ably discussed by M. Chavannes in the essay oil the God of the Soil appended to his Le T'ai Chan (Paris: 1910). See especially pp. 501-506, 520-525.

194 This name is one of the most famous in the literary annals of China. Han Yu lived 768-824,, and was canonized as Han Wen-kung.

Buddhist China

It does not seem to have been known to the author of our inscription that the unfortunate monk who declared that the anti-Buddhistic Han Yu had become identified with the t'u-ti or local tutelary god was only giving expression to a widely-current popular belief. Every village, every graveyard, every temple, is supposed to have its own particular t u-ti, or patron divinity, who, strictly speaking, is nameless [195]; but there is a tendency to regard each t'u-ti as a local manifestation of a single divine personage in whom all t'u-ti are unified, and it is a curious fact that in many parts of China this divine personage has come to be identified, in some unexplained way, with Han Yu. It was certainly rash, however, on the part of a Buddhist monk to make an open boast of the fact that the famous Han Yu, who hated Buddhism in his lifetime, had been obliged to become the tutelary guardian of the site of a Buddhist monastery after his death; and we need not be surprised that the Confucians made an example of him.

Chou Pin on Buddhism

The remainder of the inscription is devoted to a reasoned and temperate defence of Confucianism, as a guide of life, against the claims of Buddhism, which, if they were made good, says our scribe, might destroy the bases of society. He argues that Confucianism, with its insistence on the sanctity of the human relationships (ruler and subject, husband and wife, parent and child), makes for social stability. Not only so, but Buddhists themselves are dependent on Confucian ethic even while they try to supplant Confucianism. By abandoning the world and its ambitions, and by extolling the merits of a celibate life, the Buddhists exercise an influence which, if not checked, would obviously be disruptive in its effects on society; if Confucian discipline were not maintained in the State, the result would be a moral and social anarchy in which Buddhism itself would be overwhelmed. The hostility shown by Buddhism to Confucianism recoils on Buddhism itself, which is rejecting its own sources of life and strength. Confucians who refuse to accept Buddhism are merely cutting themselves off from a religious system which they can take or leave as they choose, and which is in no wise essential to their well-being; whereas Buddhists who are hostile to Confucianism are acting

---

195 For an account of village t'u-ti in Shantung, see Lion and Dragon in Northern China, pp. 371-377.

suicidally, by unconsciously trying to deprive themselves of things which are really necessaries of life. Moreover, Confucianism is universal in its appeal, Buddhism speaks only to the few. That is to say, the whole world might become Confucian, and the world would be all the better for having done so; whereas Buddhism aims at isolating its own adherents and leaving the rest of the world outside its fold. Who would feed and clothe the Buddhist monks if there were no Confucians left? And if all became monks and celibates, who would be the fathers and mothers of the Buddhists of the future?

Prospects of Buddhism

Such, in crude outline, is the argument of the scholarly Chou Pin. It is not original, for similar views have been urged again and again by Confucians of the past, but is interesting as a summary of some of the reasons which have always prevented Buddhism from becoming a really national religion in China. The case against Buddhism is plausible, but by no means conclusive. It does not take account of the fact that Buddhism has a message for laymen as well as for the monkhood, and that man does not live by ethical systems alone. The Chinese Buddhist, moreover, does not admit that his religion is incompatible with Confucianism, though it tries to provide a solution for some of those mysteries which Confucianism confessedly leaves unsolved. He takes pride in being a Confucian as well as a Buddhist, and all the Confucian virtues are inculcated in his books. The institution of a celibate monkhood seems inconsistent with the duties which a man owes to his family, especially in connection with the rearing of offspring to carry on the ancestral cult, but the inconsistency is more apparent than real. No one is allowed to accept ordination unless he has obtained his parents consent, and very few men will seek admittance to a monastery unless the continuation of the ancestral rites of his family has been already provided for. It is extremely rare in China for an only son to enter the monkhood unless, indeed, he is already the father of a healthy family.

It should be added, however, that a considerable proportion of the ordained Buddhists of the China of to-day entered the monasteries as children, and cannot, therefore, be said to have adopted a religious life from personal choice. The motives whereby parents are sometimes impelled to devote their boys to the service of Buddha are various.

Buddhist China

Sometimes they do it in fulfilment of a religious vow, sometimes on account of extreme poverty. It seems probable that the dawn of a progressive era in China and the spread of popular education will sooner or later have the effect of extinguishing the supply of children for the monasteries, and it will be interesting to observe whether Chinese Buddhism possesses a sufficient reserve of vitality to enable it to meet the difficulty. There is reason to believe that the outlook for Buddhism is not hopeless, provided the developments in secular education are met by a revival of learn ing in the monasteries, and provided Buddhism makes a serious and continuous effort to identify itself with the moral and intellectual, as well as the spiritual and artistic, interests of a progressive China.

Reginald Fleming Johnston

X. Monks And Monasteries Of Chiu-Hua

Resuming our ascent from the "Half-way-to-heaven" pavilion, and passing by several monastic buildings of no special interest, we come to the Ch'i-yuan Monastery, which is named after the famous park and vihara which were given to Buddha by prince Jeta and the disciple Sudatta. In the reign of Chia-ch'ing (1796-1820) the monastery prospered greatly under the rule of a monk named Lung-shan. This abbot died at the age of eighty-four, and in view of his spotless life and high reputation for sanctity his disciples embalmed and gilded his dead body, and set it up in a shrine in the monastery temple, so that in death he might continue to preside over the religious services which he had so long conducted in life. There the wizened features of the dead monk are still to be seen by all comers, and are regarded with awe by countless pilgrims every year. The monastery, we are told, was utterly destroyed by the T'ai-p'ing rebels, but the gilded mummy escaped injury, and was set up again in its old shrine as soon as the buildings had been restored. The restoration was effected through the exertions of a zealous monk named Ta-ken ("Great Root"), who, says the chronicler, proved himself to be a most devoted son of Buddha, and no less worthy of praise and honour than Buddha's own disciple Sudatta.

Buddhist Mummies

There was nothing very exceptional in the enshrining of the preserved body of the old abbot Lung-shan, for this procedure has been adopted in the case of ancient and revered monks in many parts of Buddhist China. In most cases the preserved corpse might pass for an ordinary gilded or lacquered image, and it is with something of a shock that the Western visitor learns (or sometimes discovers for himself) that the object before him was once the body of a living man. The usual, though not universal, method of disposing of the dead bodies of ordinary monks is by cremation. The practice of mummifying and exposing the bodies of distinguished abbots and other saintly persons is a highly disagreeable one, and will soon, it is hoped, become extinct. In Tibet the bodies of the Grand Lamas are preserved in the manner described, and it was possibly from Tibet that the practice was borrowed, for there seems to be no evidence that the

Buddhist China

custom is of great antiquity in China. Embalmed and robed and seated cross-legged in the attitude of a Buddha, the Lamas of Lhasa and Tashilhunpo are exposed to public veneration for a considerable time after their death, and each body is finally enclosed in a gilded tomb, or chorten, which is thenceforward regarded with the same reverence that was previously accorded to the embalmed body itself[196].

The Ch'i-yuan Monastery derives part of its prosperity and reputation from the fact that it is a publishing house for Buddhist books and tracts. Here the Ti-tsang-pen-yuan-ching the Sutra of the Vow of Ti-tsang is never allowed to go out of print, for there is always a demand for it among the pilgrims.

Mountain Clubs and Colleges

A little higher up we come to the place where Chin Ti-tsang was cured of his wound. The stream of water which his fairy-nurse caused to issue from a rock is still flowing, and is known as the Lung-nu-ch'uan, or "Spring of the Water-nymph." Close by the stream there once stood a building which was formerly one of the chief attractions of the mountain, though nothing now remains of it but the fragment of an in scribed stone. Here it was that the poet Li Po dwelt when he paid his memorable visits to Chiu-hua. After 762, the year of the poet's death, the cottage was neglected and gradually became a total ruin. In course of time grass grew over the site, and it came to be used as the burial-ground of a family named Chang; but in 1237 the district-magistrate, a man of culture named Ts'ai Yuan-lung, caused the ground to be excavated. Having discovered the foundations of the poet's cottage, Ts'ai proceeded to erect on the same ground a kind of scholars club, or meeting-place for students and poets and other persons of artistic tastes. It was dedicated to the memory of the great poet, and named T'ai-po Shu-t'ang, or School of Li Po. Establishments of this kind are, or were, to be found on many of China's famous mountains; some attained great celebrity and attracted large numbers of students, for these little mountain-universities were often the resort of some of the most distinguished philosophers, artists, and men of letters of their time[197]. The club, or college, founded by Ts'ai flourished

---

196 See E.R.E., iv. 611. The reader who is interested in this curious subject may also be referred to a valuable paper by Dr W. Perceval Yetts entitled Notes on the Disposal of Buddhist Dead in China " in J.E.A.S., July 1911 (see especially pp. 709-725).
197 The most famous was the College of the White-deer Grotto, Lu-shan.

for several centuries. The buildings underwent periodical restorations, of which the most elaborate took place between the years 1476 and 1479. The T'ai-p'ing rebels did not treat Li Po's college with any greater respect than they showed to the Buddhist temples, and nothing remained of it when they had worked their will but a heap of ruins.

We now arrive at a mountain-village chiefly consisting of shops and booths, which exist solely for the convenience of pilgrims. The goods sold include children's toys, sweatmeats, Buddhist books and images, and such miscel laneous articles as visitors like to carry away with them as souvenirs of their pilgrimage. Fortune-tellers are numerous, and their methods are as various as those practised in the West. The palmists show a degree of skill which is only surpassed by their remarkable self-confidence. The telling of fortunes takes place, as a rule, in the open air and within view and hearing of a large body of interested spectators and auditors.

Of several monastic buildings and temples situated in the immediate vicinity of the village the most important is the Hua-ch'eng-ssu. This monastery, as we have seen, is the oldest foundation on the mountain, and has a continuous history from the eighth century of our era. Whether Sheng Yu and his companions were its original founders, or whether it dates from the days of Pei Tu, between three and four centuries earlier, cannot now be determined. But there is no doubt that its special sanctity is due to its association with the name of the prince from Hsin-lo, the incarnate Ti-tsang. The buildings have undergone many restorations in the centuries that have elapsed since his time. In the monastic chronicle special mention is made of the work done by the monk Fu-ch'ing in 1435; and another distinguished monk was Liang-yuan, who in the reign of Wan-li (1573-1619) went to Court and was received with favour by the emperor, who not only presented title-scrolls for some of the temple buildings, but also bestowed purple robes on Liang-yuan himself. This emperor was a zealous patron of Buddhism, and it was in his reign and under his patronage that a new edition of the whole of the Buddhist scriptures was published. Sets of this edition were presented to all the great monastic centres of the empire, including the "Four Famous Hills." A special pavilion was erected behind the main buildings of the Hua-ch eng Monastery for the reception of the set which had been presented to Chiu-hua.

Buddhist China

CHIU-HUA-SHAN
(*From the north-west.*)

CENTRAL CLUSTER OF MONASTIC BUILDINGS, CHIU HUA.
(*From the Eastern Ridge.*)

Imperial Patronage

In the eighteenth century the monastery was twice honoured by imperial notice. K'ang-hsi in 1705 presented to it an autograph scroll bearing the words Chiu-hua sheng ching "the holy region of Chiu-hua"; and in 1766 a similar scroll was presented by the Emperor Ch'ien-lung. In 1857 the monastic buildings were destroyed by the rebels, but the Library[198] of Wan-li remained intact. "There cannot be any doubt that it was preserved by a miracle," remarks a recent writer named Liu Han-fang, who goes on to observe with evident satisfaction that subsequently the rebels who had taken part in the temple-burning were defeated with immense slaughter and thrown into the Yangtse River. "Thus was divine justice vindicated before men's eyes." The restoration of the Hua – ch'eng Monastery was not put in hand till 1889.

Opposite the monastery is a fish-pond, said to have been originally constructed by Sheng Yu. The majority of large Buddhist monasteries possess a pond of this kind, which is intended to afford a practical illustration of the Buddhist commandment, "Thou shalt not take the life of any living creature." It is regarded as an act of merit to supply the fish with scraps of food.

There are several monastic buildings in close proximity to Hua – ch'eng, but the only one to which special reference need be made is a temple which, though it is only an adjunct of Hua-ch eng, is the crowning glory and the most sacred shrine of Chiu-hua the Ju-shen Pao-tien. This "Holy Palace of the Mortal Body" is a temple and tomb combined, for here rest the remains of the incarnate pusa Ti-tsang, before whose gilded image incense is burned by thousands of pilgrims every year.

Prayers to Ti-Tsang

The prayers and vows uttered by the pilgrims when they reach this shrine, and the ceremonies performed by them or by the monks on their behalf, are of various kinds, but they chiefly relate to death and the next world. He who wishes to pray for the soul of a lost parent or other relative obtains from the monks (in return for a small donation) a sheet of yellow paper, on which is printed a prayer to Ti-tsang or to both Ti-tsang and

---

198 Tsang-ching-lou.

Amitabha. Blank spaces are left for the insertion of names and dates. The form of words is to the following effect:

We pray that you will have compassion on the soul of ____ aged ____, who was born on the day of the year, and whose soul has now taken leave of its earth-life and has rejoined the immortals. Alas! time passes all too quickly. We weep when our thoughts turn to the loved one we have lost. We implore you to take him from the place of pain and to lead him to happiness.

This day, the ____ day of ____ we have carried out the proper ceremonies on behalf of the dead. We implore that he may be admitted to joy and peace until such time as he may be born again into the world of men. In the name of the Buddhas, we implore you to save his soul.

When the form has been duly filled in the suppliants kneel before the image of Ti-tsang and set sticks of lighted incense on the altar. The paper is then ceremonially committed to fire, whereupon the written prayer passes to the region of spirit.

Thus we find that from the point of view of the superstitious multitude, who, like the unlettered adherents of every religion, know little and care less about the spiritual meaning underlying the formal doctrines of their faith, Ti-tsang is simply a god of the dead, who, if suitably petitioned, will procure the release of souls from hell, and will set them on the path that leads to Amitabha's heaven. The main object of great numbers of pilgrims to Chiu-hua is, therefore, to offer prayers to Ti-tsang that he will manifest his love and pity towards their beloved dead. It will be observed that the circumstances are precisely of the kind that give priestcraft its opportunity; and though the term "monk" is in general a far more appropriate description of an ordained Buddhist in China than the term "priest," we need not be surprised to find that the Buddhist clergy have not omitted to establish themselves as intermediaries between the lay masses and the divine beings whose sympathy is to be invoked on behalf of the living or the dead. Buddhist monks have never obtained (except in regions where Lamaism prevails) the exclusive privileges and dangerous prerogatives of priest hoods elsewhere; partly because Buddhism has never in China proper succeeded in establishing itself as the sole religion of the State, and partly because it has kept itself free to a remarkable degree from the taint of political or worldly ambition. This religion has seldom, if ever, tried to coerce men's bodies or enslave men's minds; and if it has often derived profit from the ignorance and credulity of the masses, we may at least say for Buddhism that the forms of superstition which its priests have countenanced or fostered are absolutely unessential to the religion itself. It may be suggested that it is hardly fair for Christianity, which in our own time is undergoing a somewhat drastic process of readjustment and reinterpretation, to emphasize the crudities of a Buddhism which has not yet been submitted to a similar modernizing process. The superstitions which are associated with Buddhist beliefs in China to-day are no more essential to Buddhism than were and are the ecclesiastically patronized superstitions of Europe to the teachings ascribed to the Prophet of Nazareth.

The Shrine of Ti-Tsang

The guardianship of the holy shrine of Ti-tsang is vested in the abbot of the Hua-ch'eng Monastery, and it is that dignitary who examines the credentials of pilgrim-monks and stamps their papers with the monastic seal in attestation of the fact that the object of their pilgrimage has been attained. The shrine was burned and pillaged by the T'ai-p'ing rebels, and was one of the first buildings on the mountain to be restored. The work was completed in 1867.

According to the local belief, the entombed body of Ti-tsang is incorruptible. The name of Ju-shen-tien, which is given to the building, implies (if we may judge from the use of the term elsewhere) that the dead man's remains are not only in a state of preservation, but are also exposed to public view in the manner already described in connection with the abbot Lung-shan. But if Chin Ti-tsang's body was preserved and enshrined like that of Lung-shan, there is no evidence to prove it: for the story that his body was found undecayed three years after death is only one of a very large class of similar legends, based, no doubt, on each biographer's pious desire to offer a "proof from incorruptibility" that his hero was unmistakably a saint[199].

After the death of Ti-tsang a mysterious flame was seen hovering over his tomb. That flame, if local report may be trusted, is still occasionally visible after nightfall, and is known as the shen kuang, or "spiritual glory." It can best be seen, say the monks, from the Tung Yen ("Eastern Cliff") a long temple-crowned ridge towards which we must now make our way.

---

199 This does not mean that no such legend has any basis in fact. The bodies of hermits who lived rigidly ascetic lives, and reduced themselves to a state of extreme emaciation, may resist decay for a long time, even without preservative treatment.

Buddhist China

EASTERN RIDGE AND T'IEN-T'AI, CHIU-HUA.

THE PAI-SUI MONASTERY, CHIU-HUA.

A gradually ascending path leads us past four or five temples before it brings us to the end of the ridge at a distance of rather less than three miles from the shrine of Ti-tsang. Here we come to a monastery known as the Pai-sui-an. Pai-sui means "a hundred years old," and the name commemorates a monk named Wu-hsia ("Spotless"), who wandered to Chiu-hua from the Mountain of Wu-t'ai in the reign of Wan-li (1573-1619). Selecting the edge of the precipitous Eastern Ridge for his dwelling-place, he made himself a thatched hut, and gave himself up to tranquil meditation. He died peacefully at the age of over one hundred, crooning hymns to himself as he was dying; and his disciples gave the name of Pai-sui to the monastery which they erected on the site of the old man's hut. In 1879 a monk named "Precious Body [200]" travelled to Peking in order to obtain for his monastery some token of imperial recognition. At present it is one of the most flourishing establishments on the mountain.

Austerities of Buddhist Monks

Visitors to Chinese monasteries will some times hear of monks who have taken a vow of silence, or have voluntarily condemned themselves to solitary confinement in a cave or cell, or have adopted some form of self-torture such as sitting in a spiked cage. Such penances are often technically known as tso kuan, which literally means "to sit gated" the gating process being of a severer type than is customary at English universities. The motives that impel Chinese monks to these acts of austerity are no doubt as various as those which prompted Christian hermits to similar acts in the Middle Ages[201]. In some cases the main object is to extract alms from the pious laity or to obtain donations towards the restoration of a temple; in others the motive force seems to be nothing nobler than a desire for notoriety. But there is no reason to doubt that sometimes the purpose in view is that of the genuine religious ascetic the annihilation of carnal desires and the attainment of self-purification and spiritual enlightenment.

On 22nd May 1908 a monk of the Pai-sui-an, named "Bright Moonlight,[202]" entered upon three years voluntary incarceration. A few

---

200 Pao-shen.
201 See Lecky, European Morals, chap, iv., for hideous details of the practices of Christian hermits.
202 Lang-yueh.

months of this period had already elapsed when I paid my first visit to this monastery in the autumn of that year. The door of his cell was sealed with the monastic seal, and he received his food through a hole in the wall. Judging from his appearance (for it was possible to catch a glimpse of him through the hole) he was well and happy; but when I spoke to him he only touched his lips, for "Bright Moonlight" was vowed to silence.

The Pai-sui-an may be regarded as almost on the summit of Chiu-hua-shan proper, though the peaks of T'ien-t'ai stand a good deal higher[203]. The views from the neighbourhood of the monastery are very striking. On the western side of the ridge may be seen the winding path by which we ascended the mountain, and at our feet lies the large group of temples in the neighbourhood of Ti-tsang's shrine. On the eastern side of the ridge we have a deep, wooded ravine, and beyond it the steep slope which culminates in the line of fantastic peaks of which T'ien-t'ai is one the peaks which kindled the imagination of the poet Li Po as he lay in his boat on the Yangtse nearly twelve hundred years ago.

The Tower of Heaven

Ti-tsang's shrine is, indeed, the holiest spot on the mountain, but no Western visitor will disagree with the Chinese literary pilgrim who declared that to shirk the ascent to the "Tower of Heaven" (T'ien-t'ai) is to remain half ignorant of Chiu-hua. The climb is a steep one. Starting from the Pai-sui-an, it is necessary first to descend the Eastern Ridge on the side remote from the Hua-ch'eng Monastery to a distance of several hundred feet. This brings us to a narrow glen, shaded with trees and bamboos, through which flows a bright mountain stream. On crossing the stream the ascent begins abruptly, leading us past the Temple of "Tinted Clouds"[204] and several other buildings, and finally bringing us to the hermitage of "Ten Thousand Buddhas,"[205] which is situated on the Kuan-yin Peak[206] of the summit of T'ien-t'ai-shan. Here we find our selves on a lofty ridge commanding a magnificent view in almost every direction.

---

[203] According to my own measurement (by b.p. thermometer), the height of the Pai-sui-an is 2,350 feet above sea-level; but I cannot guarantee the accuracy of this. The height of T'ien-t'ai is about 3,000 feet.

[204] Hua-yun-an.

[205] Wan-Fo-ssu.

[206] Kuan-yin-feng.

At T'ien-t'ai, as at the Hua-ch'eng Monastery, pilgrims may have their certificates stamped with an authenticating seal. Protective charms against devils and other noxious things may also be obtained here, and are highly prized by the humbler classes of pilgrims.

The T'en-t'i buildings are small and of no great antiquity. The most important of them was founded in 1368, and after its destruction by the rebels was restored in 1890. The restoration of the smaller temples was carried out chiefly by certain enthusiastic monks, of whom one was named P'u-ch'ing ("Universal Purity") and another Sung – ch'uan ("Pines and Fountains").

Strange Hermits of Chiu-Hua

The famous names associated with Chiu-hua are not only those of monks and hermits. The poet Li Po, as we have seen, loved to ramble over its romantic slopes, and even leaders of armies and busy politicians have sought care-free seclusion in its spirit-haunted glades. The most distinguished of these lovers of Chiu-hua was Wang Shou-jen (1472-1528) a great soldier, statesman, and man of letters of the Ming dynasty. He saw much active service against rebels and barbarian tribesmen, and achieved high rank and distinction. On more than one occasion, however, the machinations of his enemies put him under an official cloud, and at such periods he would seek a congenial resting-place on Chiu-hua. At that time the mountain was a favourite resort of many noted scholars, but Wang Shou-jen seems to have found pleasure chiefly in the society of the mountain-hermits. One of these was an unkempt person who was known to his limited circle of friends by the name of "Shock-headed Ts'ai" or "Ts'ai of the Tangled Hair ";[207] another, who was nameless, was usually referred to as the "Queer fellow who lived in Ti-tsang's cave and ate raw vegetables." Wang's interest in him was aroused by the report that he was in the habit of lying on a bed of pine-needles and used no fire for cooking purposes; wherefore in 1501 Wang paid him a visit. He had to scale a precipice to find him, and when he reached the "Queer-fellow's" den he found him fast asleep. Wang sat down beside him and, so says our chronicler gravely, tickled his toes till he woke up. When he espied Wang, all he said was: "How on earth did you get here? The path is very

---

207 Ts'ai P'eng-t'ou.

dangerous!" But the two were soon on the best of terms with one another, and there, at the edge of a cliff, they proceeded to talk philosophy. And below them rolled the mountain mists.

Wang Shou-Jen

Wang was a practical man of the world, and also a sincere Confucian, but there was a mystical side to his nature which caused him to take a rather unorthodox interest in the doings of Taoist adepts and mountain wizards. He himself studied the occult wisdom of the Taoists for a time, and devoted special attention to the art of regulating the breath[208]. So successful was he in the cultivation of his psychic powers that he developed the faculty of foretelling the future; and he startled people, so we are told, by the remarkable accuracy of his prophecies. It was commonly supposed that he had reached Tao the central truth of Taoist mysticism [209]; but Wang himself gradually awakened to a sense of the futility of a great deal of Taoist magic, and concluded his studies in that direction with the exclamation, "This frittering away of one's energies is not the Tao for me." So he reverted to Confucian orthodoxy, which warns men to venerate the spirits but to keep them at a respectful distance.[210]

---

208 Chuang-tzu, the brilliant Taoist mystic of the third and fourth centuries B.C., said that the purified man draws his breath from the uttermost depths, ordinary people only from their throats. The value of deep and regular breathing is of course taught by many systems of mysticism besides Taoism and Tantric Buddhism. For Buddhist literature on breath-regulation (prana-yama), see, e.g., B.N. 543 (17), Har. xii. vol. i. pp. 29-34. See also Oldenberg, Buddha, p. 306; Spence Hardy,, Eastern Monachism, pp. 267^.; S.B.E., xxxv. 130-1; Poussin, Bouddhisme, p. 395.

209 What Tao really is only the successful mystic can say or, rather, he knows, but will not speak. The Tao that can be discussed and defined is not the real Tao -so we learn from the Tao-t-ching.

210 Among the works of Wang Shou-jen is to be found an interesting anti-Buddhist essay written (about 1515) in the form of a Remonstrance " addressed to the Emperor Cheng Te of the Ming dynasty, but apparently never actually presented (see ninth chuan of his collected works, pp. 13 ff.). It challenges comparison, of course, with the more famous memorial addressed by Han Yu to the Emperor Hsien Tsung of the T'ang dynasty in the year 819. Its arguments are to a great extent similar to those of Chou Pin (see above, pp. 224-9), who probably had the essays of both Han Yu and Wang Shou-jen in his mind when he penned his own little essay.

Reginald Fleming Johnston

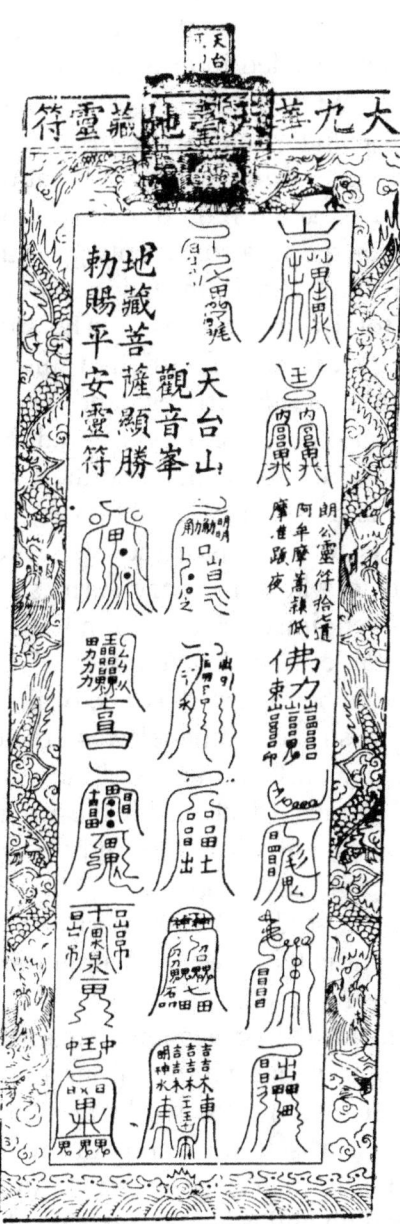

PROTECTIVE CHARMS FROM T'IEN-T'AI, CHIU-HUA-SHAN

Buddhist China

In 1519 Wang Shou-jen was sent to cope with a rebellious prince named Ch'en Hao, and succeeded in crushing the rising after a campaign of only thirty-five days. Wang's brilliant successes in war and at Court made him an object of jealousy, and some of his enemies reported to the throne that he was plotting to bring about a revolution. This resulted in his temporary disgrace, and he again retired to his favourite haunts on Chiu-hua, where he lived care-free in a rustic cottage. The emperor sent secret emissaries to spy upon him, and from their reports satisfied himself that the accusations were totally ground less. "The man is a philosopher!" exclaimed the emperor. "It is not of stuff like this that rebels are made." So Wang was reinstated in his offices, and his loyalty and splendid abilities brought him many new honours, in cluding the rank of a noble. He is known to fame not only as a gallant soldier and wise statesman, but also as a scholar, poet, and essayist. He achieved, moreover, the glory of "canonization [211]" that is to say, his name was enrolled among those of China's honoured dead to whose memory shrines are erected and before whose "spirit-tablets" religious or commemorative rites are officially performed. In 1584 his tablet was elevated to the Confucian temple, which means that he had come to be regarded as one of the holy men or saints of the Confucian system. A shrine or chapel was erected in his honour near the Hua-ch'eng Monastery on Chiu-hua, and the magistrate of the district was made responsible (in accordance with the usual practice) for seeing that the commemorative ceremonies were duly carried out in spring and autumn[212]. Hero-worship of this kind is an aspect of Chinese religious life which has been very little studied by Western writers on China; yet the subject is one of exceptional interest and importance, and deserves far more attention than it has received.

It is not only for historical or academic reasons that the career and personality of Wang Shou-jen are worthy of our attention. He is one of the few Chinese writers of his age whose works are read with avidity in both China and Japan to-day. He is studied and admired even by those young Chinese republicans who, in their eagerness to equip themselves and their country with all the learning and science of the West, are only too apt, as a rule, to turn their backs on the wisdom of their own sages. The writings of

---

211 Under the name of Wen-ch'eng.

212 In view of the distance of the mountain from the district city (Ch'ing-yang),, it was arranged that the ceremonies should be per formed at temporary shrines erected for the purpose twice yearly within the walls of the city.

Wang Shou-jen are approved of by young China, not because they are revolutionary in tone for indeed they are far from that but because they reveal the character and embody the ideals of a strong man of action, a single-minded patriot, a courageous and skilful leader in war, an incorruptible statesman. It is through lack of such men as this that China has been brought in recent years to parlous straits; it is such men as this who must be forthcoming in the near future if the country is to be saved. It is a sign of good omen that Wang Shou-jen's writings make their strongest appeal to the eager young patriots in whose hands will lie the making or marring of the new China. But they will do wrong if they imitate and applaud only the practical and utilitarian side of his teachings and fail to understand and appreciate what we may call their spiritual side. Let them not ignore the significance of the fact that Wang Shou-jen, whose words sound like fife and clarion in the ears of the active reformers and patriots of to-day, drew much of his moral energy from his solitary reveries under the starlit skies; that he was not only a leader of men on the field of battle, but also the dreamer of dreams on the silent hills. Chinese patriots hope and believe that their country is about to step into a splendid material heritage which will enable her to occupy one of the loftiest places among the nations of the earth; it will be a bitter misfortune for China and the world if they allow the spiritual heritage of their race to be cast aside as a thing of no account.

Mountain Lovers

We must content ourselves with the briefest glances at a few of the other well-known mountain lovers whose names are associated with the history of Chiu-hua.

Of a Cantonese scholar named Chan Jo-shui, who lived in the fifteenth century, we are told that he earned for himself the sobriquet of Professor Kan – ch'uan because he loved the beautiful scenery of Chiu-hua and carved on a rock the two characters kan-ch'uan, which mean "sweet waters." He had many devoted pupils, and one of the students reading-rooms on the mountain was founded in his memory and endowed with a little estate of land. One of his disciples was Lu Chung-mu, who himself became an admired teacher of ethics, and emphasized sincerity, loyalty, and filial piety as the foundation of all sound morals. He too was a lover of our mountain. "Of all the hills of the Chiang-nan provinces," he said, "none is more beautiful than Chiu-hua."

Fei Kuan-ch'ing belonged to a much earlier date than Professor "Sweet-waters," for he lived in the first half of the ninth century of our era. He was noted for his filial affection, and (in accordance with several classic precedents) he built himself a hut beside his mother's grave. When an official post was offered him he said with a sigh: "A Government appointment is useful when it enables one to support one's parents in comfort. My parents, alas, are no more; of what use would a Government appoint ment be to me?" So he declined the offer, and finally decided to make a solitary home for him self under the shadow of the peaks of Chiu-hua.

Wang Tsung-su (ninth century) also belonged to the T'ang dynasty. He always showed a keen distaste, we are told, for the pursuits that bring fame and wealth, and though circumstances compelled him to enter the official arena for a time, his happiest days were spent on Chiu-hua as a roaming student. There one day he met a strange man who handed him certain charms which enabled him to perform various Taoist miracles, such as levitating the body. Popular fancy credited him with a controlling power over the dragons that regulate the rainfall a power which he seems to have exercised beneficently. His hermitage was afterwards known as the Wu-hsiang Monastery.

Poets of Chiu-Hua

Next to Li Po, the greatest of the T'ang poets who celebrated Chiu-hua in their verse was perhaps Liu Yu-hsi (772-842). In an introduction to his little song he observes that only the great distance of Chiu-hua from the capital has prevented it from being properly appreciated, wherefore he has written a poem about it so that it may receive its due meed of praise at last.

Of the Sung dynasty names, one of the fore most is that of Chou Pi-ta, who was a great scholar and successful statesman as well as a poet and prose-writer. He, like Wang Shou-jen, was ennobled and canonized. An essay of his is preserved in which he gives a gossiping account of his visit to the mountain in 1167 and describes a meeting with an ancient monk of the "Twin-peak" Monastery (Shuang-feng-ssu) who was eighty-six years of age, and had not descended from his eyrie for twenty years.

Sun Mien (Sung period) was one of the numberless men of official rank in China who have found the "call of the wild" and the joys of literary seclusion more seductive than the sweets of office even though in Sun's case the office in question was the prefecture of Su-chou (Soochow), a gay and brilliant city which for centuries shared with Hangchow the reputation of being a "heaven upon earth." After his with drawal to Chiu-hua the Court tried its best to induce him to return to official life, but unsuccessfully.

A Wizard of Chiu-Hua

Tales of enchantment and wizardry are told of Chiu-hua as of all other famous hills in China. A typical story is that of a peasant named Ning Ch'eng, of the sixteenth century, who one day on the slopes of Chiu-hua encountered a queer old man who handed him half a peach. It should be observed that in China the peach is regarded as a fairy fruit. Numerous strange tales, including legends of the Rip Van Winkle type, turn on the eating of a magic peach, and even on the wonderful properties inherent in the peach blossom. Ning Ch'eng ate the half-peach, and then the old man led him to a cliff and tapped it. The rock opened, and Ning followed his guide into a strange dwelling-place, such as mortal man never saw before. There he lived an enchanted life; but after some time he remembered his old mother, and asked the wizard to let him visit her. During the journey he was told to shut his eyes, so he could see nothing of the devious path through which the wizard was leading him, though he heard the rushing of tumultuous waters. Ning's house was soon reached, but before he was allowed to enter it the wizard thumped his back, and lo! out of Ning's mouth came forth the half-peach[213]. The wizard told Ning that they would meet again on a date which he named, and then disappeared, leaving Ning to rejoin his family and resume the humdrum life of a simple peasant. After his mother's death some one saw him wander off in the direction of the cliff which had formerly opened at the wizard's touch, and from that day Ning was seen on earth no more. His disappearance took place in the twenty-fourth year of Wan-li (1596) in the month and on the day foretold by the wizard.

---

213 The meaning is, of course, that his connection with fairyland was now severed.

Buddhist China

The Rain Maker of Chiu Hua

The Chinese, like the people of many other lands, are laudatores temporis acti they draw their best examples of nobility, heroism, self-control, spiritual insight, religious achievement, from the well-stocked treasure-house of the "good old days." There is a Chinese saying which aptly satirizes the tendency to glorify the past at the expense of the present: "The mountains of our own times are not so lofty as the mountains of the days of old.[214]" Yet if we must look to the chronicles of the Han dynasty or the legends of a yet earlier date for accounts of the doings of the mightiest of the Taoist wizards, we may sometimes find, in the comparatively prosaic annals of the dynasty that has just expired, stories of mystery and magic which would not disgrace even the golden age of wizardry and enchantment. Teng Yu, for example, of whom some remarkable feats are recorded, lived as recently as the middle of the nineteenth century. We are told of him that he began life as a woodcutter, and that one day while pursuing his occupation on Chiu-hua he met a mysterious stranger who handed him a treatise on magical arts which enabled him to create storms, to cause rainfalls, to cure human ailments, and to extirpate the evils caused by witchcraft. All these things he would do without payment of any kind. In the sixth month of the year corresponding to 1844 there was a great drought in Ch'ih-chou-fu (the prefecture in which Chiu-hua is situated), which resulted in the drying of the wells and the withering of the crops. The prefect, knowing of Teng Yu's skill in dealing with calamities of this kind, invited him to exert his magic powers on behalf of the suffering people. He obeyed the summons, and erected an altar, at which he offered up prayers for rain. He had no sooner stretched forth his hand and uttered the thunder-spell than there was a sound of rumbling in the heavens. This was quickly followed by the gathering of clouds and the downfall of rain. Then he turned towards the east and blew softly, whereupon dark masses of cloud began to move in that direction. The prefect asked his reason for sending rain-clouds to the east, and Teng Yu explained that there was a drought in the east also, and that he was sending some rain thither in order to solace the anxious hearts of the people of the thirsting district of Ch'ing-yang. Subsequently word was brought from Ch'ing-yang that dark clouds had approached from the

---

214 Chin shan pu chi ku shun kao.

west, and resulted in a much-needed fall of rain just at the time when Teng Yu was uttering his incantations. After the happy conclusion of the rain-making ceremony the prefect wished to send Teng Yu home in luxury, and offered him a carriage-and-four; but when the carriage arrived it was found that he had already floated away by himself. This benevolent wizard passed a peaceful existence on Chiu-hua, and no one knows what became of him at last.

Perhaps of all the wise men of Chiu-hua few can have had a more interesting personality than the nameless hermit of the Eastern Cliff, who became an expert in the manipulation of clouds. Besides acquiring the art of discriminating between the various kinds and tints of clouds, he was also in the habit of collecting specimens. He used to be seen running up and down the misty slopes of Chiu-hua chasing clouds as if they were butterflies. His practice was to catch them in a crockery jar, which he held upside-down over the cloud he was pursuing. When his jar was full he would take a piece of dry parchment and fasten it down over the neck of the jar; and if friends came to see him, he would take a needle and prick a hole in the parchment, whereupon the captive cloud would come curling out, so that in a brief space of time it would fill the room. Apparently he would even go so far as to feed his guests on clouds, though whether the dainty fare satisfied their hunger or not is an unanswered question. The great poet Su Tung-p'o (1036-1101) in a sportive hour composed some lines on the subject of the cloud gatherer. "Of late," sang the genial poet, "there is one who has learned the art of cloud-catching; and he is going to give me a bag of clouds as a parting present."

Southern Slope of Chiu-Hua

The southern slope of Chiu-hua that is, the side remote from the Yangtse is often neglected by pilgrims from the north; but the beauty of its woods and waters makes this side of the mountain no less attractive than the northern, and it should not be left unvisited. The temples are small and of no special interest, but they are all situated amidst charming scenery. Starting from the Pai-sui Monastery, and retracing the path that leads from Ti-tsang's shrine for a distance of about a mile, we come to a parting of the ways. Following the new path in a southerly direction, we soon reach the Fa-yun Temple, whence the road descends to the "Third Gate of

Heaven [215]" and to the "Diamond Hermitage,[216]" behind which is a small cave-temple[217]. Lower still is the "Holy Buddha" Monastery[218], the Yung-sheng Monastery, the "Second Gate of Heaven[219]" and the "First Gate of Heaven.[220]" Here we reach the foot of the mountain. The last of the temples, situated by the side of a stream spanned by a picturesque bridge, is a supernumerary "Gate of Heaven;[221]" and thence the road winds through a beautiful gorge to a small cultivated plain and to the village of Nan-a-wan. A short walk thence brings us to the village of Pao-chia, close to which stands a white five-storied pagoda the Pao-chia-t'a, or "Pagoda of the Pao Family."

We have now come to the end of our exploration of Chiu-hua-shan; and it remains for us either to return to the Yangtse (which we can do by following a somewhat circuitous route that skirts the base of the mountain) or to proceed through Southern Anhui to the city of Hui-chou. This town stands at the head of a navigable tributary of the Ch'ien-t'ang River the stream that flows into Hangchow Bay; and the four days journey from the Pai-sui Monastery to Hui-chou will take the traveller through one of the most beautiful tracts of country to be found anywhere in the neighbourhood of the lower Yangtse. The villages are poor, for the country has not yet recovered from the ruin caused by the T'ai-p'ing rebels. Almost the only indication of the former prosperity of the province consists in the admirable stone bridges which cross the numerous water-courses. The finest of these is the sixteen-arch bridge at Hui-chou. The total distance from Chiu-hua to Hui-chou is about eighty-three miles. Hui-chou is a prefectural city, and before the T'ai-p'ing rebellion it was one of the wealthiest in this part of China; but it is now of small dimensions, and its wall is dilapidated. A neighbouring city, Hsiu-ning, is the seat of the manufacture of the best Chinese inks, and Hui-chou is the principal mart for their sale.

The water journey from Hui-chou to Hangchow can be accomplished comfortably in native boats. The rivers first the Hsin-an and subsequently

---

215 San T'ien-men.

216 Chin-kang ch'an-lin.

217 Chuan-shen-tung.

218 Pao-Fo-ssu.

219 Ku Erh T'ien-men.

220 Ku I T'ien-men.

221 Ku T'ou T'ien-men.

the Ch'ien-t'ang wind through a wooded fairyland throughout the whole length of a journey which on an average occupies about seven days. The time varies according to the state of the water, but few travellers are likely to grudge the days spent in restful contemplation of the entrancing river scenery of Western Chehkiang.

HUI-CHOU CITY AND BRIDGE.

ON THE CH'IEN-T'ANG RIVER, CHEHKIANG.

Reginald Fleming Johnston

XI. Puto-Shan And Kuan-Yin Pusa

Of the four sacred hills of Buddhist China, the one which has the shortest religious history, yet enjoys the greatest prosperity to-day, is Puto-shan. Puto is, strictly speaking, not a mountain, but an island[222]. It is one of the group known to Europeans as the Chusans, which lie off the north-eastern coast of Chehkiang, and it is therefore within easy reach of both Shanghai and Ningpo. Puto lies about two miles to the east of the large island which gives its name to the archipelago. The name of Chusan is not strange to the annals of English history, for during the wars of the nineteenth century it was twice occupied by British troops.

Puto is an irregularly-shaped island of nearly four miles in length, varying in breadth from a few hundred yards to about three miles. It is very hilly, and rises at its highest point ("Buddha's Peak") to nearly one thousand feet. The coast line is deeply indented, and diversified with rocks, coves, and sandy beaches. On the western and south-western sides the water is shallow, and the receding tide uncovers a border of dark mud; but on the eastern side, which is by far the more attractive, the rocky headlands slope into deep water, and the bays which lie between their protecting arms are fringed with firm yellow sand. A little pier has been built at the southern extremity of the island, and this is the landing-place of the crowds of visitors who in the pilgrim-seasons of spring and summer come in their thousands to kneel in adoration before the shrines of the holy pusa Kuan-yin.

The position of Puto near the estuaries of two great rivers the Yangtse and the Chien-t'ang is responsible for the dun colour of the seas that lap the coasts of the sacred isle. In other respects Puto fully deserves all the praises that have been lavished upon it by enthusiastic Chinese Buddhists. It is an island of singular charm and beauty an island which, if we may transfer to Puto the words of an English poet, is in very truth "a small, sweet world of wave-encompassed wonder."

---

222 The Chinese word shan ("mountain") is often used to denote a small, hilly island. With regard to the word Puto, which is perhaps better known to Europeans as Pootoo

Buddhist China

Gutzlaff at Puto-Shan

Puto is so easily accessible, and has been so often visited by Europeans, that there is no lack of literature relating to the island in English and other European languages[223]. Some of the earlier missionary writers made appreciative references to the natural beauty of the island, but their observations concerning its religious associations were apt to be much marred by that almost fanatical in tolerance of alien faiths which in past years has been and still is, to a limited and diminishing extent so ugly a feature of Christian missionary enterprise.

One such visitor was Charles Gutzlaff, who landed at Puto in February 1833. He describes "a temple built on a projecting rock, beneath which the foaming sea dashed," and which "gave us the idea of the genius of its inhabitants, in thus selecting the most attractive spot to celebrate the orgies of idolatry." He observes that "to every person who visits this island it appears at first like a fairyland, so romantic is everything which meets the eye "; but the images of Kuan-yin "and other deformed idols" give him much distress, and Puto, for all its beauty, turns out to be nothing better than an "infamous seat of abomination.[224]"

The old-fashioned denunciations of heathenism may strike us in these days as merely whimsical, and perhaps as a trifle ludicrous, but we should not forget that the intolerant zeal of the Christian pioneers was, unfortunately, not confined to the writing of books and papers for the edification of their Western supporters, but also displayed itself in countless acts and words of gross discourtesy (to say the least) towards a

---

[223] By far the best account of Puto in any European language is a recently published German work by Ernst Boerschmann, Die Baukunst und Religiose Kultur der Chinenen Band i.: P'u-t'o-shan (Berlin, 1911). Unfortunately, it appears that Mr Boerschmann had no opportunity of consulting the principal Chinese authority for the history of the island -the P'u-t'o-shan-chih. The only Chinese authority which he quotes is the great encyclopaedia, the T'u-shu-chi-ch'eng, which gives extracts from the Chih, but takes them from a now superseded edition. His book is nevertheless of high value owing to its careful and thorough study of the epigraphic and architectural features of Puto.

[224] See Gutzlaff's Journal of Three Voyages, 1834, pp. 438 ff., and China Opened (i. 116). The descriptions contained in Hall and Bernard, The Nemesis in China, 1847 ed., p. 306, reveal a similar readiness to praise the beauty of the island,, coupled with a detestation of the "gross idolatry" practised there. The authors apparently con curred in the rather churlish remarks of a well-known missionary (W. H. Medhurst), whose words they quote. "All its inhabitants," says Medhurst, " are employed in no other work than the recitation of unmeaning prayers and the direction of useless contemplations towards stocks and stones; so that human science and human happiness would not be in the least diminished if the whole of Puto., with its gaudy temples and lazy priests, were blotted out from the face of creation." (Cf. also Williams, Middle Kingdom, i. 124-6, for similar ill-tempered remarks.) Robert Fortune, a well-known botanist of the middle of the nineteenth century, has also left a description of Puto; of this, however, there is very little reason to complain, for Fortune's temperament was tolerant and sympathetic, and his books may still be read with pleasure and profit.

people with whom courtesy and tolerance of others foibles are among the first of virtues. Those acts and words were to a great extent responsible, not only for many of the anti-foreign outbreaks that used to be so frequent, but also for the pitiful misunderstandings which have so long prevented East and West from getting to know and appreciate one another's good qualities.

Early European Visitors

Long before the days of Gutzlaff, Puto was probably seen, though it was not actually visited, by a French Jesuit priest named Le Comte. Writing of his voyage from Amoy to Ningpo, he thus describes the charming scenery of the Chusan archipelago:

"I never saw anything so frightful as that infinite number of rocks and desert islands through which we were obliged to pass.... We also steered through a pretty wide bay, in which the Chinese observe a profound silence, for fear, they tell us, of disturbing a neighbouring dragon; we were constrained to follow their example. I know not how they call it; as for us, we named it the Dumb Man's Bay.[225]"

He goes on to say that, having spent some time among "those horrid rocks," he arrived at last at the port of Ting-hai, in the Island of Chusan. It is evident that this isle-studded sea, which is now becoming the resort of enthusiastic tourists from the West, gave small pleasure to our seventeenth-century Jesuit. Here we have a good example of that strange insensibility to the beauty of wild nature which until comparatively recent times was so curious a characteristic of civilized Europe.

Perhaps, however, the good father's indifference to the picturesque was partly due to the uneasiness caused by a violent storm from which his little vessel had but lately emerged. The dreadful omens, he tells us, increased as his ship approached the Chusan Islands. Fortunately, however, he remembered in good time that the great missionary Saint Francis Xavier had already wrought many miracles in those waters, and he resolved to appeal to that holy man to manifest his protecting power on behalf of the storm-driven ship.

---

225 Le Comte's Memoirs (English trans., 1738, p. 11). The journey described was made late in the seventeenth century.

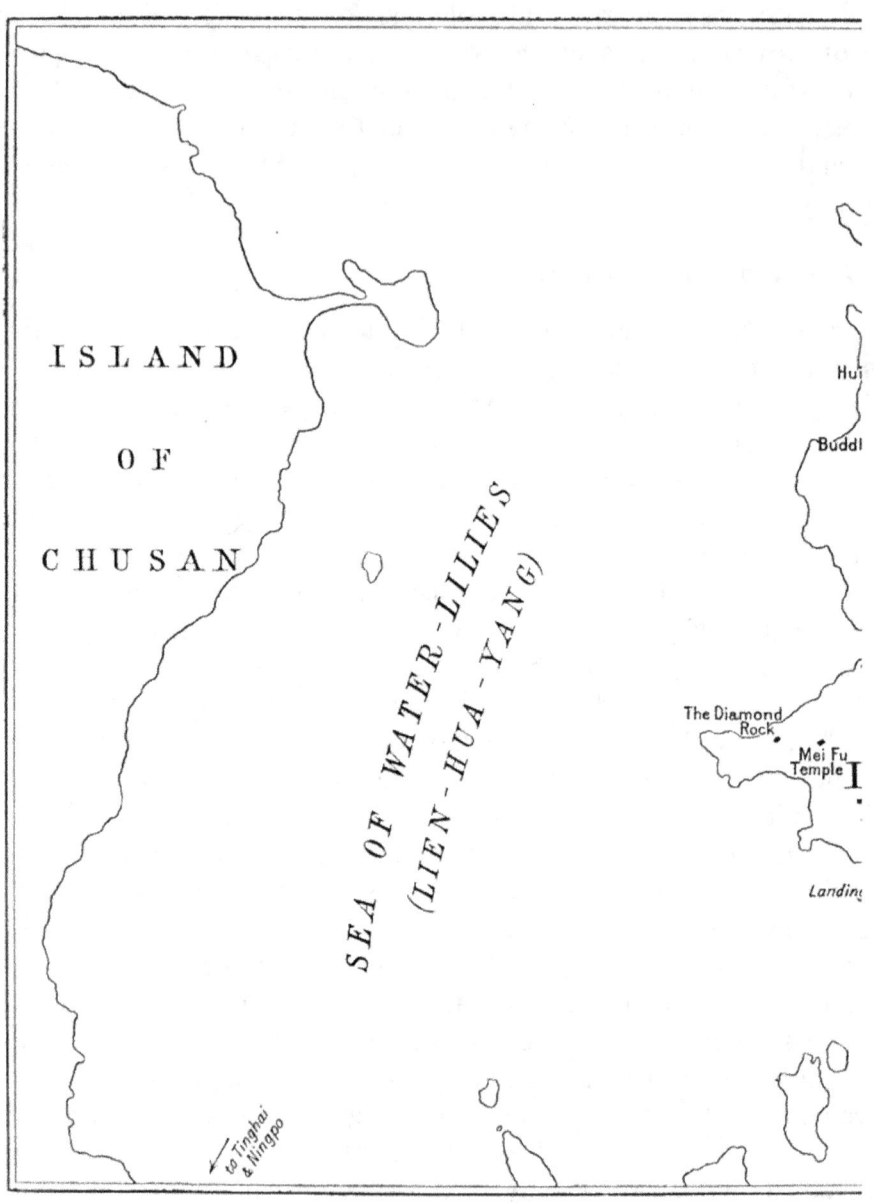

Puto Shan

"We prayed him," he says, "to divert the tempest, and enforced our prayers by a vow. Scarce were we off our knees, but, whether by a miracle or the ordinary course of nature, there blew a favourable gale of wind, which carried us through some islands into our desired port."

It might have surprised, and possibly disgusted, the Catholic father if he had been told that St. Francis Xavier had a miracle-working rival in the channels of Chusan. Indeed it is not unlikely that at the very time when the Western missionaries were addressing their supplications to St. Francis the heathen members of their crew were simultaneously addressing theirs to Kuan-yin. And who is to decide whether it was the Christian saint or the Buddhist pusa who really stilled those raging waters? However this may be, we shall shortly find that Puto and the neighbouring seas were the scenes of Kuan-yin's miraculous activities six hundred years or more before the "Apostle of the Indies" was born[226].

Chusan Islands in Chinese History

Of the island's pre-Buddhistic history next to nothing is known. A passage in the "Tribute of Yu" in the Shu Ching refers to the "wild islanders[227]" and their tribute of "grass-woven garments," and some Chinese commentators have suggested that this passage (which deals with events of the third millennium B.C.) may refer to the Chusan islanders. Coming down to times of which we have more reliable historical record, we find that between two and three thousand years ago the inhabitants of all the Chusan Islands were people of aboriginal (possibly Annamite or Shan) race, and formed part of the population of the semi-barbarous principality of Yueh, which for a time in the fifth century B.C. was the most formidable military power in Eastern China. Even as late as the Han dynasty the islanders were undoubtedly of non-Chinese race.

At that time they were known as Chien-t'i-jen, the character for t'i being a combination of the sign for "fish" and that for "barbarian." During the short-lived rule of the Ch'in dynasty (third century B.C.) there was a certain wizard named An-ch'i Sheng, who among his other attainments possessed the power of making himself invisible. Indeed, according to a popular legend he was never really seen by any one, as he lived in the

---

226 St. Francisco de Xavier was born about 1506 and died in 1552.
227 Tao I.

undiscoverable fairy islands which lay somewhere in the region of the rising sun. There is, however, another version of the legend, from which we learn that An-ch'i Sheng in his easterly wanderings never got any farther than the island we now know as Puto, which possibly he mistook, pardonably enough, for the fairyland of his dreams. He was a skilful artist; but his artistic methods were peculiar to himself, for when he wished to draw he used no brush or other implements, but merely upset his ink-slab, and without further perceptible activity on his part the blots of ink so created would take the form of exquisitely drawn peach-flowers. His skill was thus at least as remarkable as that of Wang Hsia, a painter who used to make a blot of ink and from the blot drew beautiful pictures with either his fingers or his toes. Stories of this kind, which are simply a fanciful way of describing the inexplicable and inimitable powers and achievements of genius, are often met with in the annals of Oriental art[228]. But the fact that An-ch'i Sheng's artistic instincts were associated solely with the peach was of itself a significant proof that he was a wizard: for the peach-tree, as all Chinese know, is one of the favourite products of fairyland, and its magical properties are of unrivalled renown.

The earliest Chinese name of Puto seems to have been Mei-ts'en[229] (the "Hill of Mei") a name which is still applied to a small hill in the southern part of the island. Mei Fu, or Mei Tzu-chen, was a prominent statesman and Confucian scholar of the first century B.C. About the year 6 of our era he mysteriously vanished, and it became one of the unsolved problems of biography whether he had become an immortal hsien-jen or rishi, or whether he had merely retired into voluntary exile. According to the traditions of Chehkiang, his hiding-place was no other than Puto: and his name is attached not only to a hill, but also to a modern Buddhist temple (the Mei Fu Ch'an-yuan) in front of which is a pool of water still known as Mei Fu's Well.

---

228 We are told, for example, that Kobo Daishi, the Japanese founder of the Shingon sect of Buddhism (774-834), used to take a brush and spatter ink on the wall, seemingly at random; whereupon the blots would transform themselves into beautifully traced characters. Kobo was the most famous calligraphist of his day, and calligraphy, as is well known, is regarded in China arid Japan as a fine art.
229 T'u-shu-pien ch. 64 p. 7

Buddhist China

THE FA-T'ANG, SOUTHERN MONASTERY.

T'IEN-HOU, THE TAOIST QUEEN OF HEAVEN, PUTO-SHAN.

Buddhist History of Puto

It was not till the ninth century that Puto began to acquire special sanctity in the eyes of Buddhists.[230] Its patron pusa has always been Kuan-yin (known to the Japanese as Kwannon), who, as we saw in a previous chapter, is the representative in Chinese Buddhism of the celestial bodhisat Avalokitesvara, one of the divine beings who rule over Sukhavati, the paradise of Amitabha.

In the popular religious lore of China, Kuan-yin is now always represented as a female divinity. Europeans in China know her as the "Goddess of Mercy," but she may be described more correctly as the "Pusa of Love and Pity." Her full title in Chinese is Ta-tzu ta-pei chiu-k'u Kuan-shih-yin tzu-tsai wang p'u-sa, which may be translated, "the All-compassionate Uncreated (or Self-existent) Saviour, the Royal Bodhisat who hears the cries of the world."

Various suggestions have been made as to how the Chinese came to regard Kuan-yin as a female pusa. She is in some respects the Buddhist counterpart of the deity known to popular Taoism as T'ien-hou sheng-mu ("The Holy Mother Queen of Heaven"), whose origin is also clouded in mystery. Both are worshipped as beneficent and compassionate goddesses who save men from misery and peril, especially from the dangers of the ocean; and both are regarded as the patrons and protectors of mothers and as the bringers of children. That these divinities eye one another with no unfriendly feelings may be gathered from the fact that shrines to the Taoist "Queen of Heaven" are to be found on the shores of Kuan-yin's own sacred soil of Puto[231].

---

230 Williams, in his Middle Kingdom, i. 126, says that temples were erected on the island as early as 550; but he gives no authority for this statement, which was prohahly due to a confusion on his part between the earlier and later Liang dynasties. A Chinese writer (P'u-t'o-shan-chih xvii. 2) tries to carry the Buddhist traditions of Puto back to a still earlier date (280-289 of the Western Chin dynasty); but this statement also is entirely unsupported by evidence.

231 The Shrines to T'ien-hou are in the pavilion at the entrance to the Northern Monastery and in the front hall of the Fu-ch'tian-shen Temple. The latter is near the landing-place, and close by it stands a temple (the Kuang-fu) dedicated to another Taoist deity Kuan-ti, the so-called " god of war " who is regarded by Chinese Buddhists, rather unwarrantably, as a spiritual Hu-fa, or Protector of the Faith. Popular Taoism, it may be added, possesses other female deities whose functions can scarcely be distinguished from those of T'ien-hou; and, indeed they may be regarded as local manifestations of that goddess. Such is the deity known as Pi-hsia-yuan-chun, or Niang-niang, the centre of whose worship is T'ai-shan, the sacred mountain of Shantung.

Buddhist China

Buddhism and Catholicism

If an enquirer into Buddhist origins wished to claim Kuan-yin as an importation from Europe, he would no doubt emphasize the fact that in the temples of Puto the pusa is frequently described as the Kuo-hai Kuan-yin ("the Kuan-yin who came across the sea")[232]. This epithet, however, probably contains a reference to the pusa's functions as captain of the hung-Ja, the broad raft, or "Bark of Salvation," on which the souls of the saved are borne across the sea of life and death to Amitabha's paradise. It is, of course, by no means impossible that the conception of a sea-crossing Kuan-yin has some remote connection with similar myths which we find embedded in other religious systems[233]. It is well known that in the devotional literature of the Church of Rome the Mater Dei is often referred to as a kind of sea-goddess. The song Stella Maris[234] ascribed to the eighth century, "has been breathed up in numerable times," as a recent writer observes, "by sailors who in storms sought help from the mild goddess who was the Star of the Sea, and who for those in peril opened a window in the dark and threatening skies.[235]" There are similar possibilities in respect of Kuan-yin's functions as the bestower of children, in which capacity she may be compared with the Babylonian Ishtar (Mylitta)[236]. The Sung-tzu Kuan-yin, like the Sung-tzu Niang-niang of Taoism, is often represented as carrying a male infant in her arms. The belief that she is able to grant prayers for children is founded on a passage in the Lotus of the Good Law.[237] But it does not require much daring to suggest that there was a child-carrying goddess worshipped in China long before the Sung-tzu Kuan-yin was ever heard of[238].

Chinese Buddhists acknowledge that the original seat of Kuan-yin's worship was at a great distance from China. According to one of the interpreta tions of the name of Avalokitesvara, it means the Lord (Isvara) who looks down from a height. The "height" is the sacred mountain of

---

232 Sometimes the term used is P'iao-hai ("sea-borne").

233 Cf. J. M. Robertson, Christianity and Mythology, 1910, pp. 213-215, 331.

234 Ave Maris Stella, Dei Mater Alma, etc.

235 Him, Sacred Shrine, pp. 465-6, 470.

236 Hastings, E.R.E., ii. 116, 290.

237 S.B.E., xxi. 409. Russian peasants believe the same of the Virgin.

238 On the subject of the very wide extension of the cult of the mother-and-child, see J. M. Robertson, op. cit., pp. 166-172.

Potalaka, a place which is always associated with the worship of this bodhisat. Where the original Potalaka was is a disputed question. It is usually assumed to have been a rocky hill to the east of the Malaya Mountain, in Southern India, near the harbour of Cape Komorin[239]. If this identification is correct, it seems highly probable that the deity worshipped there was of non-Buddhistic origin; and, indeed, there is evidence to associate her (or him) with the worship paid to Hindu deities such as Siva[240]. However this may be, the cult of Avalokitesvara spread not only to China, but also to Tibet. A second Potalaka was created at Lhasa, and that palace-crowned rock remains to this day the head quarters of the Dalai Lama, who is himself regarded as an incarnation of the divine bodhisat. The Buddhists of China decided that they too must have a Potalaka for their Kuan-yin, and the place selected by them was no other than our island of Puto, of which the unabbreviated Chinese name is P'u-t'o-lo-ka, or (in the Hua-yen sutra) Pu-ta-lo-ka. "Puto" is thus merely a shortened form of "Potaloka."

The Little White Flower

A writer of the Yuan dynasty says that in the T'ang period (618-906) Puto was known as Hsiao-pai-hua-shan, which means "the Island of the Little White Flower.[241]" This delightful name was probably given to it by the Buddhists, for it is still in common use by them; indeed they assert that the name is equivalent to, or is a rendering of, the original word "Potalaka.[242]" The name of Hsiao-pai-hua is certainly an appropriate one, inasmuch as Puto is famous for a certain beautiful and fragrant white flower which grows wild all over the island. This flower is the gardenia florida.

---

239 See Waddell, Lhasa and its Mysteries, 1905, pp. 364 and 388; Hastings, E.R.E., ii. 259; Watters, Yuan Chwang, "ii. 228-232. A description of the hill may be found in the Hua-yen sutra (B.N. 88), ch. 68 (see Har. i. vol. iv. p. 33). The Shan-ts'ai who is mentioned there, and figures prominently in the sutra, is commemorated by a cave " named after him in the eastern peninsula of Puto-shan. Of course neither the original author of the sutra nor the translator into Chinese makes any specific reference to the Chinese Potalaka, of which neither had any knowledge.

240 See Poussin in E.R.E., pp. 258 ff. Poussin believes that "the Chinese transformation of Avalokita into a woman had probably been already effected in India."

241 See Ming-shan-sheng-kai-chi, vol. xx. ch. 18. The same writer says that the Tung'I ("Eastern Barbarians") used to come for trading purposes to Ting-hai, the capital of Chusan. The Tung'I were probably the Japanese, whose intercourse with this part of China goes back to the Chou dynasty, when Chehkiang and the neighbouring regions were under the rule of the princes of Wu and Yueh,

242 See Eitel, Handbook, s.v. Potala.

Buddhist China

When did the cult of Avalokitesvara, or Kuan-yin, take root in China? This is a difficult question to answer, especially when we observe that there are two Buddhistic cults, more or less distinct, with which Avalokitesvara is associated. In the Amidist cult Avalokitesvara is one of a triad of divinities who rule the Western Paradise and act as the saviours of mankind. This cult may be said to have its scriptural foundation in the "Pure-Land" sutras, which were translated into Chinese between the second and fifth centuries. But there is also the Avalokitesvara of the Hua-yen and Fa-hua scriptures, who may be worshipped for his own sake, irrespective of his association with the Buddha Amitabha. One of the scriptural bases of this cult is a concluding chapter of the Lotus of the Good Law, a sutra which was first translated into Chinese about the end of the third century[243]. In Puto Kuan-yin takes precedence of every other divinity, and this pusa's image occupies the place of honour in the principal hall of nearly every temple[244]. This does not imply, however, that the Amidist theology is ignored or repudiated. On the contrary, Kuan-yin's position as one of the rulers of Amitabha's paradise, and as spiritual Son, or Word, of the glorious Amitabha himself, is at least theoretically recognized[245].

The Great Bodhisats

It is not difficult to find an explanation of the undoubted fact that Kuan-yin has attained in China and Japan a popularity far exceeding that of any of the other great bodhisats. So long as Kuan-yin was still the male Avalokitesvara, his position seems to have been no more conspicuous than that of many other pusas, such as Wen-shu, P'u-hsien, Ti-tsang, and Ta-

---

[243] This is the Saddharmapundarika, of which several translations (apparently from at least two different Sanskrit texts) were made into Chinese between the years 265 and 601. The earliest was made between 265 and 316. This is the Cheng Fa-hua-ching, translated by Dharmaraksha (B.N. 138, Har. xi. vol. ii. pp. 1-57). In this translation the name of Kuan-shih-yin is given as Kuang-shih-yin. The most popular translation is that of Kumarajiva, made between 384 and 417 (B.N. 134, Har. xi. vol. i. pp. 6-54). B.N. 136 and 137 are only fragments. A third complete translation of the sutra is B.N. 139 (Har. xi. vol. ii. pp. 57-106). The sutra has been translated into English (from the Sanskrit) by Kern, S.B.E., vol. xxi. For the section on Kuan-yin, see pp. 408 ff.

[244] It is for this reason that the principal pavilion or chapel of the monasteries of Puto is described as Yuan-t'ung Pao-tien, not as Ta-hsiung Pao-tien. Ta-hsiung, usually translated ee Great Hero," is an epithet of akyamuni Buddha, whereas Yuan-t ung ("One of comprehensive understanding") is an epithet of Kuan-yin.

[245] When Kuan-yin's image is associated with that of Amitabha, it is Amitabha who, even at Puto, occupies the central position, Kuan-yin supporting him on one side and Ta-shih-chih on the other (see above, p. 100). Many of the images of Kuan-yin are represented with a miniature image of Amitabha Buddha in the front of the crown or head-dress. The yin of Kuan-yin signifies Sound or Voice. For some interesting observations on Kuan-yin as Voice or Word of the divine Buddha Amitabha, see Beal, Catena, pp. 387-8.

shih-chih, and at one time he was probably regarded as distinctly inferior to Mi-lei (Maitreya), whose unique position as the bodhisat who is destined to be the next Buddha (hence sometimes referred to by Europeans as the "Buddhist Messiah") is vouched for in the Pali canon[246]. That the change of sex should have intensified Kuan-yin's popularity will not be a matter of surprise to those who have followed the course of dogmatic developments in other faiths. Writing of the cult of the Virgin in Christendom, an English critic of our own day remarks that Mary "is frankly an idealization of womanhood; she is worshipped simply because that is the sort of being which people feel it good to worship," although she is "admittedly a creature of the imagination.[247]" Kuan-yin, too, is worshipped in China and Japan as an idealization of womanhood, and she has gained popularity because the ideal is one which touches people's emotions and lessens the gap between the merely human and the unapproachably divine[248].

Sex of Kuan-Yin

It has been said by certain European writers that Kuan-yin was not recognized as a female until the early part of the twelfth century[249]. It may be true that the recognition did not become general until that time, but there is ample evidence that at a much earlier date Kuan-yin was sometimes, at any rate, regarded as a female pusa. The best proof of this is perhaps to be found in various extant examples of pictorial art. A high authority on Oriental art assures us that there are Chinese paintings of Kuan-yin of the seventh and eighth centuries which are "markedly feminine "; though he admits that there are other paintings of the same era

---

246 We should note, however, that the pilgrim-monk Fa-hsien, who flourished about 410, was a worshipper of Kuan-yin, and regarded her (or him) as the pusa to whom prayers should be offered for deliverance from shipwreck.

247 Henry Sturt, Ideal of a Free Church, 1909, p. 243. Cf. F. M. Cornford, From Religion to Philosophy, 1912, p. 113. "The really living objects of Christian cult are the figures of actual men and women the Virgin, her Son, the saints, and martyrs " (see also Miss Eckenstein, Women wider Monasticism, ch. i.).

248 With regard to the question of possible Western influences, it may be noted that Nestorianism has been suspected (though with doubtful justification) in the form of the liturgical services of Kuan-yin. For a description and translation of the liturgy, the reader may be referred to Beal, Catena, pp. 396 ff. , and to his Buddhism in China, 1884, pp. 133 ff. Beal did not quite realize that the qualities and functions ascribed to Kuan-yin (especially as Saviour or Redeemer) are regarded by Buddhism as common to all the great pusas; the position of Kuan-yin is therefore not unique, as he supposed it to be. Kuan-yin like Amitabha and Ti-tsang and others innumerable, commenced their careers as bodhisats by uttering great " vows " to save mankind. Kuan-yin is sometimes said to have uttered twelve such vows. Amitabha registered over forty.

249 See Edkins, Chinese Buddhism, 1893 ed., p. 382, and Prof. H. A. Giles, Glossary of Reference, s.v. Kwan-yin.

Buddhist China

which represent the pusa as a male[250]. Among the miscellaneous notes and disserta tions which have been given a place in the Chronicle of Puto, there is an essay that contains an elaborate, almost luxurious, description of Kuan-yin's personal appearance [251]; and this essay, which assumes that Kuan-yin is a female, has been attributed to the poet Wang Po, who died in 676[252]. According to the scholarly editors of the last edition of the Chronicle, the inferior literary style of the essay proves that it cannot have been written by Wang Po; but even if we assume that it was only the work of an unknown member of Wang Po' literary circle, it affords corroborative evidence that Kuan-yin's change of sex was recognized in literature, as in pictorial art, long before the twelfth century.

The womanhood of Kuan-yin does not contradict, and is not inconsistent with, the Mahayanist scriptures. All the bodhisats may, in the course of their age-long careers as saviours of the world, appear on earth in female form. We have already had occasion to notice that Ti-tsang did so in more than one of his "incarnations." There is also a passage in the Lotus of the G-ood Law which expressly says that Kuan-yin will appear in female form when that form is appropriate to circumstances[253]. An educated Buddhist, and especially a genuine mystic of the Ch'an school, brushes all these notions aside as of no real importance. The true Kuan-yin, he says, is by nature both sexless and formless, but is capable of assuming, or of appearing to assume, all forms[254].

Western students of Buddhism may ask how it was that Chinese Buddhists, wishing to do reverence to a female divinity, selected an imaginary being such as Kuan-yin, when they might have chosen the real

---

250 See Fenollosa, Epochs of Chinese and Japanese Art, 1912, i. 105 and 124; ii. 49, 50. In vol. i. p. 122, may be seen a reproduc tion of a painting by the Chinese artist Yen Li-pen, of the seventh century. This figure seems to be a female, whereas the Kuan-yin of Wu Tao-tzu (eighth century), reproduced on p. 132, is distinctly male.

251 Chih, ch. xx. pp. 19-20.

252 He was a well-known poet of the T'ng dynasty, and, like Shelley, was accidentally drowned in his twenty-ninth year.

253 It may be noted that there evidently is a Sanskrit text which contains a shorter list of Kuan-yin's "transformations" than that contained in the text, or texts, from which B.N. 134 and 139 were translated. Kern's translation (S.B.E., xxi. 410-411) is from a text which does not mention Kuan-yin's female transformations. I find by examination that the earliest extant Chinese translation of the sutra (B.N. 138) omits them also. Kern's Sanskrit original seems to have been the text which was also followed by the first translator into Chinese (Dharmaraksha). The technical term to express the (transformations " of Kuan-yin is sui-chi-ying-hsien.

254 Fenollosa correctly says that c a great bodhisattva is in its own nature indeterminate as to sex, having risen above the distinction, or rather embodying in itself the united spiritual graces of both sexes. It is a matter of accident which one it may assume upon incarnation. It just happens that T'ang thought, or preferred to think, of Kwannon (Kuan-yin) as a great demiurge or creator, while Sung preferred to lay stress upon the element of motherhood " (op. cit., i. 124).

mother of the historical Gotama. The explanation probably lies in the unwillingness of the Buddhist creed-makers to bring about an "entangling alliance" between matters of faith (or perhaps we should say religious reverie) and matters of historical fact. On this topic it is perhaps unnecessary to add to the observations already made in an earlier chapter, though the subject is one which in view of recent tendencies in Christian apologetic will probably be found by Western theologians to be worthy of close attention.

The Mother of Buddha

It would be erroneous, indeed, to suppose that Maya, the mother of Gotama, has not been regarded with deep reverence by all Buddhists. The doctrine of Buddha's virgin birth is not canonical, and was probably borrowed from one of the numerous religions in which we find traces of a similar doctrine, or from the general stock of current religious theory. But the belief in Maya's exceptional purity and holiness is common to the Buddhists of all schools[255]. The Hmayana, as we should expect, refers to her as a being who, though honoured above all others of her sex, was nevertheless the human mother of a human son: for Gotama, be it remembered, was not born a Buddha; he became one during his life on earth. In many of the Mahayana sutras Maya occupies an exalted place among the celestial beings who assemble to do honour to the deified Buddha, and there must have been a possibility at one time that a glorified Maya the Mayadevi would eventually be elevated to a heavenly throne near that of the glorified akyamuni, her divine Son[256]. We have seen that, according to a Mahayanist theory, Maya is "the eternal Mother of all the Buddhas," though this theory loses some of its significance when we find that she is not the only divine being to whom this exalted title has been accorded[257]

---

255 The Nativity of Buddha was a favourite subject with Indian sculptors, especially of the Gandhara school (nee Pl. xxix in Vincent A. Smith, History of Fine Art in India and Ceylon).

256 Among the sutras in which Maya receives prominence, cf. B.N. 153 and 082, in addition to the Ti-tsang sutra dealt with above (see p. 175). According to some Buddhists, Maya has been reborn in one of the heavens as a male deity, and rules there as king.

257 The title has also been given to the pusa Wen-shu the personified Wisdom of Buddhahood.

PAVILION IN FRONT OF SOUTHERN MONASTERY.

COURTYARD IN FRONT OF GREAT HALL OF KUAN-YIN, SOUTHERN MONASTERY.

Marichi

There is one rather mysterious deity in whom we may possibly discern a deified form of Gotama's mother. This is Chun-t'i (Chundi-devi), who is also sometimes described in Chinese as "Holy Mother" (sheng-mu) and as the "Mother of Buddha" (Fo mu}. This being plays a far more important part in Tantric Buddhism (that is, the Buddhism of word-mysticism and magic) than in the ordinary Buddhism of monastic China. Her image, however, is often seen in Chinese Buddhist temples. She is usually represented with eighteen arms, and sometimes with a third eye in the middle of the forehead[258]. By some authorities Chun-t'i is identified with the Marichi of Brahmanic mythology, and also with the Chinese T'ien-hou ("Queen of Heaven"), the Taoist deity already mentioned. Marichi, however, appears in Chinese Tantric literature under her own name, of which the Chinese form is Mo-li-chih. It has been daringly suggested that the name Marichi was derived from "the name of the holy Virgin Mary.[259]" This cannot be correct, because Marichi is mentioned as a divine being in pre-Christian Brahmanical literature[260]. Marichi was one of the "ten great sages, lords of created beings." Sometimes among Chinese Buddhists Chun-t i is identified with Kuan-yin, but the identification does not appear to be authorized by the books[261].

On the whole, we may say that the Buddhists in their religious meditations have generally treated the figure of the human mother of the historical founder of their faith in a manner that does credit to their imaginative delicacy and good taste; and in China and Japan they have found solace for this self-imposed restraint in the rapturous contemplation

---

258 The illustration is from a tablet-rubbing. Such artistic monstrosities as these are of Indian, not Chinese, origin. "The artists," as a leading authority on Indian art rightly observes, " under take to reproduce literally in stone or bronze the descriptions of the deities as given in the books, with little regard to aesthetic con siderations, and no form is regarded as too monstrous for plastic representation. The result too often is merely grotesque and absurd, when looked at by anybody who is not steeped in the notions of Hindu symbolism, but occasionally is horrible... Such forms, of course, have their meaning for the Hindu or Mahayanist Buddhist instructed in the mysteries of his faith, and may be used by him as aids to devotion, but from the artistic point of view they are... indefensible" (Vincent A. Smith, op. ait., p. 182).

259 Georgi, quoted by Eitel, Handbook, p. 98; and see Beal, Catena, p. 412.

260 Cf. the Bhagavadyltd and the Laws of Manu, S.B.E., viii. 19, 88, 387; and xxv. 14, 19, 112. See aho Vincent A. Smith, op. cit., pp. 182, 186, 188.

261 For the Chinese sutras on Chun-t f i, see B.N. 344, 345, 346. These sutras all appear to have been translated into Chinese during the seventh and eighth centuries.

Buddhist China

of the infinite graces of their ever-loving and compassionate Lady, the pusa Kuan-yin.

The recognized sutras contain innumerable references to the earthly and heavenly activities of the great pusa, but there is what we may call a romantic story of Kuan-yin as well as a scriptural one; and it is the romantic story which is nearest to the hearts of the Buddhist laity. This narrative, which is much too long for insertion in these pages, is simply a religious fairy-tale, and narrates the noble and virtuous deeds of the pusa and the terrible persecutions to which she was subjected during the life which she spent on earth (in the days of the Buddha Kasyapa) as the youngest of three princesses, daughters of a certain great king[262].

According to the writers who contribute pre faces to modern editions of the story, it was originally composed in the year 1102 of our era, in the reign of the emperor Hui Tsung, of the Sung dynasty, by a monk named P u-ming. It is perhaps the knowledge of the date of this story which gave rise to the belief that Kuan-yin was not recognized as a female pusa till the twelfth century. It is, indeed, by no means unlikely that the great popularity of the story hastened the general acceptance of the theory that Kuan-yin was a female, but it is certainly incorrect to regard the story as the sole origin of the theory.

Story of Kuan-Yin

The monk P'u-ming, we are told, once spent three months in solitary meditation, and was then visited by a strange apparition in the guise of an ancient hermit. After commending his religious zeal, the hermit bade him employ his time by writing down a full account of the wonderful life and acts of the blessed Kuan-yin, so that all who read or heard it might be brought to a full knowledge of the saintly career of that divine pusa and thereby become partakers of the heavenly bliss promised to all who should take her for their guide and saviour. P'u-ming reverently and obediently accepted the task im posed upon him by his ghostly visitor, and thereafter spent many industrious days in writing down the story of Kuan-yin's life on earth. When he had reached the last page and had laid down his pen he was rewarded by a glorious vision of the radiant pusa herself. P'u-ming

---

262 The germ of the story may possibly be found in the tale of the heretical king and his two Buddhist sons, which forms the subject of a section of the Lotus sutra (see B.N. 138, Har. xi. vol. ii. pp. 54-6; B.N. 134, Har. xi. vol. i. pp. 51-2; B.N. 139, Har. xi. vol. ii. pp. 104-5; 8.B.E. xxi. 419 ff.).

and his fellow-monks for she was visible also to them prostrated themselves in adoration, while like a floating cloud she passed before their eyes. Her figure was clad in rainbow-tinted vesture, and in her hands she bore her well-known emblems the drooping willow and the vase of heavenly dew.

P'u-ming's romantic story of Kuan-yin's life as an earthly princess is written in direct and simple language which renders it suitable for public recitation. There are some preliminary directions, indeed, which indicate that the work was intended to be read aloud in the Buddhist temples to lay audiences on the occasion of the pusa's birthday, which is celebrated on the nineteenth day of the second (Chinese) month. The reader or reciter (who would naturally be one of the monastic fraternity) should prepare himself for his sacred task by ceremonial fasting and purification, and by donning clean robes. He opens his discourse by reminding his audience that this day is the blessed anniversary of the birth of the loving and compassionate pusa Kuan-yin. He draws near to the altar, he says, in order that he may utter, in the hearing of all the assembled faithful, the precious words in which the life of the pusa is recorded. The congregation is enjoined to sit down and to maintain decorous silence; to avoid idle chattering, and to put away frivolity; to be orderly, quiet, and reverential. All must follow carefully the mean ing of what they hear, and having hearkened diligently to the truths that are promulgated, they must strive to give effect to them in their own lives. In the scriptures it is written that the pusa bears the name of Kuan-shih-yin (the "One who looks upon the world and hears its cries"), because if any living creature who is in trouble or in pain addresses a prayer to this pusa, and in true faith calls upon her name, then will the pusa immediately hearken to his cries and bring him deliverance from his woes[263]. If any living creature clings for support to the potent name of Kuan-yin, he may be thrown into a raging furnace, but the flames will leave him unscathed; he may be in peril from sharp swords, but the steel will break in pieces; he may be in danger of death from drowning, but the blessed pusa will come to his rescue and set him in a place of shallow waters[264].

---

[263] The scriptural passage referred to is in the Lotus of the Good Law (see S.B.E., xxi. 400 /.; and Beal, Catena, pp. .389 ff.).

[264] Pictorial illustrations of these and other miracles performed by Kuan-yin are often to he seen in Chinese temple frescoes.

Buddhist China

Religious Faith

The student of religion will pause before he ridicules or condemns these extravagant utterances. It is not difficult to catch a glimpse of the truth that lies behind such crudities of language. The I Buddhists, like the adherents of other creeds, have discovered that intensity of religious faith will enable a man to rise superior to all pain and to despise all danger. The limitations and imperfections of the flesh are powerless to curb the freedom of the mind. You may chain a heretic to the stake, but you cannot put fetters on his soul; you may throw a martyr to the lions, and they may tear flesh from bone, but they cannot violate the texture of his spirit. Let it not surprise us, then, to find that the Buddhist stories of the miraculous efficacy of faith in Kuan-yin stories which are based on the records of actual experience are paralleled in Christian hagiology. Maximinus orders St. Catherine of Alexandria to be broken on the wheel, but the wheel itself is shattered in pieces; Blandina is sent to the amphitheatre, but the wild beasts refuse to touch her; Herman of Cologne is condemned to death as a felon, yet faith in St. Elizabeth restores him to life; the judge Paschasius puts St. Lucy in a furnace that blazes with oil and pitch, but the saint stands unhurt amid the flames. Of the undeniable truths which are but thinly disguised in such stories as these, psychological analysis may have one explanation to offer, religious experience another. Perhaps neither is wholly right and neither wholly wrong.

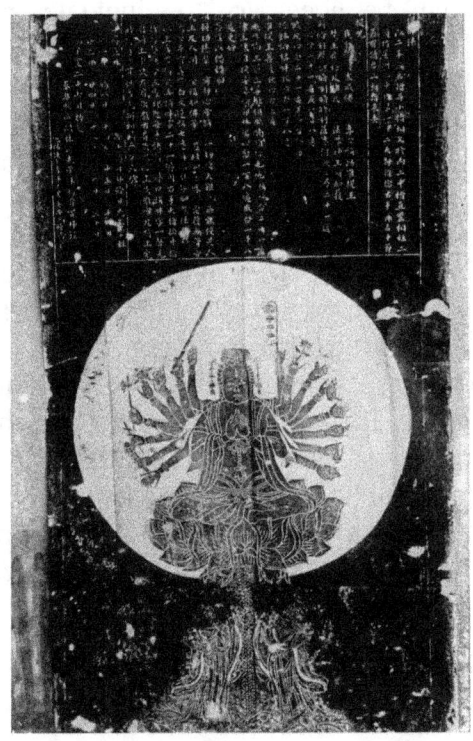

CHUN-T'I

A HERMIT OF PUTO AT THE DOOR OF HIS HERMITAGE.

Buddhist China

The Emblems of Kuan-Yin

A few words may be necessary to elucidate the reference to the willow-branch and the vase of heavenly dew, which were mentioned as Kuan-yin's favourite emblems. The vase is known in Chinese as the ching-p ing, which means "pure vessel," and the term is understood to be the equivalent of a Sanskrit word which means "the vase of immortality.[265]" The ching – p'ing was known in China in pre-Buddhist days. It was then a shallow dish, which was intended to catch the dew, and with this object it was usually placed in the outstretched hand of an image or statue. Some times, apparently, it was simply a cup-like hollow scooped out of a rock on the summit of a mountain. The dew collected by this means was believed to confer immortality on those who used it to moisten their lips and eyelids[266]. In the hands of Kuan-yin the vessel is usually represented as a narrow-necked phial (kalasa), from which the pusa sprinkles heavenly dew on her worshippers, and so endows them with the promise of endless bliss in the Western Paradise, or from which she pours upon them the celestial incense which accompanies the consecration (abhisheka) of every bodhisat[267].

With regard to the other sacred emblem carried by Kuan-yin, we may notice in the first place that the pusa's Indian prototype, Avalokitesvara, is represented as holding, not a willow-branch, but a lotus-flower hence the epithet padmapdni ("lotus-bearer"). The lotus, as we know, is to Buddhists a sacred plant, and perhaps we need look for no other reason for its presence in the hand of a holy bodhisat[268]. But it seems difficult to understand why in China Kuan-yin has come to be associated with the willow instead of the lotus. Perhaps we may find an explanation in the fact that the willow has been put by the Chinese to various magical uses, and is

---

265 Cf. Beal, Buddhist Records (1906 ed.), ii. 137, 172; and Walters, Yuan Chwang, ii. 50.

266 Cf. the European folk-lore concerning the washing of the face with dew on May morning.

267 According to another theory, healing waters issue from the pusa's finger-tips. This is a more pleasing conception than the Hindu notion of the sacred Ganga River,, which Hows from the toe of Vishnu. It may be mentioned that the phial is often seen in the hands of other pusas besides Kuan-yin, and it is sometimes carried by the Buddha Amitabha.

268 See pp. 103-9. Poussin observes (Hastings, E.R.E., ii. 260) that "already at Sauchi the 'lotus' is represented in the hand of a great many personages as an offering intended for Buddha. Those who carry lotuses are not all Avalokitas, for Maitreya is among them." Possibly Avalokitesvara as padmapdni may be connected with the post-Vedic Indian goddess Laksmi or Sri, the wife of Vishnu. This goddess was associated with the sea, from which she, like Aphrodite, is said to have arisen; and as goddess of beauty she is also associated with the lotus (see H. Jacobi, in Hastings, op. cit., ii. 808; Of. also Kern, S.B.E., xxi. 253, footnote 2).

regarded with special favour as a rain-charm[269]. Water which has been merely touched by a willow-branch is supposed to be endowed with miraculous healing properties[270]. In Buddhistic literature religious truth is often poetically referred to as a reviving rain that descends upon the parched earth. The phrase fa yu "the rain of the Law (of Buddha)" is constantly used by religious writers, and it has been chosen, as we shall see, as the name of one of the great monasteries of Puto. Thus to the worshipper of Kuan-yin it is a very natural and appropriate thing that the divine pusa, who brings succour to the distressed and sheds upon them the dew of immortal bliss (or "the wine of the sweet dew [271]"), should carry in her hand a magic willow, with which she charms down from heaven the "Rain of the Good Law.[272]"

Iconography

To follow the symbolism and iconography of the cult of Kuan-yin into all its branches would take us far beyond our prescribed limits. We may note, however, that she is sometimes described as ch'ien-shou ch'ien-yen (the "pusa of a thousand hands and a thousand eyes"), who (to quote the words of a hymn often recited in the temples of Puto) is "ever ferrying the souls of men safely across the ocean of misery, prayed to in a thousand places and in a thousand places respond ing to the call."[273] Tantric Buddhism, again, has a six-armed Avalokitesvara (perhaps to be identified with the six-armed Marichi) whose sculptured image seems to have been

---

269 Lion and Dragon in Northern China, pp. 187 and 346.

270 Such water is known as willow-water " (yang-chih-shui).

271 Kan-lu-chiu.

272 It is perhaps not impossible that Kuan-yin's spray was originally not that of a willow (Chinese yang) but that of an Indian tooth-stick tree (Chinese ch ik-mu), which seems to have been a kind of acacia. On this subject see Takakusu's I-Tsing's Records, p. 35; Watters, op. cit., ii. 171; and Beal, Records, i. 68,, ii. 173. It should be mentioned that the tamarisk (tamarixv chinensis, L.) has also been associated with Kuan-yin indeed, it is sometimes known as the Kuan-yin liu, or " Willow of Kuan-yin." It is interesting to note that a vase and a plant sometimes appear in the paintings of Western artists in association with the Virgin and the angel Gabriel (see Him, Sacred Shrine [1912], pp. 281-2). In these paintings the flower has usually been a lily; but the willow has also been applied to the purposes of Christian symbolism (see Duchesne, Early History of the Christian Church [Eng. trans., 1910], i. 167-8). This passage about the willow-wand which decays or remains green in accordance with the moral state of its owner may remind us of the belief of the Amidist that each man while living on earth is represented in paradise by a lotus, which flourishes or languishes according to his spiritual condition (see above, pp. 108-9).

[273]千处祈求千处应；苦海常作度人舟

worshipped in North western India in the eighth century of our era[274]. Sometimes we find in the chapels dedicated to Kuan – yin's worship the figures of what appear to be thirty-two different deities; but they are all manifestations of the one pusa exercising in different capacities her various functions of helper and saviour[275]. Sometimes, too, we find her image associated with eight different kinds of danger or suffering (the pa nan) from which she is engaged in extricating mankind[276]; and sometimes, as we know, she appears as co-ruler with Amitabha and Mahasthamaprapta (Ta-shih-chih), over Sukhavati, the Western Paradise, although it is correct to regard her, when acting in this capacity, not as the female Kuan-yin, but as the male Avalokitesvara of the scriptures of the Pure Land.

An epithet of Kuan-yin which is frequently met with by the student of Chinese Buddhist literature is Pai-i Ta-shih ("The Great Teacher robed in white"). An English writer has ventured to emphasize this epithet as one of several indications of a connection between the Buddhists and the Essenes, who appear to have been known as a white-clothed sect[277]. The theory that the Essenes were a sect of Buddhists has not commended itself to later scholars, though many have admitted that the religion and philosophy of the Essenes may have been partly derived from Oriental (perhaps Persian) sources. As for the white robes, they were worn not only by Essenes, but also by the Therapeutae in Egypt (assuming that they existed outside the mind of the author of the De Vita Contemplativa), and by initiates in the Orphic Mysteries[278].

---

274 See Vincent A. Smith, op. cit., p. 185. It may be unnecessary to remind the reader that the frescoes and statues of Avalokitesvara which have been found in Turkestan by Stein, Le Coq, and others are not only of characteristically Indian, Tibetan, and Chinese type, but also (more especially) of that Graeco-Indian type which has left an indelible impress on Asiatic religious art from Gandhara to Japan.

275 These are the thirty-two hsiang or " transformations " (sui-chi-ying-hsieri) of Kuan-yin and they include her appearances as a female. The thirty-two hsiang are all mentioned in thesutras (see B.N. 13-i and 139). Some of the hsiang (including the female ones, as already stated) are wanting in B.N. 138 and in the text used by Kern.

276 Strictly speaking, these are eight states or situations in which it is impossible to hear the Law of Buddha (and therefore difficult to attain salvation). 八处众生不得闻法故名八难

277 Beal, Buddhist Literature in China, 1882, xv. xvi. 159-166. A. E. Suffrin suggests the ethnic term is equivalent to Essauites, or Idumaeans, or at least a clan of Idumaea. He is strongly of opinion that the sect was non-Jewish, though on the Jewish borderland.

278 See the closing lines of the Cretans of Euripides.

The Dea Syria

But if it be unjustifiable to trace any connection between Kuan-yin and the Essenes, it is perhaps permissible to suspect Syrian influences of another kind. The cult of the Dea Syria was carried, as we know, to the extreme west of Europe; but the traders of Hierapolis had relations with the East as well as the West, and there is no difficulty in supposing that some knowledge of this goddess reached China through Persian or other channels. We may readily understand that the cult itself, with its orgiastic revelries and barbarities, could never have had the slightest chance of winning support in a land which had already submitted to the moral sway of Confucianism. Yet it will perhaps be conceded that in some respects Kuan-yin may not unfairly be regarded as a refined and moralized Atargatis[279].

Kuan-Yin as a Fish-Goddess

We know that this Syrian goddess was believed to have the control of "sacred life-giving waters,[280]" a fact which recalls Kuan-yin with her vial of vivifying rain or dew. But more significant is the fact that both divinities are associated with fish. The same, indeed, may be said of deities who have little else in common with one another such as Orpheus and Vishnu; and it is also true that Buddhism itself makes a symbolic use of fish quite irrespectively of the cult of Kuan-yin[281]. It must be admitted, moreover, that no special significance necessarily attaches to the fact that tanks of "sacred fish" are a characteristic feature of all properly-equipped Buddhist monasteries, as they were of the temples of Atargatis, for it is usually supposed (whether rightly or wrongly) that the fish in the monastery ponds were never regarded as "sacred," but are merely

---

279 It would not be the only instance of the adaptation to China of deities that originally belonged to the West. The famous Hsi-wang-mu ("the Western Queen-mother"), who occupies a prominent place in the fairy-lore of China, has recently been identified (by Prof. H. A. Giles) with the goddess Hera. Is it not possible, too, that a connection exists between the Mahayanist Amitabha who is not only the Wu-liang-kuang (the deity of Infinite Light or Space"), but also the Wu-liang-shou (the deity of " Infinite Age or Time") and the Zrvan akarana, or "Endless Time" of Mithraism?

280 See Dr T. K. Cheyne, in Encycl. Biblica coll. 1530-1.

281 Reference need only be made to the mu-yu, or " wooden fish " which occupies a prominent place in every Buddhist temple. There are three supposed characteristics of fishes which appear to have led to their being regarded in many parts of the world as sacred. One is their quietness: they are the "silent ones," even as the gods to mortal ears are silent. Another is their wakefulness: they are believed to need no sleep. The third is their fancied perpetual virginity.

supposed to serve as a permanent reminder of the strict Buddhist commandment to refrain from the deliberate slaughter of any animal[282]. But unless we adopt the hypothesis of some actual contact between the cults of Atargatis and Kuan-yin, it is difficult when we remember that the former was partly a goddess of fishes to explain why Kuan-yin in one of her manifestations should also be regarded as a fish-goddess. In this capacity she is known in Nepal as Matsyendranath, or "Ruler of Fishes"; and in China she is described as Ao-yu Kuan-yin ("The Kuan-yin of the Big Fish"). Painters of the T'ang dynasty if not those of an earlier time sometimes represented her as carrying a fish in her right hand. Certain artists of the Sung dynasty gave still bolder expression to the idea of Kuan-yin's association with fishes by clothing her in the garb of a fisherman's daughter. Occasionally, indeed, the fish notion was, from the artistic point of view, over emphasized. A Western critic, who assumes that Kuan-yin's fish is merely "a symbol of spiritual sustenance," complains that it is too large, too much in evidence[283].

If there is any justification for the suggestion that the Syrian fish-goddess Atargatis, long ago expeUed from her splendid shrine at Hierapolis, still carries on a fragmentary and ghostly existence in the person of the "fisherman's daughter" of Chinese Buddhism, we need not be surprised to find that the waters surrounding the island of Puto are theoretically regarded as an inviolable sanctuary for fishes, and that disaster is supposed to be in store for all impious fishermen who defy the commands of the Ao-yu Kuan-yin by letting down their nets in those holy waters. That the rule receives no official support, and is to-day practically a dead letter, does not affect the significance of the religious taboo.

Extension of Cult of Kuan-Yin

There is a quaint Chinese legend which associates a sudden advance in the popularity of the cult of Kuan-yin with a miraculous incident which occurred in the second quarter of the ninth century. According to this legend, the emperor Wen Tsung, of the T'ang dynasty, who reigned from 827 to 840, was inordinately fond of oysters, and the fisher-folk were obliged by imperial decree to furnish the palace with enormous and

---

282 Hence such ponds are known as fang-sheng-ch'ih ("life-sparing ponds"). Fish are not the only animals whose lives are thus ostentatiously preserved. Some large monasteries take charge of cattle and pigs as well.

283 See Fenollosa, Epochs of Chinese and Japanese Art, i. 133.

regular supplies of this delicacy, for which, however, no payment was made from the imperial exchequer. One day the emperor's eye was gladdened by the sight of an oyster-shell of exceptionally large size, and his Majesty anticipated an unusual treat. The shell, however, was so hard that all efforts to break it proved unavailing; and the emperor was about to put it aside when suddenly it opened of its own accord, and disclosed to the astonished gaze of the court a miniature image of the pusa Kuan-yin. The awe-stricken emperor gave orders that the treasure was to be carefully preserved in a gold-inlaid sandal-wood box, and he then sent for a noted Buddhist monk named Wei Cheng, who knew everything that was worth knowing on the subject of miracles, in order to obtain an authoritative explanation of the prodigy.

"This matter," explained the man of wisdom, "is not devoid of significance. Kuan-yin is the pusa who extends love and compassion to all living beings; and the pusa has chosen this means of inclining your majesty's mind towards benevolence and clemency and filling your heart with pity for your oppressed people."

The emperor, concludes the chronicler, took the hint in good part, and not only abolished the forced tribute of oysters, but issued an edict to the effect that an image of Kuan-yiri was to be admitted into every Buddhist temple throughout the Empire[284].

Whether we believe this story or not, it points to the fact that a great extension of the cult of Kuan-yin took place a very few years before the time when Puto-shan began to be recognized as that pusa's principal seat of worship in China. The oyster-loving emperor died in 840; the Buddhist history of Puto opens in 847. In that year, according to the annals of the island, a certain Buddhist ascetic from India came to Puto and worshipped Kuan-yin at the Ch'ao-yin Cave. This seems to show that Puto must have been known, even at that early date, as a favourite haunt of Kuan-yin, though there is no direct evidence that such was the case. According to the story, the Indian pilgrim attested the sincerity of his devotion by burning

---

284 It seems a pity to throw any doubt on the credibility of this story as it stands, but in the interests of truth the reader's attention must be drawn to a prosaic statement which occurs in Dr Wells Williams's description of the shell-fish and insects of China. In Chehkiang the natives take a large kind of clam (Alasmodonta) and gently attach leaden images of Buddha under the fish,, after which it is thrown back into the water. Nacre is deposited over the lead, and after a few months the shells are retaken, cleaned, and then sent abroad to sell as proofs of the power and presence of Buddha " (Middle Kingdom, i. 350-1). In view of these facts it must regretfully be admitted that where the interests of religion were at stake the Chinese monks of the ninth century seem to have shown themselves no more scrupulous than their European contemporaries.

all his ten fingers, and when he had borne this horrible torture without flinching, he passed into a state of ecstatic rapture, in which he not only saw the form of the glorious Kuan-yin, but also heard her voice.

Buddhist Austerities

If the pusa were true to her functions as a "Teacher of the Good Law," we must assume that her object in appearing before her Indian worshipper was not to signify her approbation of his conduct, but rather to express her extreme displeasure. Such deeds of religious fanaticism (records of which are painfully frequent in the annals of other religions besides Buddhism) are totally irreconcilable with the spirit of the Buddhist faith, and are contrary to the express teachings of its founder. Gotama himself, like the German fourteenth-century mystic Henry Suso, began his religious career by subjecting himself to the most rigid rules of a cruel asceticism. Like Suso, long after him, he made the discovery that painful bodily austerities were not the necessary conditions of healthy spiritual progress, and he thereafter followed a via media which he never ceased to recommend to his disciples[285]. Unfortunately, however, owing to a false interpretation of a section in the Lotus of the Good Law, it came to be believed by certain Mahayanist schools, among which the T'ien-t'ai school was conspicuous, that there was scriptural warrant, not only for a rigid asceticism, but even for self-immolation by fire.

It is a significant circumstance that the worshipper who burned his ten fingers at Kuan-yin's Cave is described as a native of India, for it was largely the example of the flesh-torturing sadhus of India that led many of the Buddhist monks of China to inflict cruel punishment on the body for

---

[285] O. Zockler has pointed out that though we cannot " regard asceticism as an element of the religious and moral life belonging exclusively to the essence of Christianity, or prescribed in its original body of doctrine as necessary to salvation,, the ascetic principle early made way for itself in the development of the Christian Church." Mutatis mutandis, the same observation may be made concerning the asceticism which we find associated with both Islam and Buddhism. Mrs Rhys Davids points out that Buddhism "claimed at its very inception, in the Buddha's first sermon,, to be a Middle Path, opposed equally to the extremes of sensuous and worldly indulgence on the one hand, and of self-mortification on the other... But in the sense of the Greek askesis, or way of life, in which some channels of activity are barred and others developed by special training, Buddhism was thoroughly ascetic... The bodily culture of the Order amounted very much to what would now be called 'the simple life.'... There does not appear, in the canonical books, any glorification of the intellectual or spiritual at the expense of the corporeal." Similarly, J. H. Bateson truly observes that though "the constant endeavour and ultimate hope of the Buddhist is to escape from corporeal existence, Gotama clearly teaches that the body is to be cared for. Desire for the pleasures, and the formation of good habits, which minister to the real self, are inculcated; and pursuit and conduct which contribute to this end are to be cultivated" (Hastings, Encycl, Rel. Ethics, ii. 70-1, 74, 759).

its proneness to rebel against the sovereignty of the spirit. Besides being opposed to true Buddhism, such proceedings are also directly antagonistic to the cardinal Chinese virtue of Hsiao ("filial piety"), which bids men maintain their bodies in a state of physical health and fitness in order that they may fulfil all their duties and obligations both to their parents and to their descendants.

Yet in condemning the harsh self-discipline of the ascetics of India and China we should beware of assuming, as the "plain man" is apt to assume, that the mortifications of the flesh which a religious enthusiast inflicts upon himself under the influence of ecstasy or intense emotion are necessarily the cause of acute physical agony. There is abundance of evidence to show that in very many cases there is no suffering whatever, all the pain being dissolved in the flames of a rapturous joy. Thus we may console ourselves with the reflection that our finger-burning ascetic may have been as free from physical pain as was Catherine of Siena or Bernadette of Lourdes, in very similar circumstances[286].

Sutras Written in Blood

Nowadays, whether as a result of a slackening of religious zeal or from some more meritorious cause, it is comparatively rarely that a Buddhist monk inflicts physical pain or injury upon himself. Few submit to any severer discipline than that known to Christian monks as inclusio voluntary self-confinement in a monastic cell for a term of months or years[287]. Others withdraw from the fellowship of the fraternity to which they belong, and take up their abode, sometimes under a vow of silence, in solitary hermitages[288].

---

286 The mystic trance appears to be frequently accompanied by a state of anaesthesia (see E. Underhill, Mysticism, pp. 429 and 435). "Credible witnesses report that Bernadette, the visionary of Lourdes, held the flaming end of a candle in her hand for fifteen minutes during one of her ecstasies. She felt no pain, neither did the flesh show any marks of burning. Similar instances of ecstatic anaesthesia abound in the lives of the saints." With regard to the wilful " creation of pain-sensations " as " a desperate device for enhancing the intensity of the emotional state," see Hirn's Origins of Art, chap. v.

287 For a case of this kind at Chiu-hua-shan, see above, p. 242. The similar practices of Tibetan anchorites are of a much severer type than anything of the kind in Buddhist China (tsee Sven Hedin, Trans-Himalaya, ii. 7 ff.}.

288 Cf. the Laura of Western monasticism.

Buddhist China

KUAN - YIN PUSA.
*Drawn in blood by a **Hermit** of Puto-shan.*
(*Much reduced in size.*)

Several such hermitages exist in Puto to this day. There are some anchorites, again, who maintain a practice which has been very widespread, and seems to be of great antiquity in China that of writing sutras or drawing sacred pictures with their own blood[289]. The only act of bodily mortification involving acute pain which is practised by ordinary monks is associated with the rites of ordination. This is the process known as jan-hsiang, or chiu-hsiang, which consists in the cauterization of the scalp with burning moxa-pastilles made from the artemisia chinensis[290]. Strictly speaking, submission to this painful ordeal is not an ascetic act that is to say, it is not done with the object of chastening the body in the interests of the spirit; it is a symbolic act, whereby the candidate for ordination signifies his willing ness to walk in the way of the bodhisats, even to the extent of sacrificing his body, if need be, for the good of his suffering fellow-creatures.

The Sacred Cave

It was mentioned that the place where the Indian pilgrim performed his act of devotion and gazed upon the divine form of Kuan-yin was the Ch ao-yin Cave. Since that time the pusa is said to have manifested herself to the eyes of her worshippers on many different occasions, but of the three "caves" in which these divine manifestations have taken place, the Ch ao-yin is that which has been most frequently hallowed by the pusa's presence, and is therefore regarded as the most sacred[291]. It is visited by all pilgrims, and all go in the strong hope that when they gaze into the cavern's dark recesses they will be favoured with a view of the pusa "clothed in white samite, mystic, wonderful.[292]" Perhaps those who are strong in faith do not often go away disappointed.

---

289 In such cases the blood is usually drawn from the tongue. A reproduction (on a reduced scale) of a portrait of Kuan-yin, drawn in blood by an anchorite of Puto whose name is Shou-ch ing, appears in this book. The technical expression for writing sutras with one's blood is tz'u hsueh shu ching.

290 For full description of the ordination ceremonies, see De Greet, Le Code du Mahayana en Chine (Amsterdam: 1893). The jan-hsiang is described on pp. 217 ff.

291 The other two are the Fan-yin and Shan-ts'ai caves, which are in the eastern peninsula, beyond the " Flying Sands." 常显现处潮音梵音善财三洞

292 The author may as well confess at once that in spite of many visits to the cave he heard or saw nothing hut the wild water lapping on the crag.

Buddhist China

As a cave the Ch'ao-yin-tung is disappointing, for it is merely a perpendicular rent in the rocks by the sea-shore, and would attract no particular attention but for its sacred associations. At times the tidal waters rush into it with resounding roar and dashing spray, and the waves, says a monkish chronicler, lash the cliff walls like the tossed mane of a wild animal. If the critical Western enquirer insists upon extorting a prosaic explanation of the ghostly appearances of Kuan-yin, he may perhaps find one in the fact that at certain times, when atmospheric and tidal conditions are favourable, a shaft of sunlight streams into the cave through a gap in the roof called the t ien-ch uang, or "heaven's window," and strikes athwart the flying foam. The cave then seems to be filled with a tremulous haze, in which the unbeliever sees nothing but sunlit spray, but which to the devout worshipper is a luminous veil through which the "Pusa of Love and Pity" becomes visible to the eyes of her faithful suppliants.

Close by the cave stand two little temples, the Lohan-tien, or "Hall of Arahants," and the Ch ao-yin-tung-tien, or "Hall of the Cave of the Tide-waves." A little stone image, one or two empty shrines and incense-jars, an iron railing, and a rock bearing the inscription Hsien-shen-ch'u, indicate the spot from which the visitor is invited to gaze into the so-called cave. This spot is known as the Ch'iu-hsien-t ai the terrace whereon the pilgrim kneels and prays. Here may also be seen a sacred well or pool known as Kuang-ming ("Lustrous and Bright"), and also as Hui-ch'uan or "Spring of Wisdom." Miracles of healing are said to have been wrought by the waters of this well[293]. In the spring of the year 1266, for example, a high official named Fan was afflicted with blind ness, and sent his son to offer up prayers on his behalf at the Cave of Kuan-yin. The son carried out his father's behest, and from the well he brought home a bottle of holy water with which he washed the blind man's eyes. As a result Fan recovered his eyesight, and he then ordered his son to make a second journey to Puto to return thanks. In front of the holy cave the young man knelt down to pray, and no sooner had he finished his prayers than the pusa made her appearance below "heaven's window." Her form, we are

---

[293] It is curious to find healing wells associated with a sacred cave in the extreme west of the Euro-Asiatic continent as well as in the extreme east. I refer to the wells which exist in the vicinity of the holy cave of St. Medan in Luce Bay Scotland. It has been "the immemorial custom of the peasantry a custom not wholly obsolete to day to bathe in these wells at sunrise on the first Sunday in May, for the purpose of curing themselves of various diseases " (D. MacRitchie, in E.R.E., iii, 268).

told, was dimly outlined within a cloud of shimmering vapour, and a scarf of jade-green gauze streamed from her shoulders.

As late as the first quarter of the sixteenth century the curative properties of Kuan-yin's well were still recognized by the highest personages in the land, for we are told that an empress of the Ming dynasty sent a special emissary to Puto to offer up prayers at the holy cave and to draw healing waters from the well. Indeed, it was in recognition of the miraculous cures wrought by the waters of this well that the name "Lustrous and Bright" was conferred upon it by imperial patent.

A Story of Kuan-Yin

It is not only amid the salt spray of Puto's sea-caves that the divine Kuan-yin has made her self visible to men's eyes, nor has she revealed herself only to those who have bent the knee before her sacred image. There is a graceful little tale which describes the wonderful experience of two devout women who were in the habit of going on pilgrimage to Puto year after year. One of these was an unmarried girl, the other her married relative. On one occasion as their boat approached the island the girl was seized with a slight sickness, and was unable to go ashore. She therefore remained in the boat, alone and melancholy, while the elder woman spent the day on the island visiting the shrines and performing the customary rites of worship. Her religious duties, unfortunately, caused her to forget the needs of her companion, who had no means of providing herself with food. The girl became very hungry in the course of the day, and was therefore much relieved when a stately lady, carrying a basket of food, suddenly appeared on the sea-shore. The boat was moored some distance off the shore, but the strange lady made a little causeway by throwing stepping-stones into the water, and by this means she reached the boat without worse misadventure than slightly wetting the edge of her robe. She fed the girl with delicious food, and then, without having spoken a word, returned to the shore. After some time the elder woman, having finished her devotions, returned to the boat and expressed a fear that the girl must be hungry. "Not at all," was the reply; "I was fed by a strange lady." So saying she pointed to a remnant of the food which still lay on the deck. Her companion on hearing the details of the story made up her mind that the girl's silent hostess must have been a divine being, and she returned to the principal temple to give thanks. Looking up reverently at

Buddhist China

the stately image of Kuan-yin seated on the lotus throne, she noticed that the hem of the pusa's robe was glistening with water.

Idolatry and Symbolism

It may be pointed out, perhaps, by some keen-eyed critic that the conclusion of this little story affords conclusive proof that the Buddhists of China, whatever they may be in theory, are in practice mere "idolaters." He may assert that in spite of the moral elevation and philosophical profundity of many Buddhist doctrines, the religion as actually practised by the people of China has come to be little more than a systematized image-worship. This, however, is scarcely true. Let us beware of supposing, when we watch the people burning incense before the great gilded images of the Buddhas and bodhisats, that all Chinese Buddhists are mere worshippers of stocks and stones. In the East, as in the West, there are many people who are, or believe themselves to be, incapable of dispensing with all sensuous aids to the religious imagination, and who find in outward signs and emblems a means of preserving undimmed within their hearts and minds the light of a lofty spiritual ideal. It is only the most ignorant of Buddhists, as it is only the most ignorant of Christians, who regard the images before which they kneel in prayer or adoration as the real and ultimate objects of their pious devotion. To the enlightened Buddhist, as to the enlightened Catholic, the image or sacred picture is merely a symbol of divinity. Christian and Buddhist are both well aware that among the untaught and unimaginative masses the symbol is, unfortunately, apt to usurp the place of the thing symbolized; and yet there are count less earnest adherents of the one faith and of the other who would feel spiritually impoverished if the symbol were withdrawn.

With regard to this question of "idols," a touching story is told by a Japanese Buddhist priest, Tada Kanai, who has published a little volume of sermons which would not discredit any Western pulpit[294].

---

294 The book is named Shodo Kowa 修道讲话 and has been translated into English by the late Rev. Arthur Lloyd under the title The Praises of Amida (Tokyo: 1907).

Reginald Fleming Johnston

Filial Piety

During a period of political unrest in Japan a number of young men of knightly rank samurai were imprisoned on a charge of participation in a revolutionary disturbance. All the prisoners, with one exception, were filled with fierce anger and resentment against their jailors, and even went so far as to assault the official who brought them their daily food. The exception was a mere child, a boy of twelve or thirteen years of age, whose patience under suffering and quiet dignity of bearing won him the sympathy and goodwill of his jailors and fellow-prisoners alike. The authorities noticed that their boy-prisoner possessed two little lay figures, which at first were supposed to be only dolls, and they wondered at a high-spirited boy caring for such childish things; but careful observation revealed the fact that he treated them not as toys, but as objects of respect and reverence. Every morning he would set them up before him and greet them as if they were living beings. "Good morning, father, good morning, mother!" he would say; and when dinner-time time came he would always place the tray in front of them and go through a form of reverent salutation before he began to ply his chopsticks. He treated the dolls, in fact, as a dutiful and respectful son (in Old Japan or in Old China) would treat his living parents; and his jailors gradually came to realize that the toy figures were largely responsible for the child's grace of manner and sweetness of disposition. The hardships of the jail failed to embitter his temper, for to him it was no jail, but rather a beautiful temple or something yet more sacred a home. To him, in very truth, stone walls were no prison, iron bars no cage; for he was free to hold spiritual communion, through the medium of his little images, with those whom he loved and honoured above all others, and he wanted no greater freedom than that.

Our Japanese preacher is not content with emphasizing the lesson to be drawn from this little story in respect of the virtue of filial piety a virtue which, by the way, seems likely to lose its hold in both Japan and China in indirect consequence of the substitution of Western for Eastern ideals in social and political life. He goes on to remind us that human life itself is a prison into which we have all been cast as fettered captives[295]. Passion and ambition, ignorance and vanity, indolence and selfishness, all the

---

295 Our Japanese Buddhist would accept the Orphic and Pythagorean notion that the hody is a prison arid the soul a prisoner. Of. Plato, Phado, 81-4, and Gorgias, 493. Cf. also the well-known words in Romans vii. 24: " O wretched man that I am! who shall deliver me from the body of this   death? " Cf. Matthew Arnold, ff For most men in a brazen prison live," etc.

limitations and weaknesses of our physical and moral natures these are the chains with which we are fast manacled throughout the whole term of our imprisonment, a term which lasts from birth to death. We, too, have dolls that we play with, idols that we worship. Let us not be ashamed of our idolatries, provided only that these idols of ours stand as symbols of something true and beautiful outside our prison walls. The boy-prisoner of Japan used his idols as a means of communion with his loved ones who were far away: and they gave his spirit wings. Some of us have idols of a baser kind, idols that hypnotize our faculties and teach us to hug our chains, so that the music of the spheres grows faint, and the range of our spiritual vision is restricted to the boundaries of our dungeon. The spirit will beat against her mortal bars in vain if our idols are such as these.

Use of Prayer in Buddhism

There is a curiously prevalent impression among Europeans that the "idolatries" practised in Buddhist China are quite incompatible with anything like prayer in the Christian sense, and that the whole of the liturgical worship of the Buddhist temples is a meaningless mummery, chiefly consisting in the recitation of transliterated Sanskrit texts and formulas which are totally devoid of meaning even to the officiating priests. Such notions as these are a survival from the bad old days when it was considered a proof of Christian zeal to heap contempt and abuse on the faiths of all non-Christian peoples; but they are notions which no person who can read Chinese is likely to entertain for a moment after he has glanced at some of the pages of the prayer-books which are in daily use in the great monasteries. Such compilations as the favourite Ch'an-men-jih-sung[296] include prayers for use by both monks and laymen in connection with all such circumstances of daily life as can be brought into relationship with religious observance[297]. There are, of course, prayers for use on saints days that is, on the days specially consecrated to the worship of the great pusas. There are burial services for monks and laymen, services for the ordination of monks, services in commemoration of pious founders and benefactors and "spiritual ancestors." There are prayers for use before and after child-birth, prayers for fair weather, for rain, for deliverance from plague and famine, for the divine guidance of rulers and

---

296 " Prayers of the Ch'an (Jhana) School for daily recitation."

297 Another popular compilation is the Ch'an-lin-shu-yu or (" Prayers of the Jhana Grove").

magistrates. There are prayers to be used before taking food, prayers for those in danger or difficulty, prayers for those at sea, prayers expressing repentance for sin, prayers for the sick and dying. Such books also contain many superstitious survivals, such as sacred words and charms which are supposed to have a controlling power over the forces of nature, and there are prayers for purely material benefits, such as wealth and worldly prosperity, and rituals which correspond more or less closely with Christian masses for the dead.

To the non-Buddhist, perhaps a more interesting feature of these religious miscellanies is the large section which is devoted to selected "sermonettes" or homilies by distinguished leaders of religious thought. These as a rule consist of moral exhorta tions which, though based on Buddhist ethics, are so free from credal or dogmatic assumptions that they might almost be regarded as the utterances of free-thinking moralists and, indeed, rightly so, for Buddhism is perhaps the only great religious system which, if it does not actually welcome and encourage the free thinker, sees no reason to make provision for his excommunication. Expulsion from the monkhood is, indeed, not unknown; but the punishment is inflicted, not for free thought or "infidelity," but merely for offences against morals or discipline. The fate of those who, if no longer subjected to physical torture, are still driven unwillingly from the fold of the Christian Church would be unthinkable in Buddhism[298]. The Buddhist monk at ordination binds himself to no Articles and to no formulated Creed, and he is perfectly at liberty to use his own judgment in interpreting the sacred books and traditional doctrines of his school, though so long as he chooses to remain in the monkhood he must, of course, conform with all the disciplinary regulations in force in the monastery to which he belongs[299].

---

[298] Modernist movements in Buddhism give rise to no acute "crises " in the Buddhist Church: partly because no one is in a position to make infallible pronouncements as to what constitutes orthodoxy. We can hardly describe the Three Refuges as a Creed in the Western sense.

[299] So far as its attitude towards dogma is concerned, the Protestantism of Auguste Sabatier and his followers has much in common with Buddhism. It is quite time to let even dogma decay, in so far as it is an object of obligatory belief. Faith must be regarded as the religious element par excellence. Wheresoever faith exists, there is religion. What is called dogma is merely a symbolical interpretation always inadequate and always modifiable of the ineffable data of the religious consciousness. All religious knowledge is necessarily and purely symbolical, seeing that mystery (as the word implies) can only be expressed through symbols " (Boutroux, Science and Religion, Eng. trans., 1909, p. 226).

Buddhist China

Prayers of the Jhana School

The edition of the Prayers of the Jhana School which is in use in the monasteries of Puto contains, as might be expected, numerous prayers addressed to or associated with Kuan-yin. As an example of these we may cite a prayer which was composed by a monk who bore the monastic name of "Fruit of Great Wisdom.[300]"

Ignoring the popular notion of Kuan-yin's womanhood, he addresses the pusa as "compassionate Father of the whole universe,"[301] to whom he offers praise for the boundless love and pity vouchsafed to all living beings, and for his ceaseless efforts to bring the world to salvation.

A Buddhist Prayer

The supplicant announces that he has come, cleansed in body and mind,[302] to prostrate himself before the pusa and to implore his help and protection. He continues as follows:

"I am indeed filled with thankfulness that it has been granted to me to know the Buddha's way of salvation; but although I am a monk and have abandoned the world, I am bitterly conscious that my heart is not yet penetrated with the truth[303]. I am sorely lacking in true knowledge, and have many vain thoughts and wrong opinions. I am deficient in the moral force necessary for spiritual advancement. I study the scriptures with diligence, and yet I am incapable of fully understanding and assimilating their holy wisdom. I fear that few blessings are in store for me, that my life is destined to be cut short[304], and that I have devoted myself all in vain to the religious life[305]. I have wasted my days, and dare hope for nothing

---

300 Ta-hui-kuo.

[301] 十方慈父

[302] 清净三业

303 If the supplicant is a layman, in place of the sentence beginning (< but although I am a monk," he may use the following words: I am still immersed in the ocean of worldly life, and my mind is confused and distracted."

304 The Buddhist prays for a long life so that he may have time for the fullest spiritual development of which his nature is capable. The common Western view that the consistent Buddhist longs, or should long, for a speedy death or annihilation is quite a mistaken one.

305 Instead of this sentence the layman says: "I fear that I am making an unprofitable use of my privileges as a man" (literally, "I have obtained a man's

body in vain").

but a spendthrift's death[306]. Behold, in my longing to purify this heart of mine, I am shedding tears of anguish. In reverence and humiliation I kneel before Thee: day and night my thoughts dwell on Thy holy countenance. I hold fast to Thy holy name, and prostrate myself before Thy sacred image.[307] Incline Thy heavenly ear, O Pusa, to hearken unto me; of Thy divine love save me from misery; grant me Thy pity and Thy protection; let Thy spiritual light shine upon my body and illumine my heart. Baptize me with Thy sweet dew, so that it may wash away all stains of hatred and ill-will, cleanse me from all sin and foulness, and make me pure in thought and deed. Guard me both day and night from all evil. Be ever with me, O Pusa, when I wake and when I sleep. Grant that my understanding may awaken under the rays of Thy glory. Grant that I may increase in spiritual intelligence and discernment. Grant that when I read the scriptures the words may remain stored in my memory, and that when the sacred truths are expounded I may have wisdom to understand them. May I be endowed with good judgment and insight; may my days be long; may I attain happiness and peace; may I ever be absorbed in the contemplation of Thy truth; may evil spirits keep far from me; may I awaken to a clear perception of the futility of living through generation after generation without spiritual progress; may I walk in the way of the pusas; may I show gratitude for all mercies; may I put my trust in the Buddha, the Law, and the company of the saints; and wherever the Law holds sway, may all living beings attain union in the perfect wisdom that leads to the peace of Buddhahood"[308]

---

306 That is, I shall have squandered all my powers and talents, and shall have accumulated no store of good karma with which to face the life that is to come.

[307]稽顙投诚终日竟夜存想圣容受持圣号礼拜圣像

[308]倾大甘露灌我顶门

Buddhist China

KUAN-YIN, "THE COMPASSIONATE FATHER."

XII. The Monastic History Of Puto-Shan

As Kuan-yin's holy island contains nearly a hundred monasteries and temples, exclusive of a still larger number of solitary hermitages, it is obvious that a full description and historical account of Puto-shan could not be compressed into the space of a few short chapters. In these pages we must content ourselves with little more than a general survey of the two principal monasteries. These are the P'u-chi, commonly known as the Ch'ien-ssu, or "Southern Monastery," and the Fa-yu, commonly known as the Hou-ssu or "Northern Monastery." As this book, however, may find its way into the hands of European visitors to the island, it may not be out of place to give some brief description of its topography.

The Diamond Rock

For purposes of study and exploration the island may be regarded as divided into five imaginary sections. The first section will include all the south-western part, beginning with the landing-place. In this section there are about seventeen temples, including the interesting Kuan-yin-tung (with a cave, as its name denotes, dedicated to the pusa), and the still more in teresting Ling-shih–ch'an-lin (the "Meditation Grove of the Spiritual Rock"). This is the famous P'an-t'o (the "Huge Rock"), as it styles itself in deeply carved characters. Next to the Ch'ao-yin Cave, described in the last chapter, this is the holiest spot on the island. Just as the whole of Puto is the Chinese duplicate of the sacred Potalaka mentioned in the Hua-yen sutra as the home of Kuan-yin, so the P'an-t'o Rock is the counterpart of the Chin-kang-pao-shih (the "Holy Diamond Rock"),[309] on which, according to that sutra, Kuan-yin sat enthroned when she (or he) was visited by the angelic Shan-ts'ai.[310] The boulder is covered with various inscriptions, among which we find "the Western Heaven," "I take my refuge in Amitabha Buddha," "the place where the Great Teacher preached the Law," "the Eternal Buddha," "the world's most famous

---

[309] 金刚宝石

[310] 善财

rock," "the holy rock which guards the State."[311] On the flat top of the boulder, which is reached by means of a wooden ladder, contemplative monks may often be seen sitting in reverie. This, in fact, is a favourite spot for the practice of ch'an-na (jhana) deep religious meditation. There is another rock close by known as the "Pulpit of Kuan-yin,"[312]

but in spite of its superior position (for it commands a fine view of the west) it cannot compete with the "Diamond Rock" in fame or sanctity.

Another temple in this section, the Mei Fu Ch'an-yuan, is worth a visit on account of the curious black-bearded and emaciated figures which are understood to represent Sakyamuni, Wen-shu, and P'u-hsien. The P'u-chi-an also deserves a visit for the sake of its magnificent camphor-tree, and the Yin-hsiu temple on account of its secluded situation. At one time the printing-blocks of the island Chronicle and other literary valuables were stored in the Yin-hsiu for safety. Its sequestered position saved it more than once from the attentions of piratical visitors.

The second of the five sections, with about twenty-five temples, contains not only the Ch'ao-yin Cave, the T'ai-tzu Pagoda, the Fa-hua grottoes, the Ch'ao-yang Cave, but also, and above all, the great "Southern Monastery" -the P'u-chi-ssu. Near the Pagoda is a new boys school, supported by the monks of Puto out of their endowments. The third section, with about twenty-three temples, includes the Hui-chi Monastery on the summit of the island ("Buddha's Peak"). The fourth section, with nine temples, includes the finest and most beautiful religious house on the island the "Northern" or Fa-yu Monastery. To this section also belong the secluded little hermitage occupied by the monk K'ai-ming; the remarkable bank of sand (Fei-sha) which slopes to the sea like a glacier [313]; the Hsiang-hui Temple, which contains, among other objects of interest, an image of the patriarch Bodhidharma (Tamo); and the Fan-yin Cave, which, though only a fissure in the sea-cliff, and therefore similar in appearance to the Ch'ao-yin Cave, is a place of wide celebrity.

---

[311] 西天；南无阿弥陀佛；大士说法处；无量寿佛；天下第一石；镇国宝石

[312] 观音说法台

[313] It is said that in former days (and as late as the Ming dynasty) there was deep water in the place now occupied by the Fei-sha, and that the eastern peninsula was therefore an island. Probably the great sand embankment was created by the action of the ocean currents, which are known to be swift and dangerous in this locality.

Reginald Fleming Johnston

Relics of Buddha

According to the island-records, the Fan-yin Cave, like the Ch'ao-yin, was visited by a distinguished pilgrim from India, though at a much later date. In 1626 of our era this pilgrim, who came from Benares, is said to have deposited here certain relics, which he asserted were relics of Sakyamuri Buddha. They were placed in a casket and reverently enshrined; and when in future years they were brought out for the in spection of the faithful, it was discovered that they did not always present the same appearance to different people. Persons of inferior character saw nothing but a black object; those of higher moral standing saw a white object; to those of moderately good character the relics assumed a red appearance; and saintly people saw the figure of Buddha[314].

The fifth and last section of the island consists chiefly of lonely hills. It contains only two or three little temples, of which the most picturesque is the Hsiao-shan-tung ("Little Hill Cave"), on a rocky promontory which at high tide becomes an island.

Buddhist Ordination

The total number of resident monks in Puto is well over a thousand, the majority of whom reside in the "Southern" and "Northern" monasteries. This number is greatly swelled for a few days during the second month of the old Chinese calendar, for the nineteenth day of that month is regarded as the birthday of Kuan-yin, and the occasion is celebrated by stately services, which are attended not only by the monks in permanent residence, but also by crowds of pilgrims (monks and laymen) from all parts of China, and by numerous candidates for ordination. It is at this time that the annual ordination ceremony is performed, and the rites are conducted by the "Northern" and "Southern" monasteries in alternate years. In 1913 the ceremony took place at the "Southern Monastery "; in 1914 it will be the turn of the "Northern." The candidates who come from various parts of central China vary in number

---

314 The idea that the relics of Buddhas and pusas can be used as a test of the moral character of the person who inspects them is a fairly common one in China. The relics of the Fan-yin Cave seem to have lost their fame in this respect, if, indeed, they are still in existence; but similar relics are still to he seen in the well-known monastery of Ayu-wang (Asoka) near Ningpo. Each visitor who wishes to behold the sacred object kneels in a little courtyard in front of the shrine and takes the relic-casket into his hands. He is then asked to look inside and to report what he sees. The author regrets to say that what he saw was neither red nor white, nor was it the figure of Buddha. He ventures to question the reliability of the test.

from one hundred to three. After ordination each young monk sets out for the monastery which he has selected, or which has been selected for him, as his permanent abode.

The rites of ordination are of an elaborate nature, but it should not be forgotten that Buddhist monks are not compelled or expected to take perpetual vows. The Buddhist monk in China as in all Buddhist lands is free to return to the world when he chooses[315]. For this reason the annals of Buddhism contain no such pitiful stories as those which we sometimes meet with in the annals of monastic Christendom stories from which we obtain fitful glimpses of the sufferings endured by those to whom the convent walls had become the walls of a loathed dungeon. The monasteries and nunneries of Buddhism have never been prisons. The letter written by the saintly but pitiless Anselm of Canterbury to a lady of noble birth who had fled back to the world from her hated nunnery has no counterpart in the literature of Buddhism[316].

A Buddhist monk is of course obliged, so long as he remains a monk, to act in strict conformity with the vows taken at ordination. He must obey the "commandments" (which are practically identical with the commandments contained in every sound moral code), he must be strictly chaste, and he must confine himself to a vegetarian diet. Flesh food is interdicted to Buddhist monks, just as it was interdicted by the Regula Benedicti of Christian monasticism. In the great monasteries the abbot's word is law, and, indeed, in many cases he is legally invested with the power of inflicting corporal and other punishment. But if the rule of a Buddhist abbot is a despotism, it is nearly always a benevolent one. We never hear of Buddhist ecclesiastics exercising their disciplinary powers in a tyrannical manner. No Chinese emperor ever had occasion to issue

---

315 As Mrs Rhys Davids has observed (Psalms of the Sisters, 1909, p. xxxiii.), " in Buddhist hagiology there is no premium placed on the state of virginity as such. The Founder himself was a husband and father, and the most eminent sisters were, three-fourths of them, matrons, not virgins."

316 " A spouse of God, a virgin, thou wert chosen; and set apart to wear the dress and live the life devoted to God. What can I say thou art now, my daughter? God knoweth. . . . For it is impossible for thee by any means to be saved, unless thou shalt return to thy rejected habit and thy vow. . . . Think, and let thine heart be shattered to pieces, sorrow vehemently over thy fall. Cast aside and tread under foot the secular dress thou hast assumed, and resume the habit of a spouse of Christ which thou didst throw off... But if thou scornest to do this, all will be against thee, and I and the Church of God shall act as in such a case we know how to act. May Almighty God visit thine heart and pour into it His love, dearest daughter." The most significant and characteristic feature of the letter is the manner in which the ultimate argument the ugly threat of punishment is reserved for the last paragraph. The saint wishes his victim clearly to understand that if reproachful pity and loving persuasion cannot effect the desired result, he and "the Church of God" will act as in such a case they " know how to act."

edicts prohibiting Buddhist abbots from mutilating the bodies of disobedient monks[317].

Morals of Chinese Monasteries

It is hardly necessary to say that the great religious houses of China do not all stand at a uniform level in respect of morals and religious zeal; but the reputation of such monasteries as those of Chiu-hua and Puto, which are far from the demoralizing influences of the great towns, is in most cases deservedly high[318]. That the Chinese monasteries are the habitual resort of the vicious and depraved, and that they offer sanctuary to criminals fleeing from justice, is one of those noxious libels which like the story about the prevalence of the custom of slaughtering female infants is not likely to be repeated in these days except by those who, with the best motives, are the unconscious victims of a desire to exaggerate the moral obliquities of the "heathen Chinee." It would be absurd to deny that there are Buddhist monks of bad character, and that many have been attracted to the monkhood through very unspiritual motives. Unfortunately, there are some evils which from time to time are bound to become unpleasantly conspicuous in connection with any conceivable form of ccenobitic life, especially in an age of religious apathy or degeneration, quite irrespective of the religious creed with which it happens to be associated. It is sometimes supposed that the life of a monk or hermit is only fit for weak-minded or incompetent idlers: whereas it is just such persons as these to whom this mode of existence is pre-eminently and dangerously unsuited.

We saw in the last chapter that the Buddhistic history of Puto begins with the year 847, when Kuan-yin appeared in a vision in response to the prayers of a Buddhist pilgrim from India. The next event of religious importance took place about a decade later, when Puto was visited by another foreigner, of greater celebrity than the nameless Indian ascetic. This foreigner was a Japanese monk named Egaku[319] a name which bears the dignified meaning of "Wisdom Peak." He was in high favour at the Japanese court, and was twice sent by the empress-dowager Tachibana on religious missions to China. This epoch was one of great prosperity for

---

317 In Europe, in the time of Charlemagne, laws had to be passed making it illegal for abbots to put out their monks eyes.

318 This is an opinion which is based on personal observation and inquiry during frequent residence in many of the principal monasteries in China.

319 Egaku would be Hui-o in modern Pekingese.

Buddhist China

Buddhism in Japan, and Japanese Buddhists were constantly moving to and fro between the great court-patronized monasteries of Nara and Kyoto and the chief centres of Buddhist learning and piety in China[320]. Japanese monks, indeed, showed as much enthusiasm in making pilgrimages to the sacred mountains of Buddhist China as Chinese monks of the same and earlier periods showed in travelling to the holy shrines of their faith in Kashmir and India.

The Arrival of Egaku

In the history of Japanese Buddhism Egaku's name is a distinguished one, for to him is assigned much of the credit of having introduced into his native country from China the doctrines of the Ch'an or Contemplative school. This is a fact which should not be overlooked by Western students and admirers of Japanese artistic culture, for it is this school of Buddhism (known in Japan as the Zen) which is more closely associated than any other with the finest developments of Japanese art[321]. While in China Egaku paid two visits to the holy mountain of Wu-t'ai (known to the Japanese as Godaisan), and on the occasion of his second visit he obtained possession of a beautiful image of Kuan-yin, which he intended to take back to Japan. Starting from Hangchow Bay he set sail for home, but while his junk was passing through the Chusan archipelago it grounded on a sunken rock near the island of Puto. Everything possible was done to lighten the vessel, even the cargo being ruthlessly sacrificed; but all measures proved useless, until at last it occurred to Egaku that the trouble might possibly be due to Kuan-yin's unwillingness to be transported to Japan. The pusa had clearly inspired him with the true solution of the difficulty, for no sooner had he reverently landed his precious image on the sacred shores of Puto than the junk slid off the rock and resumed its journey without further misadventure.

---

320 The Japanese imperial court resided at Nara from about 709 to 784. In 794 Kyoto became the capital. It was during the Kyoto (or Heian) era that the great Fujiwara family established itself as the power behind, or rather in front of, the imperial throne.

321 In Japan the Zen school consists of three main divisions the Rinzai, Soto, and Obaku. The first of these is the sect which is known in China as Lin-chi, and which in that country has its headquarters at Puto. It is the Lin-chi subdivision of the Ch'an, or Jhana, school, which is associated with the name of Egaku.

INSCRIBED ROCK, NEAR SUMMIT OF PUTO-SHAN.

THE CHUSAN ISLANDS, FROM PUTO-SHAN.

Buddhist China

According to a more romantic version of the story, Egaku's junk, with the image on board, was sailing among the islands when suddenly its progress was arrested by a miraculous growth of water-lilies, which seemed to cover the whole surface of the sea. Egaku offered up a prayer to Kuan-yin, and vowed that if he and his companions were brought safely out of their present unhappy plight he would establish a shrine for the worship of the pusa at the first place to which she in her wisdom and mercy might choose to conduct them. The immediate result of this prayer was that in the midst of the water-lilies a clear way was opened for the junk, which thereupon by some mysterious agency was guided to Puto. Mindful of his vow, Egaku here left the junk and landed with his image on the south eastern shores of the sacred island, close to that rocky promontory which contains the famous Ch'ao-yin Cave.

The legend goes on to say that Egaku was hospitably received by a family of islanders of the name of Chang, who when they discovered that Egaku was a holy man, and his image a miraculous one, willingly provided their guest with food and lodging. In pursuance of his vow he forthwith converted the building provided for his use into a temple for the worship of Kuan-yin. In this temple he enshrined his sacred image which soon acquired a wide celebrity under the name of the Pu-k'en-ch'u Kuan-yin (the "Kuan-yin who refused to go away"): for, said her worshippers, the pusa had made it abundantly clear that she had no wish to go to Japan or anywhere else, but was determined to make her home in the island of the "Little White Flower."

Egaku is a historical character, and his pilgrim ages to some of the holy places of Buddhist China are well-authenticated facts. The miracle-loving chroniclers have, of course, embellished the story of his narrow escape from shipwreck, but though we must assume that the water-lilies which obstructed the progress of his junk were nothing more miraculous than the white-crested waves of a stormy sea, there is no reason to doubt that he landed, or was driven ashore, at Puto and there returned thanks to the gracious pusa who had saved him from the perils of the deep.

The Sea of Water-Lillies

To this day the Chusan Sea or rather that portion of it which lies between the principal island and Puto is known as the Lien-hua-yang (the "Sea of Water-lilies"). The idea of the water-lilies is one which has captivated the Buddhist imagination, for the monastic chronicles of Puto contain several stories in which the same motif reappears. We are told, for example, that about the year 1080 certain predatory "Dwarfs" came to China "bearing tribute" to the Sung emperor, and in the course of their return journey from Hangchow (then the capital) they landed at Puto and carried away some of the precious relics[322]. But no sooner did they attempt to resume their eastward course than they found their ship enmeshed in the tendrils of countless water-lilies, which seemed as though they were made of iron. The frightened "Dwarfs" hastily restored the sacred articles to their shrines, and the "iron" water-lilies immediately disappeared.

A Monk of Puto

A similar story is told of a Chinese official named Wang Kuei, who was sent to Puto by the Sung emperor "to worship Buddha," but showed himself "lacking in reverence." On his homeward journey his ship was held fast in an impenetrable jungle of water-lilies. Kneeling on the deck with his face towards the holy island, he humbly implored the outraged pusa's forgiveness; whereupon a white ox suddenly emerged from the depths of the sea and proceeded to get rid of the water-lilies by eating them up. The sea was soon cleared and the junk released, whereupon the ox transformed itself into a white rock, which still remains a conspicuous feature of the Lien-hua Sea, silently but unanswerably refuting the arguments of all doubters, and putting fear into the hearts of all scoffers.

If we of the prosaic West permit ourselves to see white horses in the wind-swept ocean, why may we not allow the dreaming Buddhist to see white lilies there? In any case, his notion that some miraculous agency is frequently at work in the Puto Strait will not be judged too harshly by those who from the island's western shores have observed how quickly and unexpectedly those normally peaceful waters are apt to curl themselves into white-crested breakers[323]. The Chusan islanders have a saying to the effect that the rains of this locality are like the tears of a petulant woman quick to fall, slow to cease. This saying has been adapted

---

322 "Dwarfs" is a name which the Chinese used to apply to the Japanese, just as they spoke of Europeans as ft Foreign Devils." See Lion and Dragon in Northern China, 1910, pp. 46, 48, 70. The term " tribute-bearers " was commonly applied to the members of any mission from a foreign state, not excepting the British mission under Lord Macartney in 1792. The writers of the Puto Chronicle are careful to abstain from describing Egaku either as a Dwarf or as a tribute-bearer.

323 The unromantic cause of the phenomenon is, doubtless, the shallowness of the water.

by a certain monk of to-day to the fretfulness of the Puto Strait. It is like a woman, he declares, normally gentle and peaceful, but easily roused to wrath and difficult to pacify. So, when the water-lilies appear, that same monk may not infrequently be found sitting pensively on the "Pulpit of Kuan-yin" and gazing a little wistfully, perhaps in a westerly direction over the restless waters at the misty shores of the world which he has abandoned. If roused from his reverie, he may say perhaps he may believe--that his thoughts were concentrated wholly on the Paradise of the divine Amitabha, which, he will remind you, lies also in the west, and to which the compassionate Kuan-yin, whom he has served so faithfully, will some day conduct him. Who is to chide him, indeed, if from time to time visions of the busy world of men and of women mingle with his visions of the spiritual kingdom of the saints?

The Temples of Puto

Egaku's arrival at Puto probably took place in or about the year 858. The Chinese Chronicle of the island assigns the event to the second year of Cheng Ming of the Liang dynasty, which corresponds with 916 of our era, but this seems to be certainly a mistake[324]. It seems probable, however, that in 916 the island was again "opened" to use the Chinese phrase as the tao-Ch'ang, or "Sanctuary of Kuan-yin," and that by this time all vestiges of the earlier shrine of Egaku had vanished. It is very unlikely, indeed, that Egaku made a long stay in the island. The Chronicle says that the Chang family, whom he found living there, were prompted by religious zeal to give up their own dwelling-house to Egaku so that it might be converted into a temple for Kuan-yin's image; but the information that has been handed down to us is so scanty that even the site of the temple which is known to history as the Pu-k'en-ch'u Kuan-yin Yuan (the "Temple of the Kuan-yin who refused to go away") is a matter of uncertainty. The generally accepted view is that it was close to the Ch'ao-yin Cave, where

---

[324] In this matter I accept the arguments and suggestions ably put forward by N. Peri and H. Maspero in the Bulletin de l'Ecole Francaise d Extreme-Orient, tome ix., No. 4, pp. 797 ff. Their conclusions are based on incontrovertible facts of Japanese history. It may be mentioned, however, that the writers were evidently unaware of the fact that there is a later edition of the P'u-t'o-shan-chih (the Chinese Chronicle of Puto) than that to which they refer. Their edition was of the eighteenth century, whereas that in my possession was published about 1843. It is a great improvement on the earlier editions, but it repeats the mistake about the year of Egaku's arrival at Puto. There is, however, one passage which implies that he came to the island in the T'ang dynasty. This was true if the year 858 be accepted as the correct one; whereas if he did not arrive till 916 the T'ang dynasty was already extinct. (For the passage referred to, see the Chih, ch. ix. p. 15.)

Egaku is supposed to have landed, and that its site is now occupied by the temple and small monastery known as the Tzu-chu-lin[325]. As for the famous image, we must regretfully record the fact that it belied its name by disappearing from Puto at a very early date[326].

The monastic houses of Puto have passed through strange vicissitudes. They have been so repeatedly burned and plundered by pirates that practically all the present buildings are modern, arid it is doubtful whether there is a single structure which can be assigned to an earlier date than the fourteenth century. Even of that period the only relic though it is a valuable one is the very picturesque but somewhat battered tower known as the "Pagoda of the Prince Imperial.[327]" The records tell us that this pagoda was erected about the year 1334 by a monk named Fou Chung at the expense of his patron and disciple, a pious prince named Hsuan-jang[328]. The pagoda was built of fine stone specially imported from the neighbourhood of the T'ai-hu the island sea that Persia lies to the west of the city of Soochow and the carving was executed with minute care and skill. Among the figures of Buddhas and bodhisats which adorn its four sides are the pusas of the Four Sacred Hills Kuan-yin, Ti-tsang, P'u-hsien, and Wen-shu.

---

325 See the Chih, ch. ix. p. 14. An alternative name of this temple is T'ing-ch'ao-an ("Listen-to-the-tide-waves Temple"), the reference being to the roar of the tidal waters rushing into the sacred cave. Like all the other temples of Puto., it has undergone several restorations. An autograph scroll was presented to it by the Emperor Kang-hsi in 1699. Unfortunately , the present building is not a beautiful one: it was obviously designed by an architect cursed with an exaggerated sense of the importance of mere usefulness.

326 According to one account, it was removed during one of the temporary migrations made by the monks to the mainland, and was set up in a temple in the Ningpo prefecture.

327 T'ai-tzu T'a. I do not know what Edkins authority was for his statement that this pagoda was named after the prince who subsequently became the Emperor Wan-li (Chinese Buddhism [1883 ed.], p. 265). The pagoda belongs to the Yuan, not to the Ming, dynasty; and it seems very doubtful whether the prince in question belonged to the Chinese imperial family.

328 The career of Fou Chung, who was treated with great reverence by several persons of high rank, is described in the Chih, ch. vii. pp. 4-5.

Buddhist China

THE HALL OF IMPERIAL TABLETS, SOUTHERN MONASTERY

THE PRINCE'S PAGODA, PUTO.

Monastery of Universal Salvation

The pagoda stands in the immediate vicinity of the monastic centre of the island a cluster of temples and monasteries, of which by far the greatest is the "Southern Monastery" (Ch'ien-ssu). Its correct name is Pu-chi-ssu, or "Monastery of Universal Salvation." The first building is a hall[329] which is roofed with tiles of imperial yellow and contains tablets bearing the engraved reproductions of decrees issued by emperors of the Ming and Ch'ing dynasties. In front of this hall is a lotus-pond with a picturesque archway and several graceful kiosks and bridges.

Behind the imperial pavilion we come to the bell and drum towers and to the "Hall of the Four Heavenly Kings" who are the protectors or champions of the faith in the four quarters of the universe. Behind this hall we reach a court yard remarkable for its trees, its carved balustrades, and its great incense-burners and candlesticks. It is flanked by pavilions containing images of "the eighteen lo-han" (arahants). The large building in front is the chief sanctuary of the temple the chapel of Kuan-yin. A very large image of the pusa occupies the central position, and thirty-two figures sixteen on each side represent the pusa's transformations. The large courtyard behind the great sanctuary contains the various monastic offices, guest-quarters, abbot's apartments, and refectory. The centre is occupied by the Fa-t'ang or "Hall of the Law," a two-storied building. The lower story contains images of Sakyamuni, P'u-hsien, and Wenshu. The upper storey, which is the library, contains one of the alabaster Buddhas which are to be seen in several of the temples of Puto. They are of Burmese origin, and are said to have come from Mandalay[330]. That there are Chinese monks of the present day who from religious motives gladly undertake the long and expensive journey to Burma is a fact which is of special interest when we remember that the Buddhism of Burma and the Buddhism of China are usually regarded by Western students as hopelessly irreconcilable in respect of both doctrine and practice. But a more intimate acquaintance with the traditions and ideals of Oriental religious life will convince us that nearly all forms of Buddhism are vitalized by one indwelling spirit, of which the most characteristic manifestation is a gracious and winning tolerance. Buddhism is perhaps

---

329 Yu-pei-t'ang.

330 From Peking to\Mandalay, p. 86.

the only great religion the world has known which not only teaches that the freedom of the human spirit is a desirable ideal, but achieves a more than moderate success in making its practice in this respect conform with its theory.

The residential quarters of the P'u-chi Monas tery it is unnecessary to describe. Like nearly all structures of similar character in China, they are of comparatively plain exterior and of small architectural interest. It is always the temple buildings and shrines, with their magnificent timbered roofs, and the exquisite kiosks and pavilions which shelter the scrolls and tablets of emperors and poets, that give free scope to the skill and taste of the Buddhist architect and carver.

The present name of the P'u-chi Monastery does not appear in the records of the island till the year 1699. In that year, which was the thirty-eighth of the reign of K ang-hsi, the emperor went on a "southern progress," and in accordance with a practice frequently followed by Chinese rulers before and after his time in respect of the great monastic institutions of the empire, despatched certain state officials to Puto to offer up public prayers and thanksgivings. On this occasion he made a handsome donation to a restoration fund it was not the first time he had subscribed to the monastic treasure-chest and presented the monks of Puto with various autograph scrolls, one of which bore the words P'u-chi – ch'an-ssu (the "Jhana Monastery of Universal Salvation").

Imperial Patronage

The practice of inviting an emperor to confer a new name on a monastery undergoing restoration under imperial sanction and patronage used to be a very common one throughout China. On such occasions the emperor wrote (or was supposed to write) the characters comprising the new name we must assume that as a rule the name was suggested to him and these characters, which were written on a very large scale, were transferred by the wood-engravers to an oblong board known as a pien[331]. Besides the large characters, the pien bore facsimiles of the imperial seal and the date and year-name of the emperor. After having been carefully lacquered and gilded, the pien was ready to be suspended in a t'ing (small

---

331 Piens are, of course, presented by others besides emperors, and to many buildings besides temples.

pavilion") or over the principal shrine or main gateway of the favoured temple.

The previous history of the monastery known since 1699 as the P'u-chi is somewhat obscure, partly owing to various changes of name, and partly to the fact that some of the monkish chroniclers have confused the records of this monastery with those of the Tzu-chu-lin, which, as we have seen, seems to have the best title to be regarded as the true representative of the original building converted by the shipwrecked Egaku into a shrine for "the image that would not go away."

There is evidence that numerous monks and hermits began to take up their residence in the island during the tenth and eleventh centuries. In 967 the first emperor of the Sung dynasty extended his protection to the monks; and in 1080 a court-official named Wang Shun-feng presented a report to the throne concerning certain miraculous doings of Kuan-yin, and this impressed the emperor so deeply that he became a patron of the island and authorized the principal house (we cannot be sure which it was) to adopt the name Pao-t'o-Kuan-yin-ssu[332] (the "Monastery of the Holy Hill of Kuan-yin").

A Famous Monk

At this time the "rule" of the monks was that of the Lli or Vinaya school; but in 1131 a distinguished monk named Chen-hsieh (also known as Ching-liao), a native of the province of Ssuch'uan, came to Puto and introduced the Ch'an doctrines. The Chronicle says that on this account he is regarded as the founder of the Ch'an school of Puto-shan; but though the throne was asked to authorize the substitution of the Ch'an for the Lu rule,[333] the Ch'an did not have everything its own way after this time, for we learn that it had to be re-introduced at a much later date. Chen-hsieh, however, was a learned and far-travelled monk, whose name is deservedly held in honour by Chinese Buddhists. He seems to have been one whom nowadays we should term a "revivalist," and was never weary of rambling from place to place preach ing and converting. Wu-t'ai was one scene of his labours, T'ien-t'ai was another. When he came to Puto, which he made his home for many years, he found the neighbouring islands occupied by

---

[332] 宝陀观音寺
[333] 郡请于朝易律为禅

more than seven hundred families of fishermen. We are told that as soon as they heard Chen-hsieh preach the Law they one and all abandoned their fishing-boats[334].

This striking little story can hardly fail to recall a somewhat similar one which occupies an honourable place in Christian literature [335]; but the story about Chen-hsieh and his fishermen becomes characteristically Buddhistic when it goes on to tell us that by drawing the fishermen away from their boats Chen-hsieh saved the lives of thousands of fish. The anecdote is probably intended to emphasize the righteousness of refraining from fishing in the waters of Puto[336]. But it does not imply that the fisherman wholly abandoned their occupation. The meaning seems to be that while Chen-hsieh was preaching the fishermen left their boats and came to listen to him. Whether they ever returned to their fishing or not is a doubtful question. The Buddhists of Puto answer it in the negative.

In 1214 we find a record of an imperial gift for rebuilding and restoration; and when the work was completed the emperor (one of the last of the expiring Sung dynasty) presented a pien for the principal chapel of Kuan-yin, together with gold-embroidered ceremonial robes, silver chalices, altar hangings, and ornaments of pearl and jasper. In 1248 the island was released from taxation.

The rulers of the Yuan (Mongol) dynasty, which held the throne between 1280 and 1367, were zealous supporters of Buddhism, and Puto enjoyed a large share of imperial favour. Ch'eng Tsung (Timour Khan), grandson of the great Kublai, sent officials with presents to the island four times in four successive years (1298-1301) and his example was followed by three other emperors of the same dynasty.

One of Puto's lay-visitors during the closing years of the dynasty was a well-known scholar named Ting Ho-nien (1335-1424). He belonged to a Mohammedan family which had migrated from Central Asia, under the protection of the conquering Mongols, to the province of Hupei. He led a wandering and unhappy life during the troublous times that marked the fall of the Mongols and the rise of the Ming dynasty, but he found some consolation for his woes among the temples of Puto, and he celebrated the charms of the island in poetry.

---

[334] 海山七百余家俱业渔一闻教音俱弃舟 Chih, ch. vii. p. 2.

335 Matthew iv. 18, 22. Cf. Mark i. 16-20 and Luke v. 11.

336 A similar story is told of Chih-che, a famous monk of T'ien-t ai.

Japanese Pirates

During the Ming period (1368-1643) fortune bestowed alternate smiles and frowns on the holy island. The ravages of Japanese pirates brought great misery upon the monks during the last quarter of the fourteenth century; indeed by 1387 nearly all the buildings were reduced to a state of ruin, and in that year the Chinese general T'ang Ho, who had been entrusted with the defence of the coasts of Chehkiang, deemed it necessary to remove the monks to the mainland. The only building left standing is said to have been an iron-tiled pavilion, and a single courageous monk named I-ch ieh was left in charge of the desolate sanctuaries of Kuan-yin.

The history of Puto is a blank for nearly a hundred and thirty years. It was not till 1515 that the efforts of a monk named Tan-chai resulted in the rebuilding of a small religious house. A new era of prosperity for the island seemed likely to dawn, but in 1553 the "Eastern Dwarfs[337]" again harried the coast, and the governor of the province moved the monastic establishment, such as it was, to the Island of Chusan.

In 1572 a monastery was again founded by a monk from Wu-t'ai. His name was Chen-sung ("True Pine-tree"). Two years later certain monks beheld a beautiful vision on the sea of water-lilies. From the sea mists emerged a white-robed figure seated on a golden lotus. This was regarded as a sign that days of happiness for Puto were about to return. The omen was a true one, for the vision almost coincided with the accession of the weak but pious emperor Wan-li, who proved himself a good friend to the monks of Puto. Both the emperor and the empress-dowager frequently sent emissaries to the island with gifts of money, monks robes, altar embroideries, sacred images, medicines for sick monks, and autograph scrolls. In 1586 the imperial munificence provided for the rebuilding of new quarters for fifty-three monks. In 1598 there was a disastrous fire, which necessitated rebuilding. In this work the imperial family took considerable interest, and when it was finished, in 1605, a court official named Chang Sui was sent to the island in charge of a pien bearing a new title for the restored monastery. This title was Hu-kuo-yung-shou – P'u–

---

[337] Tung Wo

Buddhist China

t'o-ch'an-ssu ("the Jhana Monastery of Puto ensuring protec tion to the State and long life to His Majesty").[338]

Feng-Shui

In this inscription we have an indication of the point of view from which emperors and state officials in China have from time immemorial defended and justified the un-Confucian recognition and support which they have intermittently extended towards Buddhist and Taoist temples and monastic communities. Temples and religious houses, like pagodas, are, or were, regarded as beneficial to the feng-shui of their neighbourhood that is, they are centres of good geomantic influences, and radiate those influences over the whole district which happens to be subject to their spiritual sway. The temples which are situated on some "sacred hill" are regarded as deserving of greater reverence than any others, because the spiritual radiations emanating from any such build ing are intensified by the sanctity of the hill itself; the benefits they confer extend throughout the whole empire, so that even the throne itself is within the sphere of their benign influence. It is believed that the main reason why the T'ai-p'ing rebels destroyed all the mountain-monasteries they came across (including, as we have seen, those of Chiu-hua-shan) and deliberately wrecked one of the empire's greatest artistic glories the exquisite Porcelain Pagoda at Nanking was because they thought that these buildings exercised an influence inimical to their cause[339]. As for the partial immunity from destruction or spoliation enjoyed by many of the great Buddhist monasteries during the various anti-Buddhistic outbreaks of Confucian officialdom, there is no doubt that such immunity has been partly due to a general belief in the truth of the theory that such institutions were productive offeng-shui favourable to the welfare of the State as a whole. Perhaps, however, the monasteries were even more deeply indebted to those numerous Confucian statesmen who spared the sanctuaries of Buddha because they themselves looked forward to spending their later years in scholarly retirement in some sequestered mountain-hermitage; and also to the innumerable artists and poets who, if

---

[338] 护国永寿普陀禅寺

[339] For a vivid account of the ruin and desolation wrought in Chehkiang and Anhui by the Society of God " (as the T'ai-p'ing rebels styled themselves) under their bloodthirsty and fanatical leader Hung Hsiu-ch'uan, who called himself a Brother of Christ, see Baron Richthofen, Letters (1870-2), 2nd ed., Shanghai, 1903, pp. 75-6.

not always confessed worshippers of Buddha, have at least been thorough Buddhists in their worship of wild nature.

Imperial Edicts

The reign of Wan-li is chiefly memorable in the annals of Buddhism for the publication of a portion of the Buddhist scriptures and for the distribution of complete sets of the whole Chinese Tripitaka (so-called) to most of the great monasteries of the empire. Under two previous emperors of the dynasty, Yung-lo (1403-24) and Cheng-t'ung (1436-49), a new edition of nearly the whole vast collection had already been printed, but apparently it was not widely distributed. The number of han then printed (each han containing several pen, or separate volumes) amounted to 637. In Wan-li's time 41 han still remained imprinted[340]. The emperor, in obedience to the wishes of the empress-dowager, decided to make good the deficiency, and as soon as the work was finished imperial edicts were issued in which the circumstances of publication and distribution were fully set forth.

"The imperial will," says one of the edicts,[341] "is as follows: We in all sincerity of heart have caused to be printed the Buddhist scriptures, and have ordered complete sets to be deposited in the capital and distributed among the monasteries of the Famous Mountains of the empire, where they are to be treated with due reverence and carefully preserved."

The monks are enjoined to guard the sacred books from all harm, to read them diligently morning and evening, and to use them to such good purpose that all the world may be brought into fellowship with the religion of Love, Compassion, and Goodness[342].

---

340 These 41 han comprised 410 chuan, or chapters.

341 They are variously dated from 1586 to 1611. Separate edicts (identical in nearly everything but the names of the monasteries concerned) were issued to the monks of each favoured mountain. Those received by Puto are recorded in the Chih, ch, xiv. Each of the two great monasteries of Puto received a complete set of the Tripitaka as issued by Wan-li. In spite of losses due to fires and robberies, the monastic authorities state that their sets are almost complete.

342 俾四海八方同归仁慈善教 The edict in which this occurs is dated 1599.

Buddhist China

THE KUAN-YIN-TUNG AND OTHER TEMPLES, P'U'TO-SHAN.

"From of old time," says another of the edicts, "the emperors and rulers of our land have modelled their methods of government upon Confucian principles. But Confucianism is not the only doctrine: there is also Buddhism. These two doctrines are like the wings of a bird: each requires the co-operation of the other."

This observation, to which an uncompromising Confucian would demur, would meet with the approval of the majority of Chinese Buddhists. Wan-li's religious tolerance, however, did not save his dynasty from disaster. In 1619 he died, and in 1643 the last emperor of the Ming line hanged himself on a tree in his palace garden.

Death of Wu Ching-Luan

That the support given to Buddhism by some of the Ming emperors did not alienate the sympathies of all their Confucian subjects is touchingly illustrated by the story of Wu Chung-luan, a scholar and statesman who rose to the position of vice-president of the Board of Rites. After the fall of the dynasty he retired to Puto, and there, for a few years, he lived the life of a recluse. In a graceful little poem he describes the consolations of this tranquil island, where the world and its sorrows can be banished from the memory, and where he can forget even his own "old self." How delightful it would be, he thought, to spend his declining years amid these quiet Buddhist groves! But his old loyal self refused to be forgotten. He was no soldier, so he could take no active part in defending his country against the armies of the conquering Manchus; but though he could not fight a hero's battles, he could die a hero's death. He waited long enough to convince himself that all reasonable hope of expelling the northern invaders was extinguished, and then, in 1651, he crossed the "Sea of Water-lilies" and landed at the port of Ting-hai, the magisterial city of the Island of Chusan. Making his way to the Sheng Miao (the "Confucian Temple") he caused a chair to be set in the courtyard, and surrounded it with faggots (bundles of sticks). He then took in his hands the Confucian p'ai-wei (the wooden "spirit-tablets" of Confucius and his principal disciples) and seated himself in the chair. The faggots were set alight and Wu Chung-luan, clasping the Confucian tablets to his breast, passed to his patriot's death[343]. The monks of Puto suffered many hardships during the

---

[343] D. J. Macgowan, in his paper on " Self-immolation by Fire " (Chinese Recorder, Nov. 1888), refers to the story of Wu Chung-luan, but assigns it to the wrong period,, and is not quite right in his facts. He says that Wu fled as a fugitive to Chusan "to escape from the T'ai-

Buddhist China

troubles which convulsed the country before the Manchu dynasty consolidated its position. Early in the new reign (1644-61) they nearly lost their library. The story, if based on fact, throws a peculiar light on the methods adopted by Japanese Buddhists to promote the prosperity of their religion in their own country. Certain Japanese monks, we are told, were very anxious to possess themselves of the Buddhist Tripitaka which, as they knew, had been presented to the monks of Puto by the Emperor Wan-li. They accordingly hired a certain pirate named Yuan Chun to rob Puto of its books and carry them off to Japan. Having effected the robbery, the pirate removed his booty to the Island of Chusan, intending to sail thence to Japan. A monk of Puto named Chao-chung went to Chusan at the head of a large company of his brethren and implored the pirate to restore the books. But Yuan treated him with contempt, and said angrily, "If you want your books, go down to the sea-dragon's palace and ask him to get them back for you." Thereupon he set sail for Japan. But a monstrous fish was it the sea-dragon himself? got in the way of the vessel and prevented it from reaching the open sea. For several days Yuan tried vainly to proceed, but the sea-monster was too much for him. Repenting at last of his sacrilegious act, he turned his vessel's prow towards Puto. The fish ceased to trouble him, and the return journey was made in less than half a day. All the monks hastened down to the shore to meet him, and joyously resumed possession of their holy books[344].

The worst calamity that ever befel the monks of Puto and their beautiful temples did not occur till the early years of the reign of K'ang-hsi, the second emperor of the dynasty; and the story of the disaster is one which no European can read without shame and sorrow.

The island Chronicle tells us that in the third year of the reign (1664), on New Year's Day, the monks beheld a wonderful rainbow, which seemed to rise from a gleaming temple roof, and to extend across the sea

---

p'ing rebels" in 1861, whereas the incident really took place more than two centuries earlier, and Wu died as a loyal servant of the vanquished Ming dynasty. He was not the only official of rank who refused to survive his fallen emperor. No such deeds of devotion seem, so far as is known at present, to have been called forth by the fall of the Manchu dynasty.

344 The Japanese monks might have pleaded intensity of religious zeal in extenuation of their felonious conspiracy. The same excuse cannot be made for certain would-be robbers of another monastic library that of "Golden Island," at Chinkiang. During one of the Anglo-Chinese wars of the nineteenth century this library "was found," says Dr Wells Williams, " by the English officers, but there was no haste in examining its contents, as they intended to have carried off the whole collection, had not peace prevented" (The Middle Kingdom, i. 103).

to a neighbouring island, "Little Puto.³⁴⁵" Suddenly on the bridge of glowing light appeared the radiant form of the white-robed Kuan-yin, her face turned away from Puto. The vision faded, but the monks felt sure it could have only one meaning the Island of the "Little White Flower" was about to suffer some terrible disaster. Their foreboding came true in the following year.

The Coming of the Red-Hairs

In the records of Puto Europeans are mentioned more than once, but no attempt is made to distinguish between the different nationalities. The names applied to them are Huang-mao ("Yellow-hairs"), or Hung-mao ("Red-hairs"). The visit which was attended with the calamitous results now to be narrated is described by the chronicler with sufficient detail to enable us to say with out hesitation that the "Red-hairs" who were the protagonists in this particular drama were Dutchmen.

Dutch Marauders

Those familiar with the history of European enterprise in the Far East will remember that in 1661 the Dutch were attacked and driven out of their settlements in the Island of Formosa by the famous pirate-king Cheng Ch'eng-kung, better known as Koxinga. The Puto Chronicle gives us an interesting glimpse of the manner in which some of the homeless Dutchmen disported them selves during the years that followed their expulsion from the beautiful island which had been their residence for nearly forty years.

The Red-hairs (it says) having been driven out of their strongholds (literally nests and dens), took to the sea as plunderers and robbers. In the year 1665, on the thirteenth day of the fifth month, two of their ships suddenly appeared off the coast of Puto. They came ashore, and the monks noticed that they had red-yellowish hair and beards. They had short muskets strapped to their backs, and used fire-stones (huo-shih) to let them off! Their aim was unerring. They also had very sharp cutlasses, and were armed with bows and arrows besides their other weapons. As soon as they came ashore they made signs to signify that they wanted food. They

---

345 This island, of which the Chinese name is Hsiao-Loka, is the island which lies to the east of Puto. It now possesses an important lighthouse. It contains four small temples., named Miao-chan, Tzu-tsai, Yuan-t'ung, and Kuan-chiao.

Buddhist China

jabbered ha-ha and uttered the one word cattle! Not daring to disobey them, the monks pointed to the hillside where the cattle were grazing, and told the sailors they could help themselves. Thereupon they fired, and killed several head. Next day they came again and spoke words of guile[346], saying that they wished to perform some act of religious merit; but having deceitfully induced the monks to go on board the ships, they proceeded to demand money and valuables from them. Then they all forced their way into the temples and destroyed the images and dug the precious stones out of them, and seized the treasures which had been accumulating for generations, including the imperial gifts of gilded Buddhas and silver chalices, jade rings, sceptres of agate and coral, embroideries, hangings, scrolls, screens, cushions not a thing of any value did they leave behind. They broke open the cupboards containing the sutras which had been an emperor's gift, stripped off the cloth in which the outside covers were wrapped, pulled the books to pieces, tied the strips of cloth round their legs, and on returning to their ships tore them off and threw them into the sea[347]. They did not sail away until they had desecrated the holy soil of Puto in a way that words cannot describe. Not only the two great monasteries, but even the quiet hermitages in the secluded parts of the island- there was not one of them that escaped spoliation or destruction by fire. Three months later the Red-hairs returned and stole some more cattle. When they appeared for a third time the monks all cut down trees and furnished themselves with spears with the intention of fighting the pirates; but on this occasion the Red-hairs did not come ashore. Alas! for the sacred home of our Pusa! To be trampled and defiled, robbed and desecrated such was the fate of our holy island.[348]"

This is not a very pleasant picture of the manner in which Europeans and Chinese, or Christians and Buddhists, became acquainted with one another. Unfortunately there is no reason to doubt the accuracy of the narrative. It occurs only in an obscure monastic Chronicle, and was certainly not written with the vain object of stirring up popular indignation against foreigners. There was nothing to be gained by exaggerating the actual facts.

---

346 Presumably they brought an interpreter with them on this occasion.
347 Of the books themselves, the vast majority appear to have been saved.
348 P'u-t'o-shan-chih, iii. 1-2, vi. 6-7 xiii. 4.

There are many pages in the history of Western relations with China which we Europeans cannot read without shame. We do well, however, to turn back to such pages from time to time, if only for the purpose of reminding ourselves that the Chinese in the days of their haughty exclusiveness were not wholly unjustified in their belief that their Western visitors were barbarians or devils.

What happened to the Dutchmen after their heroic encounter with defenceless monks at Puto seems to be a matter of uncertainty. One account says that they went off to Japan to sell their booty, for which they received large sums of money, and that on their homeward journey their ship caught fire and was lost with every man on board[349]. This story may be regarded as ben trovato; one of the ships, at any rate, seems to have reached its destination in safety, as we learn from a curious story about a stolen bell, to which we shall have occasion to refer in the next chapter.

Departure of the Monks

Harried as they were by pirates Japanese, Chinese, and European, the monks clung bravely to their devastated island until 1671, when the Govern ment compelled them once more to migrate to the mainland. After this, Puto was abandoned to solitude and decay for a period of about seventeen years. The Chronicle gives us but few glimpses of the island during that time, and they reveal a state of utter desolation. Two little stories indicate pathetic efforts on the part of the monks to convince themselves or others that in spite of all appearances to the contrary the "Little White Flower" was still under some kind of divine protection. One of these stories tells us that during this period of decay some robbers landed on the island and made a fire inside one of the deserted pavilions with the object of melting down a metal image of Kuan-yin which they found there. Suddenly the pavilion itself caught fire, and many of the sacrilegious robbers, who for some obscure reason found themselves unable to escape, were burned to death. The other story tells us that a fleet of war-junks anchored off the island and landed a large number of plunderers, who made their way to a Ta-shih-tien (a "Hall of the Pusa"). After working their wicked will there they came forth, and suddenly found themselves confronted by innumerable poisonous serpents, which opened

---

[349] Ibid., vi, 7.

their mouths and hissed. The terrified plunderers turned and tried to run away, but they were at once met by a pack of savage dogs. Escape was impossible wild dogs were in front, poisonous serpents were behind. Many of the men perished miserably, and others were grievously injured.

Puto, like Ireland, prides itself on the fact that it possesses no poisonous snakes: Kuan-yin, like a Buddhist St. Patrick, drove them all away. The appearance of serpents on this occasion means, therefore, that they were miraculously introduced for the express purpose of punishing those who had been guilty of sacrilege. It is not impossible that in this story there is preserved an old fragment of Oriental folk-lore. Serpents (sometimes in the form of dragons) have been regarded, in both China and Japan, as the specially-appointed guardians of all holy shrines. In the Nihongi the well-known Japanese Chronicle there is a legend which tells us what happened to the emperor Yuriaku, who, in the year 463 of our era, proposed to pay a visit to the temple of the god of Mount Mimoro. He irreverently omitted to submit himself to the usual preliminary rites of ceremonial purification, and the consequence was that as he drew near the shrine he was suddenly met by a serpent of most ferocious aspect. The emperor was glad to be allowed to run away and hide himself in his palace, and his proposed visit to the god was indefinitely postponed.

Restoration of Monasteries

Puto resumed the normal course of its history in 1688, when a military officer of high rank, named Huang Ta-lai, submitted a memorial to the throne, in which he reported the lamentable state of desolation to which the holy island had been reduced, and begged his Majesty to assist the forlorn monks to re-establish the glory of their old home. The result was entirely satisfactory, and Kang-hsi took so keen an interest in the work of restoration that in a few years time the temples and monasteries of Puto had recovered all their old prosperity, and the smoke of incense once more curled upwards from the altars of Kuan-yin.

A PILGRIMS' PATHWAY, PUTO.

THE LOTUS-POND OF THE "SOUTHERN MONASTERY,"

Buddhist China

The abbot of the "Southern Monastery," during the early years of the rebuilding, was an able and zealous monk named Ch'ao-yin, and it was largely owing to his energy that the temples rose again from their ashes.[350] It was under his influence, we are told, that the island abandoned the Lu (Vinaya) in favour of the Ch'an (Jhana) rule;[351] but this statement requires qualification, for the Ch'an school had been introduced into the monasteries of Puto as early as the twelfth century. The probability is that both the Lu and the Ch'an schools were represented in the island during the intervening centuries, and that the supremacy lay sometimes with the one and sometimes with the other. There appears to be no doubt, however, that since the days of Abbot Ch'ao-yin the island of Puto has been entirely under the sway of the Lin-chi sect of the Ch'an school.

Ch'ao-yin's efforts might have been of small avail had he not enjoyed the powerful friendship and support of Puto's principal lay benefactor a noted general named Lan Li (1649-1719) whose religious zeal was probably stimulated by the fact that in the year 1690 the patron pusa of the island appeared to him in a vision at the Fan-yin Cave[352]. General Lan is regarded as one of the lay saints of Puto, and a shrine was erected to him on the island after his death. He is regarded as a hu-fa ("defender of the faith"); and the monks of Puto, remembering that he had been noted during his life for his enormous physical strength and his reckless courage, elevated him to the position of ghostly champion of the Puto monkhood.

Edict of K'ang-Hsi

The benefactions of the great Emperor K'ang-hsi commenced with a gift of money in 1689. In 1696 he presented each of the two great monasteries with a portion of the Diamond Sutra written by his own hand.[353] In subsequent years he gave generous donations in money and valuables, images, altar-hangings, robes, embroideries, autograph scrolls, beads which had been "told" by the imperial fingers, and further portions

---

[350] 补陀业林就废潮音禅师从而兴之
[351] 潮公改律为禅
[352] Chih, vi. 8.
[353] 御书金刚经二函

of the scriptures written with the imperial brush[354]. Most of these treasures are still preserved in the "Northern" and "Southern" monasteries. In 1699, as we have seen, he presented the newly-restored "Southern Monastery" with an autograph pien and a new name that which it has borne ever since. In 1705 an envoy arrived at Puto with an imperial edict, which was immediately transferred to a stone tablet. This tablet is one of those which still stands in the Yu-pei-t'ang the front hall of the P u-chi Monastery.

In this interesting edict the emperor refers briefly to the history and traditions of Puto and to the cruel treatment it had received from the pirates of the Formosan seas. He describes how the island had been abandoned for several years in consequence of these outrages, and how at last a few monks returned to it, and set to work to cut down the jungle growths and clear away the brambles, and to trace out the foundations of the old buildings.

"We" (says the emperor, if we may render his own words in a slightly abbreviated form), "chanced at this time to be in Western Chehkiang, and despatched a special emissary to inaugurate the work of restoration and to make ceremonial offerings. We bestowed gifts of gold from the State treasury, that the temples might be restored to splendour, and that their cloisters and colonnades might be made lustrous and glorious with scarlet and jade. The stone and timber have all been provided at State expense: Our subjects have not been called upon to furnish either labour or material. All this We have done in the first place from motives of filial piety[355], and in the second place that happiness and prosperity might be granted by the divine Powers to all Our people. We, since Our boyhood, have been earnest students of Confucian lore, with the constant aim of learn ing the proper duties of a good ruler. We have had no leisure to become minutely acquainted with the sacred books of Buddhism: therefore We are not qualified to discuss the deeper mysteries of that faith. But We are satisfied that "Virtue" is the one word which indicates what is essential in both systems. We find, moreover, that heaven delights to give life and nourishment; the gracious and compassionate Pusa loves to bring all living creatures to salvation. The one creates, the other saves: but there is no

---

354 It has been the practice of many emperors to prove their religious zeal by copying out portions of the Buddhist scriptures. A similar custom seems to have been known outside China. Aurangzeb, one of the Mughal emperors of India, who ascended the throne at Delhi in 1659 and died in 1707, and therefore reigned contemporaneously with K'ang-hsi, twice copied out the whole Qur'an.

355 That is, as a votive offering on behalf of the empress-dowager.

antagonism, no divergence of aim. We, Heaven's suppliant, have obtained the boon of a long reign. We have ruled the empire for over forty years[356]. Now arms have been laid aside; the empire is at peace. We know, nevertheless, that Our people are not yet free from cares and sorrows. Their sufferings come not only from the imperfections of their own natures, but also from the caprices of fortune and other circumstances for which they are in no way to blame. How to promote Our people's welfare is a problem which brings Us many wistful thoughts and anxious dreams. Let us pray to the compassionate Kuan-yin, that she may of her grace send down upon Our people the spiritual rain and sweet dew of the Good Law; that she may grant Our people bounteous harvests, season able winds, and the blessings of peace, harmony, and long life; and, finally, that she may lead them to the salvation which she offers to all beings in the universe[357]. Such are the wishes of Our heart. Let what Our hand has written be engraved upon a lofty tablet, that Our decree may be transmitted to posterity."

Religious Policy of K'ang-Hsi

Thus did the largest-hearted and largest-minded of the Manchu emperors signify his gracious goodwill towards Puto and his respect for its patron saint. As the imperial pillar of Confucian orthodoxy he was often obliged to pose in his public utterances as the denouncer of all false or heretical doctrines, and among such doctrines rigid Confucianists do not hesitate to class Buddhism. But this great ruler was no tyrant and no bigot, as even the Catholic priests who frequented his Court themselves bigots of an almost fanatical type were obliged gratefully to acknowledge. Though he became a convert neither to Buddhism nor to Christianity, he treated both Buddhist monks and Jesuit priests with a princely tolerance and magnanimity which, in addition to his other fine qualities of states manship, give him a strong claim to be regarded as the wisest and best ruler of his age, and as one of the finest imperial embodiments of the ideals of Chinese civilization.

The next important building operations at Puto were undertaken during the reign of Yung-cheng (1723-35), a not unworthy successor of

---

356 K'ang-hsi died in 1722, in the sixty-first year of his reign.

357 There is nothing in the Chinese to show what view the emperor took with regard to the question of Kuan-yin's sex. It would be more correct, probably, to assume that in this prayer the pusa is the male Avalokitesvara.

the great K'ang-hsi. Both the "Southern" and "Northern" monasteries underwent partial reconstruction at this time, and the work (which was completed in 1733) was done under the emperor's patronage and with his support. One of the local officials, a Cantonese named Huang Ying-hsiung, was ordered to visit the island from time to time and report the progress of the work. He wrote an excellent topographical account of the island, and in it he makes an interesting reference to the emperor's benignant toleration of the "three religions.[358]" He remarks that his Majesty had provided for the repair not only of the Buddhist temples at Puto, but also of the great Confucian temple at Ch'u-fou, in Shantung, and the great Taoist temple on the "Dragon-Tiger Mountains" in Kiangsi[359].

The Empress-Dowager

No severe calamities have befallen the island or its monasteries since the reigns of K'ang-hsi and Yung-cheng. Restorations and renovations have been undertaken as occasion required from time to time, and several of the later emperors of the Manchu line including the great Ch'ien-lung took a practical interest in the monks and their fortunes. Among these sovereigns must also be included the ill-omened woman who through the pitiable misuse of her unrivalled opportunities must be held mainly responsible for the ignominious collapse of the most ancient of imperial thrones. Her favourite method of signifying her august good-will towards Puto was a peculiar one: it was to enthrone herself among water-lilies, and pretend that she was the divine Kuan-yin emerging gracefully from the sea. It would be difficult, if not impos sible, to find a more thoroughly inappropriate representative of the tender and compassionate "Goddess of Mercy" than the terrible old woman who threw an emperor's favourite consort down a well, who went for a picnic on the palace lake while her minions were trying to massacre the stranger within her gates, and who could find no better reason for ordering a temporary cessation of the bombardment of a foreign church than that it gave her a headache[360].

---

[358] 以全三教盛事 Chih, xvi. 66

[359] Ch'u-fou is the little town in Shantung which possesses the principal Confucian temple in the empire. The sage himself lies buried in the beautiful cemetery of the Kung family in the immediate vicinity (see above, p. 135). The " Dragon-Tiger Mountains " (Lung-hu-shan) are in Kiangsi,, and there, in the temple known as the Shang-ch'ing-kung, resides the hereditary " Pope " of the Taoists.

[360] See China under the Empress-dowager, by Bland and Backhouse,, pp. 288 and 300. Facing p. 454 of that work and pp. 284 and 316 of Mr P. W. Sergeant's The Great Empress Dowager, may be seen photo graphs of the imperial lady in the unbecoming guise of c The Pusa

XIII. The "Northern Monastery" And "Buddha's Peak"

Hitherto our attention has been directed mainly to the history of the P'u-chi-ssu the "Monastery of Universal Salvation "; but though it is the older of the two great religious houses of the island, it is equalled, or indeed surpassed, in size, and it is far excelled in beauty, by the Fa-yu-ssu, or "Monastery of the Rain of the Law.[361]"

On both sides of the winding path that leads from the southern to the northern part of the island are many temples, grottoes, and small monasteries, each of which possesses its special attractions and its own stock of legends. These little centres of Buddhist worship we must regretfully pass by, though no pilgrim will omit to visit the Fa-hua-ling-tung (the "Holy Grotto of the Flower of the Law"), celebrated for its inscribed and caverned rocks, its magic pools, and its rich and varied foliage. Beyond the "holy grotto" is a "fairy well," and close by it is a temple (the Ch'ao-yang) built over a cave which pilgrims are recommended by the monks to visit in the early morning. It contains an eastward-facing window, through which they are invited to contemplate the rising sun. In this neighbourhood are to be seen numerous inscriptions which have been carved on the rocks and boulders of the sloping hillside. One of these inscriptions consists of the five boldly-carved characters Chung-kuo yu sheng-jen ("China has its sages"). This is a truth which is perhaps rather apt to be lost sight of to-day. A pathetic little record is that left by a visitor as recently as 1910 Tieh-nien ch'ung tao ("Revisited in old age"). Of greater religious significance are the words of the well-known Tibetan charm Om mane padme hom, written in Chinese characters, and the orthodox Chinese Buddhist's Teng-pi'an ("Cross to the other shore"), and Ta-ti chung sheng ch'eng Fo ("May all beings throughout the world become Buddha").

Kuan-yin of Puto-shan." The picture is not redeemed by the fact that one of her masquerading attendants is the notorious eunuch, Li Lien-ying.

361 On account of their relative positions the P'u-chi, as we have seen, is known as the Ch'ien-ssu, or Southern Monastery the Fa-yu as the Hou-ssu or "Northern Monastery."

Rock Inscriptions

We are now on the rising ground the Chi-pao-ling which forms the southern boundary of the longest and finest beach in Puto, the "Sands of a Thousand Paces,[362]" described by a Chinese poet as "yellow as powdered gold, soft as moss." The mile of roadway which leads us from this point to the Fa-yu Monastery is known as the Yu-t'ang Road, in commemoration of a monk of the Wan-li period (1573-1619) who bore that name and was mainly responsible for its construction. Passing by clusters of small monasteries and temples, some quite recently founded or restored, we reach the Fa-yu-ssu, delightfully situated near the northern end of the long beach and under the shadow of the tree-clad hill which culminates in "Buddha's Peak." The immediate surroundings of this fine monastery are of great beauty, and the build ings themselves are, of their kind, unsurpassed in Buddhist China. The lotus-pond, with its picturesque bridge, is one which would not disgrace the noblest of English parks; and the central halls, with their curved eaves and timbered roofs, the marble balustrades and grace ful pavilions, and the fine old trees which cast a religious shade over the spacious courtyards, combine to make the monastery of the "Rain of the Law" one of the most majestic and attractive, as it is one of the most peaceful and sequestered, of Chinese monastic dwellings[363].

"Northern Monastery" Founded

To follow in detail the history of the Fa-yu Monastery is unnecessary, as the story would be little more than a repetition of that already told in connection with the sister-monastery. Though the younger of the two, the Fa-yu since its foundation has shared all the fortunes, good and bad, of the elder, and tokens of imperial favour have been showered upon it with an equally liberal hand. According to the chronicle, a monastic building was first erected on this site in the year 1580. The founder was a far-travelled monk named Ta-chih ("Great Wisdom"), who set out on pilgrimage from the holy mountain of Omei, where he founded two temples, and who, after visiting Wu-t'ai and many other sacred places in northern and central China, arrived at last at Puto. Here he decided to spend his remaining

---

362 Ch'ien-pu-sha.
363 It was within this monastery that the author resided during his two visits to Puto.

years. The story goes that he offered up prayer at the Ch'ao-yin and Fan-yin caves for divine guidance as to the selection of a site for the hermitage which he proposed to found, and that shortly afterwards, while he was walking on the beach at the northern end of the Ch'ien-pu Sands, a long bamboo pole was washed up by the tide at his feet. Regarding this as Kuan-yin's answer to his prayers, he set to work to put up a little building close to the spot where he had seen the bamboo pole; and in commemoration of the incident which led to the choice of this site he gave his foundation the name of the "Hermitage of the Tide-waves."[364]"

Ta-chih died in 1592. Two years later the little hermitage, which had grown in size and importance, was elevated to the rank of a ssu a "monastery". In 1598 it was destroyed by fire. In 1605 it was rebuilt on a splendid scale by two monks named Ju-shou and Ju-kuang, under the munificent patronage of the emperor Wan-li, who in the following year bestowed upon it the new name of Chen-hai–ch'an-ssu ("Ocean-guardian Jhana Monastery"). In 1643 it was again partially destroyed by fire; and in 1665 it shared in the ruin brought upon all the religious houses in the island by the Dutch marauders.

The Story of a Bell

In connection with that episode the annals of the monastery tell an interesting story about the loss of its great bell. This bell was cast by the founder of the monastery, Ta-chih, in the last quarter of the sixteenth century. The "Red-hairs" carried it off as part of their loot, and succeeded in safely conveying it to the gateway of their capital in "the country of Europe." There, however, it fell down, and, owing to its great weight, was left lying where it fell. Gradually sinking into the soft ground, it at last disappeared altogether, and was forgotten. But in 1723 a sound like the rolling of thunder was suddenly heard coming from the ground; whereupon the amazed people of the neighbour hood dug up the ground and discovered the bell.

---

364 Hai-ch'ao-an.

THE YU-T'ANG ROAD, SHOWING ROCK-CARVED FIGURES.

THE LOTUS-POND OF THE NORTHERN MONASTERY.

Somehow or other these events came to the knowledge of the monastic authorities. The abbot of the monastery at the time of the discovery of the bell was one Fa-tse, who happened to be a native of Fuhkien, and was acquainted with many merchants who were engaged in foreign trade. Through these merchants negotiations were opened with "the country of Europe" with a view to the recovery of the long-lost bell. The negotiations ended successfully, and in the year 1728 it was brought back to China and landed at Namoa Island, near the port of Swatow, in the Canton province. Difficulties as to its reshipment were not overcome till 1733, which by a happy coincidence was the year which witnessed the completion of a restoration of the monastery under the auspices of K'ang-his's son, the emperor Yung-cheng. To the great joy and wonder of the monks, the bell was finally disembarked at Puto on the thirtieth day of the tenth month, at the very time when a solemn service was being held in the great hall of the monastery to celebrate his Majesty's birthday.

There is no reason to doubt that the story as thus told in the annals of the monastery is substantially true; but it seems improbable that the monks were correct in their belief that the bell had actually been conveyed to Europe. The Chinese of those days had very vague ideas of geography, and the monks of Puto had evidently no very distinct knowledge of the political divisions of the "country of Europe." Perhaps the bell did not make quite so long a journey as they supposed. The suggestion may be hazarded that its resting-place during the period from 1665 to 1723 was no European town, but a city of the Island of Java. Batavia was then, as it is still, the capital of the Dutch East Indies, and though its old ramparts no longer exist, it was a strong walled town in the seventeenth and eighteenth centuries. Possibly the Chinese story of the fall of the bell at the gates of the city, and its subsequent disappearance until its presence underground was revealed by a sound like rolling thunder, is based on the historical fact that in 1699 Batavia was visited by a destructive earthquake. Thus the real course of events may have been something like this: the bell was carried from Puto to Java in 1665; it was suspended in a tower on the wall of the city of Batavia; it remained there till 1699, when the wall was destroyed by an earthquake; it lay buried under the ruins of the wall until 1723; and in that year, after it had disappeared from view for almost a quarter of a century, the removal of the debris restored it to the light of day. The inscription on the bell, we may suppose, was read by Chinese residents in Java, who learned thereby the name of the monastery to which it originally belonged. Through them the story may easily have come to the ears of the Chinese merchants of Fuhkien, who at that time controlled a large proportion of China's foreign trade.

The joy of the monks at the return of their founder's bell was tempered by their discovery of the melancholy fact that it was no longer in a fit condition to serve its proper purpose. It had been cracked and injured to such an extent that before the hearts of monks and pilgrims could again be thrilled by its mellow tones it had to be put through the process of recasting. This work was not carried out for nearly a hundred years. It hung silently in its tower till 1825, when a wealthy pilgrim named Hsu, having interested himself in its history, undertook to defray the cost of having it recast. It is the bell of Ta-chih, originally cast before the year 1592, but re-cast in or shortly after the year 1825 by the pilgrim Hsu, that hung in the present bell-tower of the Northern Monastery until it was replaced in recent years by a bell cast during the reign of the late Emperor Kuang Hsu.

The Abbot Pieh-An

The most revered of all the abbots of this monastery is neither Ta-chih nor Fa-tse, but a remarkable man named Pieh-an[365]. He was a native of Ssuch'uan, but became abbot of the "Northern Monastery "of Puto in 1687, and remained there until his death in the last year of the century. The buildings had been in a ruinous and neglected condition ever since the disastrous visit of the "Red-hairs" in 1665, and to Pieh-an fell the task of superintending their reconstruction. In the annals of his monastery he occupies a place somewhat analogous to that of Ch'ao-yin in the annals of the sister-monastery. Both were distinguished ornaments of the Ch'an school, both were largely instrumental in interesting the emperor and other influential personages in the fortunes of Puto, and both are looked upon as re-founders of their re spective monasteries. It is Pieh-an, indeed, rather than Ta-chih, who is regarded by the fraternity of the "Northern Monastery" as their spiritual "ancestor" (t'ung tsu); for Ta-chih belonged to the Lu school, whereas Pieh-an was a prominent member of the Lin-chi subdivision of the Ch'an school the subdivision which to this day claims the allegiance of the monks of Puto. One of Pieh-an's minor titles to the

---

[365] His alternative name was Hsing-t ung.

gratitude of posterity rests on the fact that he was responsible for the casting of the enormous caldron which is the pride of the monastic kitchen [366]; but his fame is built upon foundations of a more durable, or at least a more spiritual, kind than a mere cooking-pot. He was a voluminous writer on religious subjects. Among his best-known works was a continuation of a well-known collection of Lives of Buddhist Saints[367]. He had many friends among the cultured laity, and one of them, a distinguished Confucian scholar and statesman named Yang Yung-chien (1631-1704), wrote his epitaph[368]. His spiritual authority shows no signs of eclipse in these degenerate days. One of the most important "saints days" in the calendar of the monks of the "Northern Monastery" is the day on which reverence is paid to the memory, and incense burned before the "spirit-tablet," of the "patriarch" Pieh-an[369].

"The Rain of the Good Law"

In 1699, as we know, the Emperor K'ang-hsi bestowed a new name on the "Southern Monastery." He simultaneously conferred a similar favour on the "Northern Monastery" by giving it the name which it has borne ever since Fa-yu Ch'an-ssu the "Jhana Monastery of the Rain of the Law." A brief reference has already been made to the meaning of this name. The "rain" is the rain of the "good Law of Buddha," which infinite myriads of saviour-bodhisats, who are "the clouds of the Law," graciously send down to earth in order to lay the dust of ignorance and passion and impart nourishment and fertility to the soil in which men sow the seeds of their good thoughts and actions[370].

---

366 A full description of the casting of this vessel is to be found in the Chih, xvi. 38

367 See Chih, xvi. 16ff., 41ff., 54ff.

368 Chih xvi. 45. The epitaph is interesting on account of its tolerant and sympathetic remarks on Buddhism hy one who avowed himself to be a strict Confucian.

369 In the second year of Hsuan-t'ung (1910) the " winter sacrifice" to Pieh-an fell on the twenty-third day of the eleventh month Christmas Eve.

370 A similar idea is found in the Jewish scriptures. " In the Psalms, as in the Prophets observes Yrjo Hirn in his Sacred Shrine " the rain and the dew are continually used as images of blessing. God's wrath expressed itself in sending a drought on those who had not listened to His commands, but His favour sent rain upon the faithful, and His mildness sank down like a soft dew over the field." . . . "The answering of prayer and grace are a heavenly dew which sinks down over the mind to purify and refresh it. In this respect the earliest fathers follow the terminology of the Jewish writers; and the similes of the cloud, the dew, and the rain are continually used by mediaeval scholastics and mystics, no less than by modern pious writers, from Santa Theresa and Bunyan down to the modern preachers ".

The squat tower, or ko, which stands at the entrance of the monastery and forms a kind of gateway, was built at the time of the extensive restorations which took place in the reign of Yung-cheng, and therefore only dates from about the year 1733. This is the building which, as has been noted, is dedicated to the Taoist T'ien-hou, the "Queen of Heaven." This deity, as we know, may be regarded in some respects as the Taoist counterpart of Kuan-yin. As a guardian-deity of all who go down to the sea in ships she occupies an appropriate position as protectress of all pilgrims to the holy island. The story goes that on the day on which the building was completed a fairy ship was seen on the eastern horizon. Emerging from the silvery sea mists, it rapidly approached the island, with parti-coloured pennons streaming from its masts and yards and gleaming lights flashing from its prow. It disappeared from the sight of mortal eyes while it was still at some distance from the Ch'ien-pu Sands, but those who had seen the beautiful vision felt joyfully confident that it was no other than the ship of the "Queen of Heaven," who by this means had signified her willingness to accept the homage of Puto and the guardianship of its ocean-borne pilgrims.

Passing underneath the chapel if we may so call it of the "Queen of Heaven," we reach a large quadrangle with fine old maidenhair-trees and a p'ai-lou, or carved archway, and reach the T'ien-wang-tien the "Hall of the Heavenly Kings."

The Laughing Buddha

These are Hindu or Brahmanical deities, and though they occupy a place in the mythology of Buddhism, they have no essential connection with the Buddhist religion. All Western visitors to Chinese temples are familiar with these colossal figures. They occupy a special building of their own, which is always the first of the great halls of a properly-equipped Buddhist temple[371]. In the midst of this hall, facing the incoming visitor, sits the bodhisat Maitreya (the Mi-lei Pusa of the Chinese), who, according to a vague Buddhist belief, is now a resident in one of the heavenly kingdoms (Tushita), and is destined to come to earth at some

---

371 In the case of the " Southern Monastery " of Puto, as we have seen (p. 328), the first hall is the pavilion of "Imperial Tablets" and in the case of the " Northern Monastery" the first building is the pavilion of the "Queen of Heaven." But these are extra and unessential adjuncts to the temple buildings, and could therefore he placed where fancy or convenience dictated. The T ien-wang-tien (the " Hall of the Four Heavenly Kings") is always in front of the essential buildings.

period in the more or less distant future and to be the Buddha of that age. He it is to whom Europeans have given the names of the "Buddhist Messiah" and the "Laughing Buddha."

Facing the opposite direction, and with his back to Mi-lei, stands Wei-t'o (Veda), who is regarded as a pusa entrusted with the special duty of protecting all monastic buildings. To use the Sanskrit term, he is a viharapala a tutelary deity of monasteries. The Chinese regard him also as a hu-fa ("defender of the faith"), and it is for this reason that his portrait often appears on the last page of Buddhist books.

The Four Kings of Heaven

But the most conspicuous occupants of the hall are the "four great heavenly kings" (ssu-ta t'ien-wang), who sit in couples, the one couple facing the other. These enormous and grotesque figures represent the mythological kings who stand at guard in the four quarters of the universe, or on the four sides of the fabulous Mount Meru, preventing the invasion of noxious influences or evil demons, and thus preserving inviolate the sanctity of the abodes of the Brahmanical gods. Strictly speaking, they themselves are not gods they are rather "demon-kings" who have been "converted." Each is associated, after the usual fashion of religious symbolism in the East, with certain colours and "elements." The northern king, who takes theoretical precedence of the others, is the black king of water; the southern is the blue king of liu-li-lapis-lazuli; the eastern is the white king of gold; the western is the red king of silver.

A European visitor to a Buddhist temple is apt to assume from the huge size and gorgeous ornamentation of these figures, and the prominence of the position assigned to them in the temple precincts, that the beings whom they represent must occupy an important place in the religious system to which they have gained admittance. But such is not the case. Their existence, indeed, was recognized by Buddhists at an early period, and they are mentioned in several passages of the Hinayana scriptures [372]; they are mythologically associated, moreover, with time as well as space, for they are sometimes identified with the seasons, and each is supposed to be the father of ninety sons who represent the days of the

---

[372] English readers may be referred to Dr Rhys Davids, Dialogues of the Buddha, pt. ii. pp. 259, 282-3, 287-8, 373.

year[373]. This artificial division of the year into twelve months of thirty days each was a Brahmanical sacrificial year, and though it was not astronomically accurate, it was probably of greater antiquity than either the solar or the lunar year[374]. But all these myths and fancies have no essential connection with Buddhism. As far as China is concerned, the four kings seem to have been brought into association with Buddhism no earlier than the eighth century of our era. A monk from Ceylon named Amogha (or Pu-k'ung, to use the name by which he is best known in China), who came to China about the year 733, is said to have been responsible for introducing them into the country of his adoption.

Mei-Li and the Guardian Kings

It is clear, then, that in the front hall of a large Buddhist temple, such as that of the "Northern Monastery" in Puto, there is much to attract the notice of all who are interested in the comparative study of religion. There is the Mi-lei Fo ("Maitreya Buddha"), who invariably faces the outer doorway, and invariably wears the happy expression which attracts the attention of all European visitors to Buddhist temples. Strictly speaking, he is at present neither Buddha nor bodhisat neither Fo nor Pusa; but he will be a bodhisat when he appears on earth at some future time, and he will become Buddha during that earthly life. He cannot be admitted to the holy of holies the real sanctuary of the temple because he belongs to the future, not to the present. His image is therefore placed in the outer hall, which is a mere porch or antechapel in its relation to the consecrated buildings that stand behind it. Why does he face the outer doorway? Because he is waiting to welcome the coming of the next Buddha-age. Why does he "laugh "? Because he is full of the glad tidings of the Buddha that is to come.

Behind him, as we have seen, stands the viharapala Wei-t o whose face is turned in the opposite direction, towards the inner halls and chapels of the temple. The reason of this position is obvious. The future, the things

---

373 See Beal, Catena, pp. 71-3, 77, and his Buddhist Lit. in China, pp. 157-8. Beal observes that the four kings "are, under one aspect, the Horai of Homer; under another the four elements."

374 Mr F. M. Cornford, in his From Religion to Philosophy, 1912, observes that the seasonal year being probably older than the solar or even the lunar calendar, the Horai would naturally be prominent before the moon and the sun were worshipped, as the measurers of time and the givers of life" (p. 170). It is interesting to note that the ancient year of 36O days is not yet extinct, and that it is probably still used to regulate Vedic sacrifices" (Dr J. F. Fleet, in J.R.A.S., October 1911, p. 1094).

that are to come, are no concern of his. The sole duty of AVei-t o is to stand guard over the monks and their monastery; he therefore faces the ta-tien the principal sanctuary.

As for the four heavenly kings, the figures of these mighty beings should, in theory, stand at the four points of the compass. This arrangement would be inconvenient, and they are therefore placed in couples; so that if the temple faces the south (as temples in China theoretically should), two of the kings sit on the east side and two on the west[375]. Thus the Buddhist worshipper, who is bound to pass through the front hall in order to reach the main object of his devotions, is challenged, as it were, by the guardian-kings on his left and right as he enters the precincts of the temple.

It is important to note that the five principal occupants of this hall Mi-lei and the four kings are all excluded from the temple's inner sanctuaries. They are not the recipients of prayers or thanksgivings, and are not entitled to religious adoration. In front of each, indeed, is a stone incense-jar, and into each jar the pious pilgrim, as he passes, will probably insert a stick of incense; but this will merely be an act of conventional piety or courtesy, not one which can fittingly be described as an act of religious worship[376].

Behind the "Hall of the Four Kings," in the "Northern Monastery," is a series of terraces, each of which is reached by a flight of steps. On the left and right of one such terrace stand the drum and bell towers. Above them we come to the Yu-Fo-Tien the yellow-roofed hall of the so-called Jade Buddha. Beyond this is the main sanctuary the great hall of Kuan-yin. This particular hall is generally known as the Chiu-lung-tien ("Nine-dragon Hall") in consequence of the fact that when it was undergoing restoration in the reign of K'ang-hsi it was roofed with tiles which came

---

[375] The "Northern Monastery" of Puto faces due south.

[376] This matter has been dealt with at some length, because lack of sympathy,, or defective knowledge,, or a combination of both, frequently results in misrepresentations which are apt to give rise, among Western peoples, to very erroneous and unfair impressions of Buddhism. The following is an extract from an article which appeared, as recently as January 1913, in the journal of the China Inland Mission. " We proceeded to glance at the various deities in the outer court. The most striking of these were the Laughing Buddha and the Four Kings of Heaven. . . . Two of these worthies f sat very quietly for their photographs in spite of having to sustain a somewhat trying pose at the same time! From their pictures ... we can form some idea of the worshipper's first and last impressions of what Buddhism has to offer. These four door guardians, flourishing thunder-bolts and spitting fireworks, offer [no forgiveness to the sinner, no hope to the penitent, no strength to the weak, no comfort to the sorrowful, no guidance to the. perplexed, their whole attitude being one of vengeance and fury.".

from a dismantled imperial palace at Nanking. These tiles were a gift to the monastery from the emperor himself. The hall contains a very large image of Kuan-yin. In front of this great image stands a smaller one of gilded wood, said to have been brought from Tibet. There are also two other images of the pusa, the eighteen arahants, and a Wei-t o in a shrine faced with glass.

Interior of Monastery

Behind the great hall is the Yu-pei-t'ing (the "Pavilion of Imperial Tablets"); and behind this is the large Fa-t'ang, which is used by the monks for their daily services. It is only on solemn festivals that services are held in the great hall of Kuan-yin. Among numerous images in the Fa-t'ang are those of Sakyamuni, Kuan-yin, P'u-hsien, and Wen-shu. In the courtyard, on either side of this hall, are two chapels, one dedicated to Chun-t'i, the other to Kuan-ti. Kuan-ti is properly to be classed among the deities of Taoism, but he has been admitted into Buddhist temples for two main reasons. In the first place, as a "god of war" he is regarded as a valuable champion to enlist on the side of true religion; in the second place, he was a tutelary deity of the Manchu dynasty. Whether his image will tend to disappear from Buddhist temples now that the dynasty has collapsed is a question to which as yet no answer seems to have been given.
On either side of the various halls and chapels just described are the various monastic offices, guest-quarters, refectory, kitchens, monks apart ments, meditation-halls (Ch'an-T'ang] and reception-rooms. The innermost block of buildings contain the abbot's quarters, rooms for distinguished guests and pilgrims, a chapel dedicated to Bodhidharma (in recognition of his position as patriarch of the Ch'an school), and the monastic library.

Buddhist China

WITHIN THE GROUNDS OF THE NORTHERN MONASTERY.

AN ALABASTER IMAGE OF BUDDHA, PUTO-SHAN.

Reginald Fleming Johnston

Monastery of Buddha's Peak

From the "Northern Monastery" a well-made pathway leads to the summit of the island. The "Buddha's Peak" (Fo-ting) is also known as the "Pusa's (that is, Kuan-yin s) Peak." A third name is "White Flower Peak" (Pai-hua-ting), the refer ence being, of course, to the "little white flower" for which the island is famous. The height is little more than nine hundred feet, and the ascent is gradual. In the pilgrim-season many mountain-chairs are seen on the winding pathway, but these are almost monopolized by "small-footed" women and old folk, whose strength would be overtaxed even by so simple a mountain walk as this. The climb, such as it is, would be well worth undertaking if only for the sake of the magnificent view of the Chusan archipelago which is to be had from the summit; but there are also charmingly-situated temples to be visited. Of these the finest is the temple which at present ranks as third in size and importance of the religious houses of Puto. This is the Hui-chi Monastery, popularly known as the "Buddha's Peak Monastery,[377]" which stands half-concealed amid a little forest of small oak-trees. It dates from the latter years of the Ming dynasty, when it was founded by a monk named Yuan-hui. A good view of its coloured roof-tiles is to be had from the wall of the little disused lighthouse which crowns one of the summits. The setting of dense dark foliage adds greatly to the lustre and beauty of these tiles, the colours of which are yellow, blue, white, and black. The interior of the temple is scarcely less attractive than the exterior. The "Hall of the Four Kings" that which is crowned with the coloured tiles is worthy of attention on account of its remarkable ceiling, a fine example of modern Chinese wood-artistry. The main building of the temple is not dedicated to Kuan-yin but to Sakyamuni: in this respect it differs from the other large temples of the island. It is roofed with tiles of imperial yellow, and the interior is richly garnished. Sakyamuni himself, represented by a large gilded image, occupies the central position, and on either side stand the figures of Ananda and Kasyapa. In front of Sakyamuni is a comparatively small image of Kuan-yin; and along the back of the hall (not at the two sides, as is customary) are ranged the images of the eighteen lo-han ("arahants"). On a separate throne sits Ti-tsang, the saviour-pusa of Chiu-hua-shan.

---

377 Fo-ting-ssu.

Buddhist China

Near the central hall is a two-storied building. The lower room is the tsu-t'ang (the "ancestral hall"), containing the spirit-tablets of abbots, monks, and benefactors, in addition to three images, of which the central one is the image of Bodhidharma[378]. The upper room is a chapel dedicated to Kuan-yin, of whom there are three images.

A remarkable feature of this temple is that it contains a Yu-huang-tien a hall consecrated to the worship of the supreme god of Taoism. The reason for his admission to this Buddhist temple is not far to seek. The "Jade Imperial God" of the Taoists is regarded throughout China as the principal presiding deity of every mountain-summit[379]. In any other temple in Puto his image would be out of place; in the temple which stands on the hill-top even though that hill-top is "Buddha's Peak" he finds his appropriate dwelling-place.

Solar and Lunar Deities

The god is enthroned in the centre, and on right and left are ranged his attendants and disciples. At the back of the chapel, on either side of the central shrine, sit two deities, each of whom holds a circular plaque or disk. These two divine personages are Jih-kuang and Yueh-kuang the gods (or god and goddess) of sun and moon. They, like the Jade Imperial God himself, belong to the Taoist pantheon, but they are not unrecognized by Buddhism. There are many curious survivals of primitive sun worship and moon worship to be found in the different Buddhist systems, especially in

---

378 Concerning Bodhidharma, see above, pp. 83-86. It is distressing to find that the ridiculous theory, first put forward by Catholic missionaries, that Bodhidharma was the apostle St. Thomas, is for ever rising phoenix-like from the flames of destructive criticism. The theory seems to have been based partly on the fact that Bodhidharma's portrait as engraved on several stone tablets and reproduced in many a work of pictorial art reveals a countenance that is thoroughly un-Chinese in type, and partly on the fact that the name by which he is popularly known in Chinese is Tamo, which is supposed to bear a suspicious resemblance to Thomas. It is hardly necessary to remind the reader that Bodhidharma (who did not come to China till the sixth century of our era) was a native of India, which is quite sufficient to account for his foreign type of countenance, and also, it may be added, for his shaggy abundance of hair. There is no reason to doubt that the traditional pictures of Bodhidharma one of which is reproduced in this book are genuine portraits. Chinese Buddhists seem to have made no attempt to give him the appearance of a countryman of their own. As for the name Tamo, it is merely an abbreviation of P'u-t'i-ta-mo (Bodhidharma). Had the Chinese wished to write the name Thomas in Chinese script, they could easily have used characters bearing the sound To-ma. It should have been unnecessary to bring up this subject in these enlightened days, and this note would not have been written had it not been for the fact that the Tamo-Thomas theory has quite lately sprung to life again in a recent volume of travels Through Shen-kan, by R. S. Clark and A. de C. Sowerby (Fisher Unwin: 1912). It is only fair to the authors of the book to add that their authority for the theory was a missionary named F. Madeley, with whom they apparently believed it to have originated.

379 See Lion and Dragon in Northern China, pp. 32, 391, 396, 398.

the Amidist cult[380]. The worship of solar and lunar deities, it is hardly necessary to say, existed long before the rise of Buddhism. It engrafted itself upon Buddhism just as it did upon Hinduism, Taoism, Shinto, and Manichaeism[381]. According to the ancient Japanese mythology, the sun was ruled by a goddess (Ama-terasu) the great divinity who is still worshipped at Ise and from whom the emperors of Japan claim descent. The moon, on the other hand, was ruled by Amaterasu's brother, the god Susa-no-o. The nameless religion (it was not identical with Taoism), which seems to have had a zealous devotee in the Chinese emperor Ch'in Shih-huang in the third century B.C., included sun worship[382]; and, indeed, the State religion of China gave official recognition to the worship of sun and moon up to the date of the fall of the Manchu dynasty in 1912, as the altars outside the eastern and western walls of the "Tartar City" of Peking still remain to testify[383].

The Buddhist Dead

Near the Hui-chi Monastery will be found some of the finest tombs on the island. The most charmingly situated is perhaps that which was erected as recently as 1887 to the abbot of Hui-chi, whose fa-wing, or religious name, was Hsin-chen ("Trusting in the Truth"). The tombs of Puto are numerous and interesting, and if we were to do justice to them, and to the religious ideas which they symbolize or represent, we should have to devote a chapter to this subject alone. It may be mentioned, however, that they are of two principal kinds. There are the separate graves of abbots and other distinguished persons, and of these the grave of Hsin-chen is a good example. There are also the p'u-t'ung-t'a -large tombs which are used for the "universal mingling" of the ashes of monks who are not granted the privilege of separate burial. The typical p'u-t'ung-t'a consists

---

380 See De Groot, Le Code du Mahayana en Chine pp. 185 ff., 220ff; and Beal, Catena, pp. 68-70. Chandrasuryapradipa ("Moon-sun-lamp") Buddha is mentioned in various sutras. The name is rendered in Chinese by Jih-Yueh-Teng Fo, or Wen-kuang Fo.

381 With regard to Mabichaeism, the following remarks hy Mr G. R. S. Mead (The Quest, Jan. 1913, p. 360) are of interest. "It is well known that in both the cosmology and soteriology of Mani, the moon and the sun, under the figure of luminous vessels or light ships, play an important rule. In the soteriology they are connected with the purification,, respectively by water and fire, and the transportation of the souls of the righteous deceased across the ocean of the aether." (See also J.R.A.S.,, January 1913, p. 90.)

382 A shrine to the sun-god has existed from time immemorial on the north-eastern promontory of Shantung, near Weihaiwei. According to tradition, the emperor Ch f iri Shih-huang worshipped the rising sun at this spot the easternmost limit of his empire.

383 The quaint relics of moon worship which still exist among the Chinese peasantry (see Lion and Dragon in Northern China, pp. 182-4, 191) have no connection with Buddhism and no essential connection with Taoism,

Buddhist China

mainly of a massive stone structure having on each of its four or more sides a small hole a few inches square. Each of these holes is closed up by a loose block of stone, which can be withdrawn when the ashes of a dead monk are to be deposited in the interior. The bodies of monks and of lay Buddhists too, sometimes are cremated. Each monastery of any size possesses not only its own p'u-t'ung-t'a, but also its own crematorium, which is a small stone building somewhat similar in appearance to a miniature temple. A properly-constructed p'u-t'ung–t'a should have four separate cavities one for the ashes of pi–ch'iu, or ordained monks, another for those of pi-ch'iu-ni, or ordained nuns[384], a third for those of upasakas (yu-p o-sai), or lay-brothers, and a fourth for those of upasikas (yu-p'o-i), or lay-sisters.

The graves of monks, like those of laymen, usually bear inscriptions containing euphemistic expressions whereby death, it is thought, is robbed of its sting. In Puto one of the favourite descriptions of a grave is shou-yu ("the region of longevity," or the "long home"). The poetical term chun hsi ("to store away for the long night," as it has been translated) is also found carved on monumental stones.

Western visitors to Puto, who might perhaps care little for its history or religious associations, could hardly fail to be enchanted with its scenery and its flora. Many of its trees are of great beauty. The grove of evergreen oak[385] which covers part of "Buddha's Peak" consists of comparatively small trees; but the island contains fine specimens of camphor, ginkgo[386], cypress, chestnut, and sophora, besides many other trees well known in central China. Pines and similar trees seem to decay before they attain any great age or size. The Chinese say that they are injured by the salt sea winds, but it seems more probable that they exhaust the soil. There are plum, peach, and cherry trees which burst into glorious blossom in the spring; and the maple tints in autumn bring some consolation for the fading of the exquisite gardenia florida the fragrant "little white flower" for which the island has been celebrated for a thousand years. Flowering plants and shrubs are indeed abundant in Puto. Many have been

---

[384] There are no nuns or other women resident in the religious houses of Puto. The ashes of dead nuns as of lay Buddhists, male and female--may, however, be carried to Puto for burial there.

[385] Quercus sclerophylla.

[386] Salisburia adiantifolia.

introduced into the monastery gardens by the monks, who, like all Orientals, and Buddhists in particular, are lovers of flowers.

Vegetables and grain of many kinds are, of course, cultivated to the fullest extent possible, for the monastic fraternities are strictly vegetarian. The so-called Chinese potato is said to have been brought from Japan. Beans and other leguminous plants are common, and there are a few rice-fields. Fruit-trees are cared for rather for their blossom than for their fruit, but the Chinese like oranges, and of these Puto possesses at least three varieties. The island also produces a special kind of tea, which is much prized by the Chinese and is said to have medicinal qualities[387].

Fauna of Puto

As to the fauna of Puto, this is another subject to which it would be quite impossible to do justice in these few pages. There are a few small hornless deer[388] which owing to the fact that they are never hunted or disturbed by the monks are so tame that they will enter the temple gardens, and will lie basking in the sun on the Ch'ien-pu Sands even in the presence of so preposterous a creature as a Western foreigner. It is said that wild pigs, monkeys, and wild cat were common at one time, though whether they are to be seen on the island nowadays seems doubtful. According to the Chronicle, tigers used to swim from Chusan across the "Sea of Water-lilies," but they always turned and went back before they reached the shores of Puto. This may have been because their strength was no match for that of the ocean-currents, or (to mention the theory preferred by the Buddhists) because some instinct told them that the soil of the island was sacred and that the slaughter of animals was not permitted. Snakes are common, but owing to Kuan-yin's intervention they are all perfectly harmless. Those which refused to surrender their poisonous properties were banished to the mainland. A few cattle and water-buffalo are to be seen, but these are kept only for agricultural purposes. The buffalo are used for the ploughing of the rice-fields. Squirrels, goats, and monkeys are said to have been often kept as pets in the monastery grounds. The Chronicle tells us about a tame goat that belonged to the monks of Fa-yu.

---

387 It is said to be beneficial for lung-diseases and dysentery. Another of Puto's many medicinal plants is the vitex ovata.
388 Hydropotes inermis?

Buddhist China

GRAVE OF THE ABBOT HSIN-CHÊN.

A P'U-T'UNG-T'A.
(*For the reception of the ashes of deceased monks.*)

"It can understand what people say to it. If you call to it, it will follow you. If you give it food, it will bend one leg and bow its head and take the food from your hand quite gently. If you tell it to kneel, it will go down on both fore-legs. It is not often" concludes the chronicler triumphantly, "that you have the chance of seeing a goat like that! "

Poets of Puto

In reading the literature associated with the great Buddhist hills we cannot fail to notice how frequently the love and enthusiasm of monks and hermits and poets for their wild and romantic homes impel each to extol his own chosen place of retreat as the pride and glory of all holy and beautiful mountains. We need not be surprised, therefore, to learn from one of the poetic recluses of Puto that his beloved island is Chih-na ssu-shan chih kuan ("the Crown of China's Four Mountains"[389]). "Who tells you," exclaims another poet in a still more ecstatic strain, "that there is no road to heaven? This is heaven's own gate way, and through it you may pass direct to the very throne of God.[390]"

Almost equally enthusiastic is much of the verse that has been written by poets whose interest in Puto can hardly be said to have been based on religious emotion. To some of these reference has already been made. Another of those who sang the praises of the island in graceful verse was the famous scholar and statesman Wang An-shih (1021-86), who visited it during his tenure of office as magistrate of a district in Chehkiang. Another was the distinquished artist and poet Chao Meng-fu (1254-1322), who held official positions under the Sung and Yuan dynasties. A third was Ch'en Hsien-chang (1428-1500), a Cantonese poet whose tablet has been elevated to the "Confucian Temple," though by religious temperament he seems to have had closer kinship with Buddhism than with Confucianism.

The poet-monk T'ung-yuan, who was an abbot of the "Southern Monastery" in the first half of the eighteenth century, was a typical example of a class from which the Buddhist monk hood has drawn many

---

389 Chih, xvii. p. 2.

390 This occurs in a poem by the monk T'ung-hsu. Western readers, who usually take it for granted that no Buddhists recognize a supreme personal God, will be surprised to learn that a Buddhist and an ordained monk can give expression to such words as these. But there is no real cause for surprise. The fact is that the river of Buddhism, like all the great streams of religious thought, frequently breaks its own banks and flows far beyond the limits of the channel to which in theory it should confine itself.

Buddhist China

of its best recruits. A little sketch of his career, written by a friend who had known him from boyhood, is preserved in a preface to his poems. Poets, says the biographer, often have to go into quiet and lonely places before they can give fit expression to their thoughts. They must lead lives of solitude, and nest themselves in hills and woods, so that they may hold themselves aloof from worldly distractions and allow their minds to become clear and unruffled. Outward conditions must be attuned to their inward feelings before they can turn the promptings of poetic inspiration to good account. T'ung-yuan, continues the sympathetic biographer, was one of those to whom such a life as this was thoroughly congenial. As a boy he was clever, but he cared little for the noisy company of his friends. He used to steal away from them so that he might enjoy lonely quietness. When he was still little more than child his thoughts began to hanker after a religious life, for its loneliness and tranquillity attracted him. At the age of seventeen he went to Puto and became a member of one of the monasteries there. A few years later the temples were destroyed by pirates and all the monks were obliged to migrate to the mainland[391]. A long time afterwards, when the temples were rebuilt, he returned to Puto, where he spent the rest of his life in the religious and poetic meditation which his soul loved.

Incorruptible Riches

But Puto has not confined its welcome to scholarly poets and famous statesmen, from whose names it might borrow a reflected glory. It has been the tarrying-place or the home of many a poor fugitive from the battle of life, many a stricken soul whose only longing was to escape from the turmoil of a world in which he had tasted only sorrow and the bitterness of defeat. To such as these the great monasteries of China have always been havens of refuge, and Puto has not spurned them from her shores. Some times, indeed, those who have taken or could take only an inglorious part in the struggle for riches and rank have proved their ability to secure a goodly share of the only form of wealth that does not diminish by being shared with others. The riches of the spirit, the treasures that are incorruptible, have been most often secured in Buddhist China as in Christian Europe by men who have cared but little for those material

---

[391] This refers to the events of 1665-71.

successes and rewards which, to the worldly-minded, constitute the goal of all ambition.

We may guess, perhaps, that one of those meditative souls who know how to turn material defeat into spiritual victory was a monk of Puto who assumed, or was given, the significant name of Chen-cho ("Truly-stupid"). He had an alternative name Wu-neng, which means "Can't-do-anything." He, we are told, was seized with religious longings at the early age of seven. But he was an only son, and Chinese custom made it impossible for him to devote himself to the monkhood so long as no provision had been made for carrying on the rites of ancestral "worship." So when he became a young man he went on pilgrimage to Chiu-hua-shan for the express purpose of imploring Ti-tsang to take pity on his father and mother, who would be childless if he became a monk. "Can t-do-anything" proved that even if he could do nothing else, he at least knew how to move a divine being to compassion, for shortly after his visit to Chiu-hua the good news was brought to him that he had an infant brother. He was then free to follow where his spirit beckoned. In 1616 he came to Puto, where he earned the love and respect of the monks, not only for the austerity of his mode of life, but also for the unselfish zeal with which he interested himself in the welfare of pilgrims and strangers. A building to which he gave the name of the "Temple of the Sea Mists" was founded by him for the special purpose of accommodating and entertaining the pilgrim-monks who came across the waters to worship at the shrine of Kuan-yin.

Two Strange Visitors

Puto has had many strange visitors, and some of them if we may believe the testimony of those who had the best opportunity of judging belonged to a plane of existence that was more exalted than the plane of ordinary humanity. A monk of the Ming dynasty named Chen-I has a tale to tell us about a mysterious couple a man and a woman who came to Puto in 1605. They took up their abode side by side on a little hill overlooking the sacred cave of Kuan-yin, in two thatched huts which they made with their own hands. The huts were so small and so rudely put together that they afforded no proper protection against the weather, and it was impossible either to stand or to lie down inside them; moreover, the roofs leaked and the ground was damp. The wretched couple, who were supposed to be beggars, drank nothing but cold water and ate nothing but coarse herbs. For several days at a time, indeed, they took no nourishment at all, yet seemed none the worse for their abstinence. If people took pity on them and offered them food or money, they did not refuse such gifts, but always gave them away again to any hungry pilgrim who happened to pass by. The monk Chen-I took a kindly interest in the couple, and went one night to pay them a friendly visit. They seemed quite indifferent to his presence, and for a long time ignored his well-meant remarks. He raised a lamp so that he might have a better view of them, and this seemed to wake them up a little. But still the man only smiled when spoken to, and the woman only uttered interjections. They refused to tell him their names, and the only fact in connection with their past history which they were willing to communicate was that they had lived for a long time on the sacred mountain of Chung-nan in distant Shensi. Chen-I then asked them about their religious beliefs, and the response was a curious one: "Our eyes have seen the ocean; our ears have heard the wind soughing, the rain descend ing, the sea waves dashing, and the wild birds calling." Then the monk asked what their occupation was. "Sometimes," they replied, "we meditate on Kuan-yin. At other times we sit still and do nothing."

Chen-I seems to have gone away in a state of great perplexity. He was unable to make up his mind as to whether the couple were very foolish or very wise: it seemed clear to him that they must be either one or the other. They remained in their huts throughout the ensuing autumn and winter. In the second month of the following year pilgrims began to come to the island in crowds. One day, while great numbers of pilgrims were standing at the entrance to the sacred cave, the nameless couple suddenly appeared before them. "Peace be with you all,"[392] they said; and thereupon they vanished and were never seen again.

The Praises of Buddha

The answer given by these strange beings to the question about their religious beliefs was not so irrelevant as an unwary reader may be tempted to suppose. A sacred mountain or a sacred island is, to the Buddhists of China, a great altar set up to the worship of the Buddhas and pusas, and the sky is its jewelled canopy. From another point of view it is a mighty temple, whose dome is heaven. The separate shrines and sanctuaries of

---

[392]汝辈各安

Puto are but chapels within one vast cathedral. It is not only the chanting monks who utter the praises of Buddha in their great pavilions; it is not only from jars of bronze and stone that perfumed clouds rise daily to the lotus-throne of the compassionate pusa. From the sea waves also come the sounds of a mighty anthem; the rain that patters on the temple roofs is the rain of the Good Law that is poured from the unfailing vial of Kuan-yin; the winds murmur sutras in the sacred caves and in the spirit-haunted woods; the wild birds in their calling are but joining in the universal chorus of adoration; and the "little white flower" sends up to Buddha, from millions of censers not made by the hand of man, the sweet fragrance of inexhaustible incense.

Buddhist China

A MONASTERY GARDEN, PUTO-SHAN.

COURTYARD IN THE NORTHERN MONASTERY. PUTO-SHAN.

XIV. Index

Abhidharma 23, 35
Adam, James 54
Adamnan, Abbot of Iona 109
Adibuddha 68
Afghanistan 19
Agni 142
Akka 93
Akshobhya 70, 71
Al Ghazzali 53
Altar of Heaven 3
Ama-terasu 273
American Indians 146
Amidism 67, 70, 72, 74, 78, 82
Amitabha ..67, 68, 70, 71, 72, 74, 75, 76, 78, 79, 80, 81, 82, 83, 84, 86, 88, 90, 112, 127, 128, 170, 195, 198, 199, 208, 210, 211, 227, 236
Ammon at Thebes 93
Amogha 267
Amoghasiddha 70
Amoy 189
Ancestor-worship 7
Anesaki 20
Antony, St. 52
Aphrodite 208
Apis 93
Apollo 93
Apostle of the Indies 192
Apostles Creed 145
Arabic story of an ostrich 50
Aristotle 83
Art 7, 20, 200, 201, 212, 215
Ashtoreth 93
Asokan Buddhism 16
Asvaghosha 19, 20, 21, 22, 23, 26, 29, 60
Atargatis 211, 212
Augustine 33, 49, 63, 80, 89
Aurangzeb 255
Avalokita 197
Avalokitesvara 70, 74, 75, 76, 195, 196, 198, 208, 209, 210, 256
Avatamsaka-sutra 66
Avichi hell 129
Awakening of Faith 20, 26, 27, 29
Badarinath 93
Banished Angel 157

Barnett, L. D. 50
Basilides 82, 89
Batavia 262
Bateson, J. H. 214
Beal, Samuel cited . 198, 199, 203, 205, 208, 209, 210, 267, 273
Benares, five ghats of 93, 229
Bergson 90
Bernadette of Lourdes 215
Bible of the Buddhists 11
Blake 39
Blandina 206
Bodhidharma .. 21, 60, 63, 64, 228, 269, 272
Body of Bliss 56
Boerschmann's P'u-t'o-shan 188
Book of the Dead 82
Boutroux cited 223
Brahma, story of the god 44
Brahmajala-sutra 121
Brahman girl, story of the 129, 132
Brahmanical persecutions, alleged 18
Brahmanism 147
Bright Moonlight 173
Buddha's Peak 187, 228, 258, 259, 271, 272, 274
Buddhahood. 44, 49, 52, 72, 80, 84, 90, 110, 127, 128, 136, 139, 143, 201, 225
Burma, Buddhism in 12, 17, 123, 239
Caird's Evolution of Religion cited 33
Canterbury Tales, The 95
Canton 138, 262
Case, Dr Shirley 84
Catechism 84, 86
Catherine of Alexandria, St 206
Catherine of Siena, St 215
Ceylon, Buddhism in 12, 14, 17, 20, 123, 201, 267
Charlemagne 231
Chavannes 161
Cheyne, Dr T. K. 145, 211
China Inland Mission 268
China under the Empress Dowager, by Bland and Backhouse 257
Chou, Duke of 99
Christ ...27, 35, 57, 63, 74, 94, 145, 230, 244

283

Christianity 10, 12, 26, 27, 40, 42, 54, 63, 74, 75, 76, 101, 125, 144, 145, 171, 196, 214, 256
Chundi-devi 203
Clement of Alexandria 89
Clement VI., (Pope) 57
Clovis of Buddhism 23
Comte 54, 189
Confucian 1, 2, 6, 7, 9, 99, 100, 112, 139, 161, 162, 163, 176, 178, 193, 244, 247, 255, 256, 257, 264, 277
Confucianism .. 1, 2, 5, 6, 7, 9, 10, 12, 64, 82, 99, 100, 139, 161, 162, 163, 211, 247, 277
Confucius 1, 3, 5, 6, 7, 33, 99, 247
Coomaraswamy, Dr 39
Cornford, F. M 199, 267
Creative Evolution 90
Cretans of Euripides 210
Cruach Phadraig 93
Cuzco in Peru 93
Dalai Lama 197
De Vita Contemplativa 210
Dea Syria 211
Deity 89, 127
Delphi 93
Delvolve 54
Devils 235
Dhamma 110
Dhammapada 52
Dharma 110
Dharmakara 71
Dharmakaya 56, 82, 110
Dharmaraksha 198, 200
Dhyana 21, 60
Dialogues of the Buddha . 24, 32, 36, 41, 42, 44, 121, 266
Diamond Rock 227, 228
Dickinson, G. Lowes 80
Docetism 56
Dragon's Pool 160
Duchesne, Mgr. Louis 27, 209
Duns Scotus 80, 89
Dwarfs 235, 243
Eastern Cliff or Ridge of Chiu-hua. 171, 183
Eckenstein, Miss 199
Eckhart 39, 63
Edkins, J. 199, 237
Egaku 231, 232, 234, 235, 236, 241
Egypt 14, 210
Eightfold Path 48
Elements, the four (or five) 106
Elizabeth, St 206
Epirus 14
Essenes 210, 211
Evil 134
Evil Poison 134
Evolution 33
Faith 42, 79, 84, 145, 195, 223
Faith of St. Jerome 145
Famous Hills of Chinese Buddhism 104, 105, 106, 108, 110, 167
Faust 90
Fenollosa Ernest 7, 200, 212
Filial Piety 140
First Emperor 16
First Gate of Heaven 159, 184
First Gateway of Contemplation 160
Fish-ponds 211, 212
Five Buddhas 71
Fleet, Dr J. F. 20, 22, 267
Flowers 155
Formosa 249
France 6
Fuji, Mount 93
Fujiwara family 232
Gabriel, the angel 209
Gandhara 14, 19, 201, 210
Gardner, Prof. Percy 27
Geology 86
Georgi 203
Gerard, Rev. John 80
Giles, H. A. 35, 199, 211
Gobharana 100
Godaisan 232
Goddess of Mercy 75, 195, 257
Golden Island 248
Gondophares 26
Gondophernes 26
Gotama 52, 70, 113, 128, 129, 131, 201, 214
Great Vehicle the 18, 22, 52
Greek mythology 10
Gregory of Nyssa, St 97
Groot, Prof. J. J. M. De 273
Growse's Mathura 82
Haimavantas 18
Halensis, Alexander 57
Hall and Bernard's Nemesis in China 188
Hamilton, Lord Ernest cited 74
Han dynasty 106, 182, 192

Hangchow................108, 181, 184, 232, 235
Hardoon edition of Buddhist scriptures .. 6, 9
Hardy, E. Spence................................ 18, 176
Heaven....72, 79, 81, 84, 184, 195, 203, 227, 265
Heavenly Kings, Hall of the ... 132, 239, 265
Hedin, Sven 215
Hell... 80, 125
Hera 211
Heraclitus 39
Herman of Cologne 206
Hermes 146
Hermitage of the Tide-waves 260
Hero-worship.. 178
Hetuvada Causationalist school............ 23
Hibil Ziwa 146
Hierapolis 93, 211, 212
Hinayana...18, 23, 28, 29, 35, 41, 52, 57, 66, 84, 266
Hindu pilgrimages 93
Hinduism 17, 146, 273
Hirn, Prof. Yrjo 74, 151, 264
Holy Grotto of the Flower of the Law 258
Horai of Homer 267
Hugo of St Victor 63
Hui-chou... 184
Hydropotes inermis 275
Ignatius Loyola, St 61
Images, religious use of........................ 137
India..11, 14, 17, 18, 19, 20, 36, 40, 93, 100, 104, 115, 142, 146, 154, 197, 201, 210, 213, 214, 215, 229, 231, 255, 272
Indo-Scythians mission to king of Indra. 100
Infinite 211
Inspired Drunkard................................ 157
Iranian mythology 142
Ireland.. 93, 101, 252
Irrefragable Doctor 57
Ise, Japanese shrines of................. 93, 273
Ishtar... 196
Isis at Busiris 93
Islam 93, 214
Isvara.. 196
Itineraria Pilgrims Handbooks............. 109
Jacobi, H. 208
Jade Imperial God................................ 272
Jagannatha in Orissa 93
James of Compostella, St..................... 93

Japan8, 12, 24, 27, 56, 66, 67, 70, 74, 75, 84, 93, 98, 144, 178, 193, 198, 203, 210, 221, 232, 234, 248, 251, 252, 273, 275
Japanese... 20, 66, 67, 68, 74, 75, 78, 84, 88, 89, 144, 146, 193, 195, 197, 200, 212, 220, 221, 231, 232, 235, 236, 243, 248, 251, 252, 273
Java.. 262
Jesus of Nazareth................................. 42
Jeta Prince.. 165
Jhana........222, 232, 240, 244, 254, 260, 264
Jimmu Tenno 93
Jinas 68
Jizo... 144
Jodo sect 70
Johannine Gospel................................. 75
John of Damascus................................ 89
Juggernaut.. 93
Justin, Martyr...................................... 89
Kanakamuni... 70
Kanishka............. 14, 17, 18, 19, 20, 22, 26
Kapimala.. 21
Kashmir 14, 19, 22, 232
Kassapa.. 70
Kasyapa 70, 100, 113, 204, 271
Katyayani-putra 19
Kern............................. 198, 208, 210
Khema the nun..................................... 38
Khotan.. 20
Kings of Heaven 268
Kingsmill, T. W. 26
Kokka... 78
Korea 152, 153
Koxinga.. 249
Koya... 93
Krakuchandra 70
Krishna 81, 146
Kshitigarbha 124
Kuan-yin .. 65, 74, 75, 76, 81, 107, 112, 127, 138, 140, 147, 174, 187, 188, 192, 195, 196, 198, 199, 200, 203, 204, 205, 206, 208, 209, 210, 211, 212, 213, 214, 217, 218, 219, 224, 227, 229, 231, 232, 234, 236, 237, 239, 241, 242, 243, 249, 251, 252, 256, 257, 258, 260, 265, 268, 269, 271, 272, 275, 279, 281
Kumarajiva 19, 198
Kwannon.................................. 195, 200
Kyoto.. 232
Laksmi.. 208

285

Lamaism 68, 105, 170
Lao-tzu 9, 154
Laughing Buddha 266, 268
Laura of Western monasticism 215
Le Coq 210
Lecky's European Morals 173
Lhasa 166, 197
Liang dynasties 195
Lilley, Canon 6
Little, A. 104
Lives of Buddhist Saints 264
Lloyd, Prof. Arthur 26, 29, 61, 220
Loigaire, King of Ireland 101
Lokesvararaja 71, 74
Lord of Fate 136
Loretto 93
Lotus of the Good Law ... 196, 198, 205, 214
Lourdes 93, 215
Lucifer 144
Lucy, St 206
Macartney, Lord 235
Macedonia 14
Macgowan, D. J. 247
MacRitchie, D. 218
Madeley, F. 272
Mahabharata 142, 146
Mahakasyapa 21
Mahasthama bodhisattva 74, 76
Mahavibhasha 23
Mahayana ... 7, 18, 22, 26, 27, 28, 29, 41, 45,
   48, 49, 55, 56, 57, 63, 66, 78, 80, 84, 107,
   110, 112, 124, 127, 146, 201, 217, 273
Maitreya 70, 129, 145, 199, 208, 265, 267
Maitreya bodhisattva 70, 129, 145, 199, 208,
   265, 267
Malunkyaputta 32
Manchu dynasty 7, 3, 66, 248, 256, 257, 269,
   273
Mandaeism 27
Mandalay 105, 123, 239
Manichaeism 27, 273
Manjusri 128
Mantra Buddhism 68
Manu, Laws of 203
Marichi 203, 209
Martin of Tours, St 93
Maspero, H. 236
Matsyendranath 212
Maximinus 206
Maximus the Confessor 89

Maya, the mother of Buddha .. 128, 131, 201
Mead, G. R. S. 40, 273
Mecca 93
Medhurst, W. H. 188
Medina, tomb of Mohammed at 93
Meditation 66, 68, 90, 227
Mencius 99, 157
Meru, Mount 266
Meshhed Ali in Nejef 93
Messiah 42, 199, 266
Metteya 70
Milton's Comus 144
Mimoro 252
Ming dynasty ... 13, 100, 103, 152, 175, 176,
   197, 219, 228, 236, 237, 239, 242, 243,
   247, 248, 271, 279
Minucius Felix 82, 89
Miracles 42, 152, 218
Mithraism 27, 146, 211
Modernism 84
Mohammedans 18, 93
Monasteries 165
Monastery of the White Horse 100
Monasticism 199
Mongol dynasty 105, 242
Morals and religion 74, 173
Moscow 138
Mother of Buddha 203
Moule, Bishop 86
Mughal emperors 255
Muller, Max 6, 24, 52
Mylitta 196
Mysteries 197, 210
Mysticism 39, 40, 54, 61, 63, 80, 89, 125,
   215
Nagarjuna 21, 60, 66
Nagasena 35, 45, 46, 47
Nalanda 28
Nara 93, 232
Nativity of Buddha 201
Neoplatonism 89
Nepal 18, 68, 212
Nestorianism 199
Nietzsche 55
Nihongi 252
Nine-dragon Hall 268
Ningpo 187, 189, 229, 237
Nirmanakaya 56
Nirvana 18, 32, 38, 46, 48, 49, 88, 89, 90,
   110, 129, 133

Nomen est numen	82
Norfolk	95
Northern Monastery	195, 227, 258, 263, 264, 265, 267, 268, 271
Obaku	232
Ocean-guardian Monastery	260
Oldenberg	32, 38, 176
Ontake	93
Ophites	27
Origen	20, 89
Origins	29, 215
Orpheus	211
Orphism	210, 221
Osiris	82
Padmapani	70
Pagoda of the Prince	237
Paik-chyoi	153
Pali canon	17, 18, 22, 28, 199
Paradise	56, 67, 71, 72, 74, 76, 78, 79, 81, 88, 90, 112, 131, 138, 154, 198, 208, 210, 236
Paramartha	23, 24
Parsva	19
Parthia	19
Pascal, Baylon	151
Paschasius	206
Patrick, St.	101, 252
Pauch-kosi	93
Paul, St.	63
Peak Monastery	271
Peking	105, 138, 160, 173, 239, 273
Pelagius	49
Peri, N.	236
Persia	11, 142, 237
Personality	35
Peru	93
Peter, St.	145
Pilgrim Fathers	94
Pilgrim's Guide	109, 110, 115
Pilgrimages	91, 97
Pilgrims	109, 110
Pines and Fountains	175
Plato	221
Platonic methods	63
Plotinus	33
Political Futurism	16
Polo, Marco	91
Pope	57, 140, 257
Porcelain Pagoda	244
Positivists	98
Potala	49, 197
Potalaka	49, 197, 227
Potthapada	32
Poussin, L. de la Vallee	32, 53, 56, 68, 176, 197, 208
Prayers	222, 224
Pringle-Pattison, A. S.	89
Pseudo-Dionysius	89
Pulpit of Kuan-yin	228, 236
Purgatory	125
Puto	7, 49, 67, 75, 104, 105, 106, 107, 148, 187, 188, 189, 192, 193, 195, 196, 197, 198, 200, 209, 212, 213, 217, 218, 219, 224, 227, 228, 229, 231, 232, 234, 235, 236, 237, 239, 240, 241, 242, 243, 245, 247, 248, 249, 251, 252, 254, 255, 256, 257, 258, 259, 262, 263, 265, 267, 268, 271, 272, 273, 274, 275, 277, 278, 279, 281
Puto-shan	67, 75, 104, 187, 197, 213, 227, 241, 258
Pythagorean teachings	221
Quetzalcoatl	93
Qur'an	255
Rain of the Good Law	209
Rain of the Law	258, 259, 264
Ramayana	146
Ratnapani	70
Ratnasambhava	70
Ravana	146
Red-hairs	249, 260, 263
Reformers	94
Regula Benedicti	230
Reischauer, A. K.	84
Revolution	7, 4, 92
Rhys, quoted	18, 24, 32, 35, 36, 41, 42, 52, 53, 121, 214, 230, 266
Richard of St Victor	63
Rinzai	232
Rishi	154
Robertson, J. M.	196
Rock	46, 65, 160, 227
Rock of the Tranquil-Mind	160
Roman Catholic	57, 82, 92, 125
Sabatier, auguste	223
Sacred Hills	91, 94, 99, 101, 103, 104, 237
Saddharmapundarika	198
Sadhus	115
Saints	57, 110
Saivite deities	18

Buddhist China

Sakyamuni..1, 10, 14, 16, 18, 21, 48, 56, 70, 78, 113, 137, 138, 139, 145, 228, 239, 269, 271
Salette, La in Dauphine 93
Salvation Army.. 76
Samantabhadra 70
Sambhogakaya.. 56
Sanday, Dr... 35
Sangha 110
Sanskrit.22, 28, 49, 66, 68, 70, 71, 110, 120, 124, 128, 142, 198, 200, 208, 222, 266
Santi-Deva... 50, 147
Sariputta 41
Sarvastivadins.. 23
Satan 143
Saviours 88
Schiller, F. C. S. 40
Schopenhauer 54
Schrader, Dr F. Otto 38
Scotland 95, 218
Seishi 74
Sekhet at Bubastis 93
Selbie, Rev. J. A. quoted 12
Self the in philosophy 16
Self-immolation 247
Semitic pilgrimage 93
Serpent-lore 252
Sextus-Pythagoricus 33
Shakespeare 157
Shanghai 9, 187, 244
Shantung............99, 108, 162, 195, 257, 273
Shin-gon sect 68
Shinto 98, 273
Shirishu.. 70
Shock-headed Ts'ai 175
Shodo Kowa 220
Shun... 103, 241
Siam.. 12, 123, 152
Sil-la 152, 153
Siva 197
Small Vehicle 18
Smith, Mr V. A. 20, 201, 203, 210
Snakes... 275
Society of God 244
Soil 161
Soto 232
Soul 12
South Sea Islanders mythology 146
Southern branch 65

Southern Monastery227, 228, 229, 239, 254, 255, 258, 264, 265, 277
Southern Sacred Mountain 65
Spencer, Herbert 54
Sri 208
Srinagar 23
Star of the Sea 196
Stein, Sir Aurel 210
Stephen, Sir Leslie 54
Stoicism 54
Sturt, Henry 199
Sudatta 165
Suffrin, A. E. 210
Suicide Cliffs 97
Sukhavati 70, 71, 195, 210
Sung dynasty .. 106, 180, 204, 212, 241, 242
Susa-no-o 273
Suso, Henry 52, 214
Sutta-Nipata 53
Sweet Dew, Monastery of 160
Syria 14
T'ai Chan, Le, by Ed. Chavannes 161
T'ang dynasty 65, 88, 106, 155, 160, 161, 176, 180, 212, 236
Tabriz 93
Tada Kanai 220
Takakusu, J. 23
Tamo 21, 60, 61, 63, 64, 228, 272
Tantric Buddhism 176, 203, 209
Taoism ... 1, 3, 9, 10, 11, 12, 33, 82, 99, 101, 103, 104, 108, 176, 195, 196, 269, 272, 273
Tashilhunpo 166
Tathagata 38, 39
Tavatimsa Pali for Trayastrimsa 128
Taylor, A. E. 54
Tea cultivation 159
Ten Thousand Buddhas 174
Tendai School 66
Theologia Germanica 39
Therapeutse 210
Theravada School of the Elders 18
Thirty-nine Articles 74
Thomas, St. 26, 29, 272
Thompson, Rev. J. M. 42, 84
Three Holy Ones 110
Three Refuges 110, 223
Tibet 68, 107, 165, 197, 269
Timour Khan 242
Tinted Clouds, Temple of 174

288

Ti-tsang...107, 124, 125, 127, 128, 129, 131, 133, 137, 138, 139, 140, 143, 144, 145, 150, 151, 153, 155, 157, 158, 159, 166, 167, 169, 170, 171, 173, 174, 175, 183, 198, 199, 200, 201, 237, 271, 279
Tower of Heaven 174
Tracts, Buddhist...................................16, 139
Transitus Sanctae Mariae 74
Translation... 6
Trayastrimsa... 128
Treasure of the Church 57, 127
Tribute of Yu 192
Trikaya 56
Trinitarian doctrine of Buddhism 20
Tripitaka 11, 23, 24, 245, 248
Turkestan...................... 19, 20, 107, 210
Tushita Heaven............................... 129, 265
Tyrrell, George 90
Underhill, E 39, 61, 63, 215
Universal Purity..................................... 175
Upanishads 39
Vacchogotta..32, 38
Vairochana 70
Vaisali... 142
Vaishnavas of Bengal 81
Vajrapani.. 147
Vasubandhu.................................. 19, 23, 24
Vasumitra 19, 24
Veda 266
Vedanta.. 39
Vedic mythology 142, 208, 267
Vikrama era 20

Vinaya 66, 241, 254
Vishnu 93, 146, 208, 211
Visvapani... 70
Vivasat... 142
Waddell's Lhasa and its Mysteries 197
Ward James 90
Warren's Buddhism in Translations .. 32, 35, 38
Water-lilies 234, 247, 275
Water-nymph... 166
Watters, Yuan Ch'ang ... 19, 20, 23, 24, 197, 209
Way of Amitabha..................................... 88
Western Lake.................................... 67, 108
White Flower Peak 271
White-deer Grotto.................................. 166
Williams Middle Kingdom 188, 195, 213, 248
Xavier, St. Francisco De................ 189, 192
Yakshas.. 130
Yama-raja 124
Yami 142, 143
Yellow-hairs 249
Yetts, W. Perceval 166
Yogacharya.. 18
Yoshio, Noda Professor 89
Yuddhishthira 146
Yuriaku.. 252
Zen... 232
Zeus at Dodona 93
Zockler, O.. 214
Zrvan akarana 211

www.ingramcontent.com/pod-product-compliance
Lightning Source LLC
Chambersburg PA
CBHW051420290426
44109CB00016B/1368